Ernst Bloch
Georg Lukács
Bertolt Brecht
Walter Benjamin
Theodor Adorno

NLB

Aesthetics and Politics

Afterword by Fredric Jameson

Translation Editor: Ronald Taylor

Aesthetics and Politics, first published 1977
©NLB 1977

NLB, 7 Carlisle Street, London W.1.

Filmset in Monophoto Ehrhardt by Servis Filmsetting Ltd, Manchester

Printed in Great Britain by Lowe and Brydone Printers, Norfolk.

Bound by Kemp Hall Bindery, Oxford.

Designed by Ruth Prentice

ISBN 902308 38 6

Contents

Publisher's Note

The texts assembled in this volume have been selected for the coherence of their inter-relationships. Brief presentations are designed to provide the Anglo-Saxon reader with biographical and cultural background to the successive exchanges contained in them. They were prepared by Rodney Livingstone, Perry Anderson and Francis Mulhern. The translators of the texts – Anya Bostock, Stuart Hood, Rodney Livingstone, Francis McDonagh and Harry Zohn – are credited at the end of them. Ronald Taylor edited the translations for the volume. Fredric Jameson's essay forms a contemporary conclusion.

NLB

Presentation I

The conflict between Ernst Bloch and Georg Lukács over expressionism in 1938 forms one of the most revealing episodes in modern German letters. Its resonance is in part due to the criss-crossing of intellectual evolution and political destiny between its two protagonists. The main outlines of the career of Lukács are now well-known in the Anglo-Saxon world; those of his intimate friend and exact contemporary Bloch less so. Born in Ludwigshafen in the Rhineland in 1885, the son of a railway official, Bloch was educated in Bavaria at Wurzburg and Munich. He soon displayed polymathic gifts, studying philosophy, physics and music. He first met Lukács when in his early twenties, at a soirée of Georg Simmel's in Berlin, and later during a visit to Budapest. However, it was in the period of their common residence in Heidelberg, from 1912 to 1914, that the two men were drawn together into an intense philosophical partnership. Paradoxically, in view of their later development, it was Bloch who essentially influenced Lukács towards serious study of Hegel, while it was Lukács who directed Bloch towards Christian mysticism, especially the work of Kierkegaard and Dostoievsky.[1] Russia on the eve of the revolution held a magnetic interest for the two men, together with others in Max Weber's circle at Heidelberg at the time. The onset of the First World War marked their first divergence: Lukács answered the call-up in Hungary, to the incomprehension of Bloch whose much more radical rejection of the war took him to Switzerland and a form of revolutionary defeatism. However, even four years later, Lukács was still suggesting to Bloch that they collaborate together on an Aesthetic, with Bloch contributing to it on music. Bloch's first major work, *Der Geist der Utopie* (1918), a wild synthesis of religio-apocalyptic and proto-socialist ideas, contained ardent tributes to his friend.

[1] See Michael Löwy, *Pour Une Sociologie des Intellectuels Révolutionnaires*, Paris 1977, pp. 292–300, for Bloch's early relationship with Lukács.

After the war, Lukács joined the Hungarian Communist Party, fought for the Commune, and then worked in exile as a party organizer and Marxist theorist within the Third International throughout the twenties. Bloch, by contrast, did not join the KPD in Germany, remaining a heterodox sympathizer rather than enlisted militant – herald of a revolutionary romanticism that he was never to disavow. Bloch, too, was much closer to experimental and esoteric literary circles in Weimar Germany.[2] The philosophical trajectory of the two men now increasingly separated, as Lukács exalted the realism of the later Hegel and Bloch defended the irrationalist reaction of Schopenhauer to it. The Nazi seizure of power drove them from Germany. Bloch went to Prague, Lukács to Moscow. Their responses to the victory of fascism soon proved to be sharply contrasted in emphasis. Bloch's book *Erbschaft dieser Zeit*, published in exile in 1934, took the form of a kaleidoscopic set of aphoristic reflections and evocations from the quotidian and cultural life of Germany in the twenties. It sought to understand the elements of genuine protest – however irrational their guise – in the revolt of the German petty-bourgeoisie that had been captured by fascism. To extricate these and to win the pauperized petty-bourgeois masses over to the working-class was, he argued, as important a task for the revolution in Germany as the conquest of the peasantry had been in Russia. Lukács, on the other hand, had from 1931 onwards – at a time of extreme Third Period sectarianism in the Comintern – been developing literary positions that anticipated the cultural policies of the Popular Front period. Their main watchwords were to be: reverence for the classical heritage of the Enlightenment, rejection of any irrationalist contaminations of it, assimilation of modernist trends in literature to irrationalism, identification of irrationalism with fascism. After the installation of the Nazi dictatorship, Lukács's first major essay was a scathing requisitory of Expressionism as a phenomenon within German culture, published in the journal *Internationale Literatur* in January 1934.

In it, he argued that Wilhelmine Germany, increasingly a society of parasitic rentiers, had been dominated by philosophies (Neo-Kantianism, Machism, Vitalism) that conjured away the connections between ideology and economics or politics, preventing any perception or critique of imperialist society as a whole. Expressionism had been a literary reflection

---

[2] He was, for example, a friend of Benjamin, whom he once used as a personal emissary to Lukács, when the latter was living underground in Vienna. In the later twenties, Bloch and Benjamin took narcotics together, cross-annotating their impressions of the experience – a typical miniature eddy of the time.

of that obfuscation. Its 'creative method' was a search for essences pursued through stylization and abstraction. While the Expressionists professed to attain the kernel of reality, they merely gave vent to their own passions, in a subjectivism that verged on the solipsistic, since words were used not referentially but only 'expressively'. Politically, the Expressionists had opposed the War; while in other respects their confusions were a kind of cultural analogue of the political ideology of the Independent Socialists (USPD). The Expressionists voiced a general hostility to the bourgeois, but they were unable to locate bourgeois vices in any particular class. Thus they could discern capitalist symptoms in workers, and could postulate an 'eternal' conflict, beyond mere class struggle, between bourgeois and non-bourgeois. The latter were seen as an elite that should rule the nation, an illusion that eventually led to fascism.

It was these antithetical interventions by Bloch and Lukács, immediately after the victory of Nazism, that form the background to the exchange below. In 1935 the Comintern switched to the Popular Front strategy. In July, the International Writers Congress for the Defence of Culture in Paris approved a decision to create a German literary journal in exile, as a forum for anti-fascist writers and critics. The three formal editors were intended to reflect a representative spectrum of opinion: Bertolt Brecht, a Marxist without official party affiliation, Willi Bredel of the KPD, and Leon Feuchtwanger, a bourgeois admirer of the USSR. The journal was published from Moscow and since none of these writers was on the spot for long, their contribution and influence varied notably. Feuchtwanger showed the greatest enthusiasm, while Brecht remained luke-warm, confining his own contributions largely to poems and extracts from his plays. After staying in Moscow for six months, Bredel left for the Spanish Civil War. Effective control was thus exercised by Fritz Erpenbeck, a journalist and actor who had been active in Piscator's theatre. His views tallied in all essentials with those of Lukács.

Once controversial, Lukács's views had meanwhile been steadily gaining in influence and in 1937, some two years after the Seventh World Congress of the Comintern, a coordinated assault on German Expressionism was launched in *Das Wort*. The signal for it was given by Alfred Kurella – a disciple of Lukács who was later to rise to prominence in the DDR – with a violent attack on the heritage of Expressionism, manifestly inspired by Lukács's long essay three years before. Kurella's article provoked a flood of replies, only some of which could be published. Among those to appear were contributions by former Expressionists

like Wangenheim, Leschnitzer and most importantly, Herwarth Walden
– who, as the editor of *Der Sturm* (1910–32) had played a key role in
publicizing the works of the Expressionists, as well as those of foreign
schools like Cubism. Other essays were written by associates of Brecht
like Johannes Eisler, and a number of other defenders of modernism,
including Bela Balazs. The most trenchant rejoinder, however, came
from Bloch. Dismissing Kurella, he now directly engaged with Lukács as
the source of the current polemics against Expressionism. It was his
essay which brought Lukács himself into the fray, with a lengthy reply.

Why did Expressionism excite so intense a debate in the German
emigration? Expressionism as a movement had flourished from about
1906 to the early twenties. It had been composed of a series of small
groups complexly inter-related and extending over the visual arts, music
and literature. *Die Brücke* and *Der Blaue Reiter* were essentially pre-war
phenomena, though of a number of their artists survived into the thirties.
Most of the leading poets, however, had died during or even before the
war (Heym, Stadler, Trakl, Stramm), or had turned away from Expressionism (Werfel, Benn, Döblin). Its last major achievements were the
retrospective anthology of poems, *Menschheitsdämmerung* (1920) and
the plays of Toller and Kaiser. If the normal definitions are slightly
extended, Expressionism may lay claim to Karl Kraus's *The Last Days
of Mankind* and the early works of Bertolt Brecht. A number of factors
determined the demise of the movement. Among them was the War,
which the Expressionists had at first prophesied and then opposed, and
whose end rendered them superfluous. A profound disillusionment followed when their League of Nations dream of a new mankind was
exploded. Expressionism was also upstaged by more 'radical' movements
like Dada and Surrealism, while in Germany the anti-revolutionary mood
and cynical 'realism' of Neo-Objectivity (*Neue Sachlichkeit*) made their
idealism look naively theatrical. Finally, the Nazi take-over drove the
survivors into silence, exile or imprisonment. Yet, although it had
petered out in such failure, Expressionism had memorably and indis-
putably represented the first German version of modern art. The
arguments between Bloch and Lukács and their respective allies over
its fate were thus essentially a contest over the historical meaning of
modernism in general. Bloch's plea for Expressionism started with an
effective counter-attack against Lukács's remoteness from the actual
productions of the movement, especially in the field of painting, where the
most durable achievements of Expressionism (Marc had long been

admired by Bloch)[3] and the most persistent weakness of Lukácsian aesthetics coincided. Bloch went on to reaffirm the legitimacy of Expressionism, ideologically as a protest against the imperialist war and artistically as a response to the crises of a transitional epoch, when the cultural universe of the bourgeoisie was disintegrating, while that of the revolutionary proletariat was still inchoate. Finally, Bloch sought to acquit Expressionism of the recurrent charges of elitism and cultural nihilism, by stressing its latent humanism and the interest shown by its exponents in popular, traditional forms of art and decoration. Lukács remained unmoved. In answer to Bloch's reflections on the fragmentary character of contemporary social experience, he insisted that capitalism formed a unitary whole, and most visibly at precisely those moments of crisis that prompted Bloch to speak of fragmentation. The characteristic subjectivism of Expressionist art was a denial of this cardinal truth and a repudiation of the objective of all valid art, the faithful reflection of the real. Furthermore, he argued, 'popularity' in art implied much more than the idiosyncratic enthusiasms of the Expressionists. Authentically popular art was distinguished by its affirmation of the most progressive experience of the nation, and by its close ties with realism, an aesthetic form that was truly accessible to 'the people'.

Few will dissent from Bloch's comments on his adversary's critical methods. Lukács's normal procedure was to construct an ideal type of what he took to be the ideological substrate of the works in question; these were then judged collectively, in the light of his own politico-ideological positions. The results of this were often grave conflations and reductions, and sometimes, when he did venture to analyse individual works, sheer blindness – as Adorno, unconstrained by feelings of friendship as Bloch may well have been, later showed. This difference of procedure was not simply technical. For Lukács, literary history composed an ordered and univocal past whose meaning and value were fixed by the wider history that determined it; the tradition handed down to the present by the 'progressive' epochs of the past was a set of compelling norms, a mortmain that literary legatees must honour on pain of disinheritance. For Bloch, on the other hand, this history was the *Erbe*, a reservoir in which nothing was ever simply or definitively 'past', less a

---

[3] Bloch was later to recount that he had confided his enthusiasm for the *Blaue Reiter* exhibition of 1916 to Lukács, who replied that it resembled the outpourings of a 'nerve-wracked gypsy'.

system of precepts than a sum of possibilities. Thus, no work was simply replaceable by another, by virtue of its ideological exchange-value, or wholly to be discounted because of its divergence from this or that aesthetic canon. The appropriate focus of a criticism so motivated was the individual art-work, the notorious blind spot of Lukácsian criticism. At the same time, however, it should be said that Lukács's procedure was also part of the greater coherence and ambition of his work, which produced, as no other contemporaneous *oeuvre* did, the elements of a systematic history of prose narrative and a sustained account of the relations between ideology and literary form – his *Historical Novel*, written around the same time as the rejoinder to Bloch, is perhaps the strongest example.

The pivotal issue of the exchange – the relationship between Expressionist art and social reality – is not easily arbitrated. Bloch's defence of Expressionism avoided direct confrontation with the aesthetic premises of Lukács's attack. Circumventing his opponent's assumption that the proper function of art was to portray objective reality, in organic and concrete works from which all heterogeneous material, and especially conceptual statement, was excluded, Bloch chose instead to insist on the historical authenticity of the experience that underlay Expressionism. It was thus left open to Lukács simply to remind him that the subjective impression of fragmentation was theoretically groundless, and to conclude that Expressionism, as an art that typically misrepresented the real nature of the social whole, was invalid. The effect of Bloch's *démarche* was to distract Lukács's attention, and his own, from one of the most crucial issues in the exchange between them. Driven by the 'impressionistic' character of Bloch's defence to emphasize the *unity* of the social whole, Lukács failed to register its essential point: that this unity was irreducibly *contradictory*. In this way, an opportunity to debate the problems of the artistic presentation of contradiction – the absent context of Bloch's remarks on montage, and a stubborn crux in Lukács's realist aesthetics – was missed.

The explicit politico-cultural context of the exchange was the Popular Front. It may be said, indeed, that it represented one of the high points of popular-frontist cultural debate in that period. But it should also be noted that both essays are weakest at precisely that point. If Lukács was right to point out that Bloch's catalogue of Expressionism's popular interests and debts was quite arbitrary, and that modernism in general was objectively elitist and thus estranged from 'the people' in every practical sense, it seems no less clear that his own invocations of national popular traditions, especially those of Germany, were at best strained and at worst vapid. The problems of defining a 'popular' literary practice were not necessarily entirely intractable, as the example of Brecht was to show. However, final judgment of the rival theses of Bloch and Lukács in the matter should probably be referred to a wider enquiry into the cultural and political limits of popular frontism itself.[4] In that perspective, the roles of the two men in the period would probably be revealed in yet another light. For, despite the lamentable conclusion of Lukács's essay – so far below the level of his main argument, and so symptomatic of the administrative tone of official culture within the Comintern during the Popular Front – it would be a mistake to assume that Bloch was freer than Lukács from the worst deformation of the time. In fact, it was Bloch in Czechoslovakia who volunteered fulsome affidavits for the Moscow trials, complete with the official tales of Nazi-Japanese plots in the Bolshevik Party, at the very same time that he was resisting the campaign against Expressionism;[5] while Lukács in the USSR, undeceived, avoided the subject wherever he could – compromising himself far less seriously. The real history of the epoch affords no comfort to facile retrospective alignments, in either aesthetics or politics.

[4] For a pioneering study of this sort, see Franco Fortini, 'The Writers' Mandate and the End of Anti-Fascism', *Screen* 15, 1 (Spring 1974), pp. 33–70.

[5] See, in particular, the articles 'Kritik einer Prozesskritik' and 'Bucharins Schlusswort', now collected in *Vom Hasard zur Katastrophe. Politische Aufsätze aus der Jahren 1934–1939*, Frankfurt 1972.

Ernst Bloch

Discussing Expressionism

It is excellent that people should be starting to argue about this again. Not so long ago such a thing seemed unthinkable; the *Blue Rider*[1] was dead. Now we hear voices invoking its memory once more, and not only with reverence. It is almost more important that there are people who can get so worked up over a movement long since past, as if it still existed and were standing in their way. Expressionism assuredly does not belong to the present; yet can it be that it still shows signs of life?

Zeigler has represented it as at most a haunting memory in the minds of a few elderly people.[2] Such people were once flushed with the zeal of youth; now they declare their allegiance to the classical heritage, but still suffer from the after-effects of their earlier beliefs. Benn – a particularly striking exponent of Expressionism – ended up in Fascism. Ziegler observes his evolution and concludes: 'Such a development was inevitable. The other Expressionists were simply too illogical to arrive at the same goal. Today we can clearly see what sort of a phenomenon Expressionism was and where it leads, if followed to its logical end; it leads to Fascism.'

The irritation recently provoked by the Expressionists is thus not simply private; it also has a cultural-political aspect, an anti-Fascist dimension. The *Dawn of Mankind*[3] turned out to be one of the pre-

---

[1] *Der blaue Reiter*, founded in Munich in 1911, was the second important school of German Expressionist painting, after *Die Brücke*. Its outstanding members were Wassily Kandinsky, Franz Marc and August Macke.

[2] Bernhard Ziegler was the pseudonym of Alfred Kurella, whose article 'Nun ist dies Erbe zuende . . .' had been published in *Das Wort*, 1937, vol. 9.

[3] *Menschheitsdämmerung*, edited by Kurt Pinthus and published in 1920, was the most influential anthology of Expressionist lyric poetry, containing samples of the work of Trakl, Benn, Werfel, Becher, Lasker-Schüler, Heym and Stadler. The *Dämmerung* in the title was ambiguous, suggesting at once the twilight of the human race that had failed in the World War and the birth of a new, redemptive mankind.

conditions of Hitler. Unfortunately for Ziegler, just a few weeks before his research into the antecedents of Fascism was published, Hitler completely failed to recognize them in his Munich speech and at the exhibition there.[4] Indeed, seldom has the absurdity of a false deduction, a hurried negative judgement been so swiftly and so strikingly demonstrated.

But was the absurdity demonstrated absolutely, in such a way to persuade us today? To concur with Hitler in his denunciation of Expressionism must have been a shock to Ziegler, for such a coincidence of views would be lethal to any man. Yet the charlatan in Munich might have had his reasons (though what it is hard to see) for covering the tracks of Fascism. So if we are to get to the heart of the matter, we should not focus on Ziegler's chronological misfortune, or even on his article itself, but instead direct our attention to the prelude to the whole discussion cited by Leschnitzer in his earlier contribution to the discussion of Expressionist lyrics. We refer to Lukács's essay *The Greatness and the Decline of Expressionism*, published four years ago in *Internationale Literatur*. It is that essay which furnishes the conceptual framework for the latest funeral oration on Expressionism. In what follows we shall concentrate our attention on it, since Lukács supplies the intellectual foundations of both Ziegler's and Leschnitzer's contributions. In his conclusions, Lukács was indeed significantly more circumspect than they; he insisted that the *conscious* tendencies of Expressionism were not Fascist, and that in the final analysis, Expressionism 'could only become a minor component of the Fascist "synthesis"'. But in his summing-up he also observed that 'the Fascists were not without justification in discerning in Expressionism a heritage they could use'. Goebbels had found the 'seeds of some sound ideas'[5] here, for 'as the literary mode corresponding to fully-developed imperialism (!), Expressionism is grounded in an irrationalist mythology. Its creative style tends towards that of an emotive, rhetorical, vacuous manifesto, a declamatory pseudo-activism. . . . What the Expressionists intended was undoubtedly the very opposite of atavistic. But since they were unable to free themselves intellectually from an imperialist parasitism, and since they colluded in the ideological decay of the imperialist bourgeoisie without offering either criticism or resistance, acting indeed

---

[4] In June 1937, the Nazis organized an Exhibition of Degenerate Art in Munich, in which leading modernist works, plundered from the museums of Germany, were ridiculed.

[5] In 1933 Goebbels had said: 'Expressionism contained the seeds of some sound ideas, for there was something Expressionistic about the whole age.'

on occasion as its vanguard, their creative method could without distortion be pressed into the service of that synthesis of decadence and atavism which is the demagogy of Fascism'. It can immediately be seen that the view that Expressionism and Fascism are cast in the same mould has its ultimate source here. The antithesis of Expressionism versus – let us say – the Classical Heritage, is just as rigid in Lukács as in Ziegler. However, in Lukács it acquires a conceptual foundation and is not just a matter of purple-patch journalism.

However, objectively the antithesis is not so readily demonstrable. Anyone who actually looks at Lukács's essay (a procedure highly to be recommended: the original is always the most instructive), will notice at the very outset that nowhere is there any mention of a single Expressionist painter. Marc, Klee, Kokoschka, Nolde, Kandinsky, Grosz, Dix, Chagall simply do not figure at all – to say nothing of musical parallels, such as the contemporary works of Schönberg. This is all the more surprising in that the links between painting and literature at that time were extremely close, and the paintings of Expressionism were far more characteristic of the movement than its literature. Reference to the painters, moreover, would have had the additional advantage of making it harder to dismiss Expressionism so categorically, for some of their pictures have a lasting importance and greatness. But even the literary works have not received the attention they merit, either qualitatively or quantitatively – their critics being content to make do with a very limited and highly untypical 'selection'. Trakl, Heym and Else Lasker-Schüler are totally absent; Werfel's early work is only mentioned because he wrote a few pacifist verses; the same is true of Ehrenstein and Hasenclever. The early and often important poems of Johannes Becher merely attract the comment that the author 'gradually succeeded in discarding' the Expressionist manner, while quotations from poetasters like Ludwig Rubiner abound, again only for the purpose of reinforcing the charge of abstract pacifism. Significantly, a quotation from René Schickele is also introduced in this context, even though Schickele was never an Expressionist but just an abstract pacifist (like many worthy men and poets, Hermann Hesse and Stefan Zweig among them).

What material does Lukács then use to expound his view of the Expressionists? He takes prefaces or postscripts to anthologies, 'introductions' by Pinthus, newspaper articles by Leonhard, Rubiner, Hiller, and other items of the same sort. So he does not get to the core of the matter, the imaginative works which make a concrete impression in time and space, a reality which the observer may re-experience for himself. His material is second-hand from the outset; it is literature on Expressionism, which he then proceeds to use as a basis for literary, theoretical and critical judgements. No doubt Lukács's purpose is to explore 'the social base of the movement and the ideological premisses arising from that base'. But it thereby suffers from the methodological limitation that it produces only a concept of concepts, an essay on essays and even lesser pieces. Hence the almost exclusive criticism merely of Expressionist tendencies and programmes, chiefly those formulated, if not foisted on the movement, by its own commentators.

In this connection Lukács makes many accurate and subtle observations. He draws attention to the 'abstract pacifism', the Bohemian concept of 'the bourgeois', the 'escapist quality', indeed the 'ideology of escapism' in Expressionism. Again, he uncovers the merely subjective nature of the Expressionist revolt, as well as the abstract mystification implicit in its attempt to reveal the 'essence' of objects by depicting them in the Expressionist manner. But even on this question of the subjective nature of the Expressionist revolt, he does not really do these poets justice, in berating them – on the evidence of Prefaces – for their 'pretentious showiness', their 'tinny monumentality'. The same can be said of his claim that all the content of their works reveal is 'the forlorn perplexity of the petty-bourgeois caught up in the wheels of capitalism', or 'the impotent protest of the petty-bourgeois against the kicks and blows of capitalism'. Even if they had done nothing else, even if the Expressionists had no other message to proclaim during the Great War than peace and the end of tyranny, this would not entitle Lukács to dismiss their struggles as shadow-boxing or to describe them as no more than 'a pseudo-critical, misleadingly abstract, mythicizing form of *imperialist* pseudo-opposition' (my italics).

It is true that *after* the War Werfel and others of his kind transformed their abstract pacifism into a toy trumpet; in the context of revolution, the slogan of 'non-violence' became a palpably counter-revolutionary maxim. But this does not invalidate the fundamentally revolutionary character of that slogan *during the War itself*, prior to the point where the War might have developed into a civil war; and it was understood precisely in this way by the politicians who were intent on fighting on to the bitter end. Moreover, there was no lack of Expressionists prepared to come out in favour of 'virtue in arms', Christ's scourge driving the money-changers from the Temple. These ideals of brotherly love were not as naive as all that. Indeed the assertion that Expressionism never abandoned 'the general ideological assumptions of German imperialism', and that its 'apologetic critique' ultimately furthered imperialism, is not merely one-sided and distorted: it is so warped that it provides a textbook example of that schematic brand of sociologism which Lukács himself has always opposed. But as we have remarked, none of this even touches the actual *creative* works of Expressionism, which alone are of interest to us. It belongs essentially to the *Ziel-Jahrbuch*[6] and similar diatribes, now justifiably forgotten (even though under the leadership of Heinrich Mann there were at least no imperialist war cries). But there is surely no need to labour the point that in the emotional outbursts of the art of the period, with their semi-archaic, semi-utopian hypostases, which remain today as enigmatic as they were then, there is to be found far more than the 'USPD ideology'[7] to which Lukács would like to reduce Expressionism. No doubt these emotional outbursts were even more dubious than enigmatic when they had no object outside themselves. But to describe them as the expression of 'the forlorn perplexity of the petty-bourgeois' is scarcely adequate. Their substance was different; it was composed partly of archaic images, but partly too of revolutionary fantasies which were critical and often quite specific. Anyone who had ears to hear could hardly have missed the revolutionary element their cries contained, even if it was undisciplined and uncontrolled, and 'dissipated' a considerable amount of the 'classical heritage' – or what was then more accurately 'classical lumber'. Permanent Neo-classicism, or the conviction that anything produced since Homer and Goethe is not worth considering unless it is produced in their image or as an abstraction from them, is no vantage-point from which to keep one's eye on the last avant-garde movement but one, or to pass judgement on it.

Given such an attitude, what recent artistic experiments can possibly avoid being censured? They must all be summarily condemned as aspects of the decay of capitalism – not just in part, which might not be unreasonable, but wholesale, one hundred per cent. The result is that there can be no such thing as an avant-garde within late capitalist society; anticipatory movements in the superstructure are disqualified from possessing any truth. That is the logic of an approach which paints everything in

---

[6] Edited by Kurt Hiller, the *Ziel-Jahrbücher* appeared from 1915–20 (though they were banned in 1916 because of their pacifist opinions). They were the vehicle of Hiller's own utopian activism which sought to establish the hegemony of an intellectual aristocracy.

[7] The USPD (Independent Social-Democratic Party of Germany) was formed as a scission from the SPD (Social Democratic Party) in 1916, in protest against the pursuit of the War. From 1919 to 1920, it occupied a position between the Social-Democratic and Communist Parties. In 1920, its Party Congress voted to merge with the latter, but in practice most of its leaders and many of its members reverted to the former.

black and white – one hardly likely to do justice to reality, indeed even to answer the needs of propaganda. Almost all forms of opposition to the ruling class which are not communist from the outset are lumped together with the ruling class itself. This holds good even when, as Lukács illogically concedes in the case of Expressionism, the opposition was subjectively well-intentioned and its adherents felt, painted and wrote as adversaries of the Fascism that was to come. In the age of the Popular Front, to cling to such a black-and-white approach seems less appropriate than ever; it is mechanical, not dialectical. All these recriminations and condemnations have their source in the idea that ever since the philosophical line that descends from Hegel through Feuerbach to Marx came to an end, the bourgeoisie has nothing more to teach us, except in technology and perhaps the natural sciences; everything else is at best of 'sociological' interest. It is this conception which convicts such a singular and unprecedented phenomenon as Expressionism of being pseudo-revolutionary from the very beginning. It allows, indeed forces, the Expressionists to figure as forerunners of the Nazis. Streicher's family-tree now finds itself improbably and utterly confusingly upgraded. Ziegler indeed fashions a crescendo out of names which are worlds apart – separating them only by commas, and listing them in sequence as brothers, in the same 'carping' fellowship: 'Bachofen, Rhode, Burckhardt, Nietzsche, Chamberlain, Baumler, Rosenberg.' On the same grounds, Lukács even doubts whether Cézanne is of any substance as a painter, and talks of the great Impressionists *in toto* (not just of the Expressionists) as he speaks of the decline of the West. In his essay nothing is left of them but a 'vacuity of content . . . which manifests itself artistically in the accumulation of insubstantial, merely subjectively significant surface details'.

By contrast, the Neoclassicists emerge as true giants. Theirs alone is the heritage. For Ziegler this includes even Winckelmann's conception of antiquity, with its noble simplicity and serene grandeur, the culture of a bourgeoisie which had not yet disintegrated, the world of a century ago and more. In the face of such a simplification we need to remind ourselves that the age of Neo-classicism witnessed the rise not only of the German bourgeoisie but also of the Holy Alliance; that the Neoclassical columns and the 'austere' manorial style take account of this reaction; that Winckelmann's Antiquity itself is by no means without feudal passivity. True enough, the *laudatores temporis acta* do not confine themselves to Homer and Goethe. Lukács holds Balzac in the highest esteem, makes a case for Heine as a poet of national stature, and is on occasion so out of touch with Classicism that in his essay on Heine he can describe Mörike, who has always been regarded by lovers of earlier poetry as one of the most authentic of German lyricists, as a 'charming nonentity'. But in general, the Classical is seen as healthy, the Romantic as sick, and Expressionism as sickest of all, and this is not simply by contrast with the undiluted objective realism which characterized Classicism.

This is not the occasion for a detailed discussion of an issue so crucial that only the most thorough analysis can do it justice: for it involves all the problems of the dialectical-materialist theory of reflection (*Abbild-lehre*). I will make only one point. Lukács's thought takes for granted a closed and integrated reality that does indeed exclude the subjectivity of idealism, but not the seamless 'totality' which has always thriven best in idealist systems, including those of classical German philosophy. Whether such a totality in fact constitutes reality, is open to question. If it does, then Expressionist experiments with disruptive and interpolative techniques are but an empty *jeu d'esprit*, as are the more recent experiments with montage and other devices of discontinuity. But what if Lukács's reality – a coherent, infinitely mediated totality – is not so objective after all? What if his conception of reality has failed to liberate itself completely from Classical systems? What if authentic reality is also discontinuity? Since Lukács operates with a closed, objectivistic conception of reality, when he comes to examine Expressionism he resolutely rejects any attempt on the part of artists to shatter any image of the world, even that of capitalism. Any art which strives to exploit the *real* fissures in surface inter-relations and to discover the new in their crevices, appears in his eyes merely as a wilful act of destruction. He thereby equates experiment in demolition with a condition of decadence.

At this point, even his ingenuity finally flags. It is undoubtedly the case that the Expressionists utilized, and even exacerbated, the decadence of late bourgeois civilization. Lukács resents their 'collusion in the ideological decay of the imperialist bourgeoisie, without offering either criticism or resistance, acting indeed on occasion as its vanguard'. But in the first place there is very little truth in the crude idea of 'collusion'; Lukács himself acknowledges that Expressionism 'was ideologically a not insignificant component of the anti-war movement'. Secondly, so far as 'collusion' in an active sense goes, the actual furtherance of cultural decline, one must ask: are there not dialectical links between growth and decay? Are confusion, immaturity and incomprehensibility always and in every case to be categorized as bourgeois decadence? Might they not equally – in contrast with this simplistic and surely unrevolutionary view – be part of the transition from the old world to the new? Or at least be part of the struggle leading to that transition? This is an issue which can only be resolved by concrete examination of the works themselves; it cannot be settled by omniscient *parti-pris* judgements. So the Expressionists were the 'vanguard' of decadence. Should they instead have aspired to play doctor at the sick-bed of capitalism? Should they have tried to plaster over the surface of reality, in the spirit, say, of the Neo-classicists or the representatives of Neo-objectivity,[8] instead of persisting in their efforts of demolition? Ziegler even reproaches the Expressionists with 'subversion of subversion', without realizing in his detestation that two minuses produce a plus. He is quite incapable of appreciating the significance of the demise of Neo-classicism. He is even less able to comprehend the strange phenomena which emerged just at the moment when the old surface reality collapsed, to say nothing of the problems of montage. In his eyes all this is just 'junk clumsily glued together', rubbish for which he cannot forgive the Fascists, even though they will have none of it either – in fact entirely share his opinion.

The importance of Expressionism is to be found exactly where Ziegler condemns it: it undermined the schematic routines and academicism to which the 'values of art' had been reduced. Instead of eternal 'formal analyses' of the work of art, it directed attention to human beings and their substance, in their quest for the most authentic expression possible. There is no doubt that there were frauds who took over its uncertain and easily-imitable directness of tone, and that its unduly subjectivist break-throughs and vague presentiments were not always, or indeed hardly ever, to achieve a lasting authority. But a just and dispassionate evaluation must be based on the work of the real Expressionists and not – to make criticism simpler – on distortions, let alone on mere misrecollections. As a phenomenon, Expressionism was unprecedented, but it did not by any means think of itself as lacking in tradition. Quite the reverse. As the *Blue Rider* proves, it ransacked the past for like-minded witnesses, thought it could discern correspondences in Grünewald, in primitive art and even in Baroque. If anything, it unearthed too many parallels rather than too few. It found literary predecessors in the *Storm and Stress* movement of the 1770s, it discovered revered models in the visionary

[8] *Neue Sachlichkeit*, or Neo-Objectivity, represented a non-political recoil from the emotional effusions of expressionism. Typical exponents ranged from Erich Kästner to writers like Ernst Jünger. The accent on cool detachment also left its mark on Brecht.

works of the youthful and the aged Goethe – in *Wanderers Sturmlied*,
in *Harzreise im Winter*, in *Pandora* and in the Second Part of *Faust*.
Moreover, it is untrue that the Expressionists were estranged from
ordinary people by their overwhelming arrogance. Again, the opposite
is the case. The *Blue Rider* imitated the glass paintings at Murnau;[9] in
fact they were the first to open people's eyes to this moving and uncanny
folk-art. In the same way, they focused attention on the drawings of
children and prisoners, on the disturbing works of the mentally sick and
on primitive art. They rediscovered 'Nordic decorative art', the fantastic-
ally complex carvings to be found on peasant chairs and chests down to
the 18th century, interpreting it as the first 'organic-psychic style' and
defining it as a sort of secret Gothic tradition, of greater worth than the
inhumanly crystalline, aristocratic style of Egypt, and even than Neo-
classicism. We need hardly add that 'Nordic decorative art' is a technical
term from art-history, and that neither the genre nor the solemn fervour
with which the Expressionists welcomed it has anything in common with
Rosenberg's fraudulent cult of the Nordic, of which it is certainly not
an 'origin'. Indeed his Nordic carving is full of Oriental influences;
tapestries and 'linear ornamentation' in general were a further element in
Expressionism. There is one further point that is the most important of
all. For all the pleasure the Expressionists took in 'barbaric art', their
ultimate goal was humane; their themes were almost exclusively human
expressions of the incognito, the mystery of man. Quite apart from their
pacifism, this is borne out even by their caricatures and their use of
industrial motifs; the word 'man' was as common a feature of Expressionist parlance in those days as its opposite, the 'beautiful beast', is
today among the Nazis. It was also subject to abuse. 'Resolute humanity'
turned up all over the place; anthologies had titles like *Menschheitsdämmerung* (*The Dawn of Mankind*) or *Kameraden der Menschheit*
(*Friends of Mankind*) – lifeless categories, no doubt, but a far cry from
pre-Fascist ones. An authentically revolutionary, lucid humanist
materialism has every reason to repudiate such vapid rhetoric; no-one
maintains that Expressionism should be taken as a model or regarded as
a 'precursor'. But neither is there any justification for refurbishing interest
in Neo-classicism by renewing outmoded battles with an Expressionism
long since devalued. Even if an artistic movement is not a 'precursor' of

[9] A village in Bavaria where Kandinsky, one of the leading members of the *Blaue Reiter*,
had a house where he spent the summers from 1908 until the outbreak of the war.

anything, it may for that very reason seem closer to young artists than * [a third-hand classicism which calls itself 'socialist realism' and is administered as such. Superimposed on the architecture, painting and writing of the Revolution, it is stifling them. The end-product is not a painted Greek vase but the later Becher as a sort of Wildenbruch.[10]] Even a more authentic classicism is doubtless culture, but distilled, abstracted, schematized. It is culture seen without temperament.[11]

For all that, the passions of an earlier period still stir controversy. So perhaps Expressionism is not outmoded after all; might it still have some life left in it? Almost involuntarily, the question brings us back to the starting point of our reflections. The vexatious voices to be heard today certainly do not in themselves warrant an answer in the affirmative. Nor do the three problems posed by Ziegler in the conclusion of his article shed any new light. Ziegler asks, to test his own hostility to the movement, the questions 'Antiquity: "Noble simplicity and serene grandeur" – do we still see it in that light?' 'Formalism: enemy number one of any literature that aspires to great heights – do we agree with this?' 'Closeness to the people, popular character: the fundamental criteria of any truly great art – do we accept this without reservation?' It is quite clear that even if one answers these questions in the negative, or rejects them as improperly formulated, it does not necessarily mean that one still harbours 'vestiges of Expressionism' within one. Hitler – and unfortunately, when faced by questions so bluntly put, one cannot avoid thinking of him – Hitler has already unreservedly answered the first and third questions in the affirmative, but that does not put him on our side.

Let us leave aside 'noble simplicity and serene grandeur', which involves a purely historical, contemplative question, and a contemplative attitude towards history. Let us confine ourselves to the questions of 'formalism' and 'closeness to the people', however ambiguously they may have been formulated in the present context. There is surely no denying that formalism was the least of the defects of Expressionist art (which must not be confused with Cubism). On the contrary, it suffered far more from a neglect of form, from a plethora of expressions crudely,

---

[10] A minor nationalist writer of the Wilhelmine epoch who specialized in monumental historical dramas.

[11] An allusion to Zola's definition of Naturalist art as 'nature seen with a temperament'.

* The passage contained between [   ] was written into the text by Bloch when it was republished in 1962.

wildly or chaotically ejaculated; its stigma was amorphousness. It more than made up for this, however, by its closeness to the people, its use of folklore. That disproves the opinion of it held by Ziegler, who conceives of Winckelmann's view of Antiquity and the academicism derived from it as a sort of artistic equivalent of Natural Law. It is enough, of course, that fake art [*kitsch*] is itself popular, in the bad sense. The countryman in the 19th century exchanged his painted wardrobe for a factory-made display cabinet, his old, brightly-painted glass for a coloured print and thought himself at the height of fashion. But it is unlikely that anyone will be misled into confusing these poisoned fruits of capitalism with genuine expressions of the people; they can be shown to have flowered in a very different soil, one with which they will disappear.

Neo-classicism is, however, by no means such a sure antidote to kitsch; nor does it contain an authentically popular element. It is itself much too 'highbrow' and the pedestal on which it stands renders it far too artificial. By contrast, as we have already noted, the Expressionists really did go back to popular art, loved and respected folklore – indeed, so far as painting was concerned, were the first to discover it. In particular, painters from nations which had only recently acquired their independence, Czech, Latvian and Yugoslav artists about 1918, all found in Expressionism an approach that was infinitely closer to their own popular traditions than the majority of other artistic styles, to say nothing of academicism. If Expressionist art often remains incomprehensible to the observer (not always; think of Grosz, Dix or the young Brecht†), this may indicate a failure to fulfil its intentions, but it may also mean that the observer possesses neither the intuitive grasp typical of people undeformed by education, nor the open-mindedness which is indispensable for the appreciation of any new art. If, as Ziegler thinks, the artist's intention is decisive, then Expressionism was a real breakthrough to popular art. If it is the achievement that counts, then it is wrong to insist that every single phase of the process be equally intelligible: Picasso was the first to paint 'junk clumsily glued together', to the horror even of cultivated people. At a far lower level, Heartfield's satirical photography was so close to the people that many who were intellectuals thereafter refused to have anything to do with montage. If Expressionism can still provoke debate today, or is at any rate not beyond discussing, then it follows that there must have been more to it than the 'ideology of the USPD', which has now lost any sub-structure it ever had. The

† The 1937 text refers to Becher, not Brecht.

problems of Expressionism will continue to be worth pondering until they have been superseded by better solutions than those put forward by its exponents. But abstract methods of thought which seek to skim over recent decades of our cultural history, ignoring everything which is not purely proletarian, are hardly likely to provide these solutions. The heritage of Expressionism has not yet ceased to exist, because we have not yet even started to consider it.

Translated by Rodney Livingstone

Georg Lukács

Realism in the Balance

In its day the revolutionary bourgeoisie conducted a violent struggle in the interests of its own class; it made use of every means at its disposal, including those of imaginative literature. What was it that made the vestiges of chivalry the object of universal ridicule? Cervantes' *Don Quixote*. *Don Quixote* was the most powerful weapon in the arsenal of the bourgeoisie in its war against feudalism and aristocracy. The revolutionary proletariat could do with at least one little Cervantes (*laughter*) to arm it with a similar weapon. (Laughter and applause.)

> *Georgi Dimitrov, Speech given during an anti-Fascist*
> *evening in the Writers' Club in Moscow.*

Anyone intervening at this late stage in the debate on Expressionism in *Das Wort* finds himself faced with certain difficulties. Many voices have been raised in passionate defence of Expressionism. But as soon as we reach the point when it becomes imperative to specify *whom* we are to regard as the exemplary Expressionist writer, or even to include in the category of Expressionism, we find that opinions diverge so sharply that no single name can count on general agreement. One sometimes has the feeling, particularly when reading the most impassioned apologias, that perhaps there was no such thing as an Expressionist writer.

Since our present dispute is concerned not with the evaluation of individual writers but with general literary principles, it is not of paramount importance for us to resolve this problem. Literary history undoubtedly recognizes a trend known as Expressionism, a trend with its poets and its critics. In the discussion which follows I shall confine myself to questions of principle.

1.

First, a preliminary question about the nature of the central issue: is it really a conflict between modern and classical (or even neo-classical) literature, as has been implied by a number of writers who have concentrated their attack on my critical activities? I submit that this way of posing the question is fundamentally wrong. Its implicit assumption is that modern art is identical with the development of specific literary trends leading from Naturalism and Impressionism via Expressionism to Surrealism. In the article by Ernst Bloch and Hanns Eisler in the *Neue Weltbühne*, to which Peter Fischer refers,[1] this theory is formulated in a particularly explicit and apodictic way. When these writers talk of modern art, its representative figures are taken *exclusively* from the ranks of the movements just referred to.

Let us not pass judgement at this stage. Let us rather enquire: can this theory provide an adequate foundation for the history of literature in our age?

At the very least, it must be pointed out that a quite different view is tenable. The development of literature, particularly in capitalist society, and particularly at capitalism's moment of crisis, is extraordinarily complex. Nevertheless, to offer a crude over-simplification, we may still distinguish three main currents in the literature of our age; these currents are not of course entirely distinct but often overlap in the development of individual writers:

1) Openly anti-realist or pseudo-realist literature which is concerned to provide an apologia for, and a defence of, the existing system. Of this group we shall say nothing here.

2) So-called avant-garde literature (we shall come to authentic modern literature in due course) from Naturalism to Surrealism. What is its general thrust? We may briefly anticipate our findings here by saying that its main trend is its growing distance from, and progressive dissolution of, realism.

3) The literature of the major realists of the day. For the most part these writers do not belong to any literary set; they are swimming against the mainstream of literary development, in fact, against the two currents noted above. As a general pointer to the complexion of this contemporary form of realism, we need only mention the names of Gorky, Thomas and Heinrich Mann and Romain Rolland.

In the articles which leap so passionately to the defence of the rights

[1] E. Bloch and H. Eisler: 'Die Kunst zu erben', in *Die Neue Weltbühne*, 1938.

of modern art against the presumptuous claims of the so-called neo-classicists, these leading figures of contemporary literature are not even mentioned. They simply do not exist in the eyes of modernist literature and its chroniclers. In Ernest Bloch's interesting work *Erbschaft dieser Zeit*, a book rich both in information and in ideas, the name of Thomas Mann occurs only once, unless my memory deceives me; the author refers to Mann's (and Wassermann's) 'bourgeois refinement' [*soignierte Bürgerlichkeit*] and with that he dismisses the matter.

Views such as these turn the entire discussion on its head. It is high time to put it back on its feet and take up cudgels on behalf of the best modern literature, against its ignorant detractors. So the terms of the debate are not classics versus modernists; discussion must focus instead on the question: which are the progressive trends in the literature of today? It is the fate of realism that hangs in the balance.

2.

One of Ernst Bloch's criticisms of my old essay on Expressionism is that I devoted too much attention to the theoreticians of the movement. Perhaps he will forgive me if I repeat this 'mistake' here and this time make his critical remarks on modern literature the focal point of my analysis. For I do not accept the view that the theoretical descriptions of artistic movements are unimportant – even when they make statements that are theoretically false. It is at such moments that they let the cat out of the bag and reveal the otherwise carefully concealed 'secrets' of the movement. Since, as a theoretician, Bloch is of quite a different stature than Picard and Pinthus were in their day, it is not unreasonable for me to examine his theories in somewhat greater depth.

Bloch directs his attack at my view of 'totality'. (We may leave out of account the extent to which he interprets my position correctly. What is at issue is not whether I am right or whether he has understood me correctly, but the actual problem under discussion.) The principle to be refuted, he believes, is 'the undiluted objective realism which charac-terized Classicism'. According to Bloch my thought is premissed throughout 'on the idea of a closed and integrated reality . . . Whether such a totality in fact constitutes reality is open to question. If it is, then Expressionist experiments with disruptive and interpolative techniques are but an empty *jeu d'esprit*, as are the more recent experiments with montage and other devices making for discontinuity.'

Bloch regards my insistence on a unified reality as a mere hangover from the systems of classical idealism, and he goes on to formulate his own position as follows: 'What if authentic reality is also discontinuity? Since Lukács operates with a closed, objectivistic conception of reality, when he comes to examine Expressionism, he resolutely sets his face against any attempt on the part of artists to shatter any image of the world, even that of capitalism. Any art which strives to exploit the real fissures in surface inter-relations and to discover the new in their crevices, appears in his eyes merely as a wilful act of destruction. He thereby equates experiments in demolition with a condition of decadence.'

Here we have a coherent theoretical justification of the development of modern art, one which goes right to the heart of the ideological issues at stake. Bloch is absolutely right: a fundamental theoretical discussion of these questions 'would raise all the problems of the dialectical-materialist theory of reflection [*Abbildlehre*]'. Needless to say, we cannot embark on such a discussion here, although I personally would greatly welcome the opportunity to do so. In the present debate we are concerned with a much simpler question, namely, does the 'closed integration', the 'totality' of the capitalist system, of bourgeois society, with its unity of economics and ideology, really form an objective whole, independent of consciousness?

Among Marxists – and in his latest book Bloch has stoutly proclaimed his commitment to Marxism – there should be no dispute on this point. Marx says: 'The relations of production of every society form a whole.' We must underscore the word 'every' here, since Bloch's position essentially denies that this 'totality' applies to the capitalism of our age. So although the difference between our views seems to be immediate, formal and non-philosophical, one which revolves instead round a disagreement about the socio-economic interpretation of capitalism, nevertheless, since philosophy is a mental reflection of reality, important philosophical disagreements must be implicit in it.

It goes without saying that our quotation from Marx has to be understood historically – in other words, economic reality as a totality is itself subject to historical change. But these changes consist largely in the way in which all the various aspects of the economy are expanded and intensified, so that the 'totality' becomes ever more closely-knit and substantial. After all, according to Marx, the decisive progressive role of the bourgeoisie in history is to develop the world market, thanks to which the economy of the whole world becomes an objectively unified totality. Primitive economies create the superficial appearance of great unity; primitive-communist villages or towns in the early Middle Ages are obvious examples. But in such a 'unity' the economic unit is linked to its environment, and to human society as a whole, only by a very few threads. Under capitalism, on the other hand, the different strands of the economy achieve a quite unprecedented autonomy, as we can see from the examples of trade and money – an autonomy so extensive that financial crises can arise directly from the circulation of money. As a result of the objective structure of this economic system, the surface of capitalism appears to 'disintegrate' into a series of elements all driven towards independence. Obviously this must be reflected in the consciousness of the men who live in this society, and hence too in the consciousness of poets and thinkers.

Consequently the movement of its individual components towards autonomy is an objective fact of the capitalist economic system. Nevertheless this autonomy constitutes only one part of the overall process. The underlying unity, the totality, all of whose parts are objectively interrelated, manifests itself most strikingly in the fact of crisis. Marx gives the following analysis of the process in which the constituent elements necessarily achieve independence: 'Since they do in fact belong together, the process by means of which the complementary parts become independent must inevitably appear violent and destructive. The phenomenon in which their unity, the unity of discrete objects, makes itself felt, is the phenomenon of crisis. The independence assumed by processes which belong together and complement each other is violently destroyed. The crisis thus makes manifest the unity of processes which had become individually independent.'[2]

These, then, are the fundamental objective components of the 'totality' of capitalist society. Every Marxist knows that the basic economic categories of capitalism are always reflected in the minds of men, directly, but always back to front. Applied to our present argument this means that in periods when capitalism functions in a so-called normal manner, and its various processes appear autonomous, people living within capitalist society think and experience it as unitary, whereas in periods of crisis, when the autonomous elements are drawn together into unity, they experience it as disintegration. With the general crisis of the capitalist system, the experience of disintegration becomes firmly entrenched over long periods of time in broad sectors of the population which normally experience the various manifestations of capitalism in a very immediate way.

[2] See *Capital*, Vol I, p. 209, London 1976 (Penguin/NLR edition).

3.

What has all this to do with literature?

Nothing at all for any theory – like those of Expressionism or Sur-realism – which denies that literature has any reference to objective reality. It means a great deal, however, for a Marxist theory of literature. If literature is a particular form by means of which objective reality is reflected, then it becomes of crucial importance for it to grasp that reality as it truly is, and not merely to confine itself to reproducing whatever manifests itself immediately and on the surface. If a writer strives to represent reality as it truly is, i.e. if he is an authentic realist, then the question of totality plays a decisive role, no matter how the writer actually conceives the problem intellectually. Lenin repeatedly insisted on the practical importance of the category of totality: 'In order to know an object thoroughly, it is essential to discover and comprehend all of its aspects, its relationships and its "mediations". We shall never achieve this fully, but *insistence on all-round knowledge* will protect us from errors and inflexibility.'[3] (G.L.'s italics)

The literary practice of every true realist demonstrates the importance of the overall objective social context and the 'insistence on all-round knowledge' required to do it justice. The profundity of the great realist, the extent and the endurance of his success, depends in great measure on how clearly he perceives – as a creative writer – the true significance of whatever phenomenon he depicts. This will not prevent him from recognizing, as Bloch imagines, that the surface of social reality may exhibit 'subversive tendencies', which are correspondingly reflected in the minds of men. The motto to my old essay on Expressionism under-scores the fact that I was anything but unaware of this factor. That motto, a quotation from Lenin, begins with these words: 'The inessential, the apparent, the surface phenomenon, vanishes more frequently, is less "solid", less "firm" than the "essence".' [4]

However, what is at issue here above all is not the mere recognition that such a factor actually exists in the context of the totality. It is even more important to see it as a factor in this totality, and not magnify it into the sole emotional and intellectual reality. So the crux of the matter is to understand the correct dialectical unity of appearance and essence. What matters is that the slice of life shaped and depicted by the artist

[3] Lenin, *Collected Works*, vol. 32, p. 94.

[4] Lenin, *Collected Works*, vol. 38, p. 130.

and re-experienced by the reader should reveal the relations between appearance and essence without the need for any external commentary. We emphasize the importance of shaping [*gestalten*] this relation, because, unlike Bloch, we do not regard the practice of left-wing Surrealists as an acceptable solution to the problem. We reject their method of 'inserting' [*Einmontierung*] theses into scraps of reality with which they have no organic connection.

By way of illustration, just compare the 'bourgeois refinement' of Thomas Mann with the Surrealism of Joyce. In the minds of the heroes of both writers we find a vivid evocation of the disintegration, the discontinuities, the ruptures and the 'crevices' which Bloch very rightly thinks typical of the state of mind of many people living in the age of imperialism. Bloch's mistake lies merely in the fact that he identifies this state of mind directly and unreservedly with reality itself. He equates the highly distorted image created in this state of mind with the thing itself, instead of objectively unravelling the essence, the origins and the mediations of the distortion by comparing it with reality.

In this way Bloch does as a theorist exactly what the Expressionists and Surrealists do as artists. Let us take a look at Joyce's narrative method. Lest my hostile assessment put the matter in a false light, I shall quote Bloch's own analysis: 'Here, in and even beneath the flowing stream we find a mouth without Ego, drinking, babbling, pouring it out. The language mimes every aspect of this collapse, it is not a fully developed, finished product, let alone normative, but open-ended and confused. The sort of speech with puns and slips of the tongue that you normally find at moments of fatigue, in pauses in the conversation, and in dreamy or slovenly people – it is all here, only completely out of control. The words have become unemployed, they have been expelled from their context of meaning. The language moves along, sometimes a worm cut in pieces, sometimes foreshortened like an optical illusion, while at yet other times, it hangs down into the action like a piece of rigging.'

That is his account. Here is his final evaluation: 'An empty shell and the most fantastic sellout; a random collection of notes on crumpled scraps of paper, gobbledygook, a tangle of slippery eels, fragments of nonsense, and at the same time the attempt to found a scholastic system on chaos; . . . confidence tricks in all shapes and sizes, the jokes of a man who has lost his roots; blind alleys but paths everywhere – no aims but destinations everywhere. Montage can now work wonders; in the old days it was only thoughts that could dwell side by side,[5] but now things can do the same, at least in these floodplains, these fantastic jungles of the void.'

We found it necessary to quote this lengthy passage because of the highly important, even crucial role given to Surrealist montage in Bloch's historical assessment of Expressionism. Earlier on in the book we find him, like all apologists of Expressionism, making a distinction between its genuine and its merely superficial exponents. According to him, the genuine aspirations of Expressionism live on. He writes: 'But even today there is no artist of great talent around without an Expressionist past, or at least without its highly variegated, highly storm-laden after-effects. The ultimate form of "Expressionism" was created by the so-called Surrealists; just a small group, but once again that is where the avant-garde is, and furthermore, Surrealism is nothing if not montage . . . it is an account of the chaos of reality as actually experienced, with all its caesuras and dismantled structures of the past.' The reader can see here very clearly, in Bloch's advocacy of Expressionism, just what he regards as the literary mainstream of our age. It is no less clear that his exclusion of every realist of importance from that literature is perfectly conscious.

I hope that Thomas Mann will pardon me for making use of him here as a counter-illustration. Let us call to mind his Tonio Kröger, or his Christian Buddenbrook, or the chief characters from *The Magic Mountain*. Let us further suppose that they had been constructed, as Bloch requires, directly in terms of their own consciousness, and not by contrasting that consciousness with a reality independent of them. It is obvious that if we were confronted merely by the stream of associations in their minds, the resulting 'disruption of the surface' of life would be no less complete than in Joyce. We should find just as many 'crevices' as in Joyce. It would be a mistake to protest that these works were produced *before* the crisis of modernity – the objective crisis in Christian Buddenbrook, for example, leads to a more profound spiritual disturbance than in Joyce's heroes. *The Magic Mountain* is contemporary with Expressionism. So if Thomas Mann had contented himself with the direct photographic record of the ideas and scraps of experience of these characters, and with using them to construct a montage, he might easily have produced a portrait as 'artistically progressive' as the Joyce whom

---

[5] Allusion to celebrated lines in Schiller's *Wallensteins Tod* (Act II, sc. 2)
  "The world is narrow, broad the mind –
  Thoughts dwell easily side by side
  Things collide violently in space."

Bloch admires so hugely.

Given his modern themes, why does Thomas Mann remain so 'old-fashioned', so 'traditional'; why does he choose not to clamber on to the bandwagon of modernism? Precisely because he is a *true realist*, a term which in this case signifies primarily that, as a creative artist, he knows exactly who Christian Buddenbrook, who Tonio Kröger and who Hans Castorp, Settembrini and Naphta are. He does not have to know it in the abstract way that a social scientist would know it; in that sense he may easily make mistakes, as Balzac, Dickens and Tolstoy did before him. He knows it after the manner of a creative realist: he knows how thoughts and feelings grow out of the life of society and how experiences and emotions are parts of the total complex of reality. As a realist he assigns these parts to their rightful place within the total life context. He shows what area of society they arise from and where they are going to.

So when, for example, Thomas Mann refers to Tonio Kröger as a 'bourgeois who has lost his way', he does not rest content with that: he shows how and why he still is a bourgeois, for all his hostility to the bourgeoisie, his homelessness within bourgeois society, and his exclusion from the life of the bourgeois. Because he does all this, Mann towers as a creative artist and in his grasp of the nature of society, above all those 'ultra-radicals' who imagine that their anti-bourgeois moods, their – often purely aesthetic – rejection of the stifling nature of petty-bourgeois existence, their contempt for plush armchairs or a pseudo-Renaissance cult in architecture, have transformed them into inexorable foes of bourgeois society.

4.

The modern literary schools of the imperialist era, from Naturalism to Surrealism, which have followed each other in such swift succession, all have one feature in common. They all take reality exactly as it manifests itself to the writer and the characters he creates. The form of this immediate manifestation changes as society changes. These changes, moreover, are both subjective and objective, depending on modifications in the reality of capitalism and also on the ways in which class struggle and changes in class structure produce different reflections on the surface of that reality. It is these changes above all that bring about the swift succession of literary schools together with the embittered internecine quarrels that flare up between them.

But both emotionally and intellectually they all remain frozen in their own immediacy; they fail to pierce the surface to discover the underlying essence, i.e. the real factors that relate their experiences to the hidden social forces that produce them. On the contrary, they all develop their own artistic style – more or less consciously – as a spontaneous expression of their immediate experience.

The hostility of all modern schools towards the very meagre vestiges of the older traditions of literature and literary history at this time, culminates in a passionate protest against the arrogance of critics who would like to forbid writers, so it is alleged, to write as and how they wish. In so doing, the advocates of such movements overlook the fact that authentic freedom, i.e. freedom from the reactionary prejudices of the imperialist era (not merely in the sphere of art), cannot possibly be attained through mere spontaneity or by persons unable to break through the confines of their own immediate experience. For as capitalism develops, the continuous production and reproduction of these reactionary prejudices is intensified and accelerated, not to say consciously promoted by the imperialist bourgeoisie. So if we are ever going to be able to understand the way in which reactionary ideas infiltrate our minds, and if we are ever going to achieve a critical distance from such prejudices, this can only be accomplished by hard work, by abandoning and transcending the limits of immediacy, by scrutinizing all subjective experiences and measuring them against social reality. In short it can only be achieved by a deeper probing of the real world.

Artistically, as well as intellectually and politically, the major realists of our age have consistently shown their ability to undertake this arduous task. They have not shirked it in the past, nor do they today. The careers of Romain Rolland and of Thomas and Heinrich Mann are relevant here. Different though their development has been in other respects, this feature is common to them all.

Even though we have emphasized the failure of the various modern literary schools to progress beyond the level of immediate experience, we should not wish it to be thought that we decry the artistic achievements of serious writers from Naturalism to Surrealism. Writing from their own experience, they have often succeeded in developing a consistent and interesting mode of expression, a style of their own, in fact. But when we look at their work in the context of social reality, we see that it never rises above the level of immediacy, either intellectually or artistically.

Hence the art they create remains abstract and one-dimensional. (In this context it is immaterial whether the aesthetic theory espoused by a given school favours 'abstraction' in art or not. Ever since Expressionism the importance attached to abstraction has been consistently on the increase, in theory as well as in practice.) At this point the reader may well believe that he detects a contradiction in our argument: surely immediacy and abstraction are mutually exclusive? However, one of the greatest achievements of the dialectical method – already found in Hegel – was its discovery and demonstration that immediacy and abstraction are closely akin, and, more particularly, that thought which begins in immediacy can only lead to abstraction.

In this context, too, Marx put Hegelian philosophy back on its feet, and in his analysis of economic relationships he repeatedly showed, in concrete terms, just how the kinship between immediacy and abstraction finds expression in the reflection of economic realities. We must confine ourselves to one brief illustration. Marx shows that the relationship between the circulation of money and its agent, mercantile capital, involves the obliteration of all mediations and so represents the most extreme form of abstraction in the entire process of capitalist production. If they are considered as they manifest themselves, i.e. in apparent independence of the overall process, the form they assume is that of the purely automatic, fetishized abstraction: 'money begets money'. This is why the vulgar economists who never advance beyond the immediate epiphenomena of capitalism feel confirmed in their beliefs by the abstract, fetishized world that surrounds them. They feel at home here like fish in water and hence give vent to passionate protests about the 'presumption' of a Marxist critique that requires them to look at the entire process of social reproduction. Their 'profundity, here as everywhere else, consists in perceiving the clouds of dust on the surface and then having the presumption to assert that all this dust is really very important and mysterious', as Marx comments à propos of Adam Müller. It is from considerations such as these that I described Expressionism in my old essay on the subject as an 'abstraction away from reality'.

It goes without saying that without abstraction there can be no art – for otherwise how could anything in art have representative value? But like every movement, abstraction must have a direction, and it is on this that everything depends. Every major realist fashions the material given in his own experience, and in so doing makes use of techniques of abstraction, among others. But his goal is to penetrate the laws governing objective reality and to uncover the deeper, hidden, mediated, not immediately perceptible network of relationships that go to make up society. Since these relationships do not lie on the surface, since the underlying laws only make themselves felt in very complex ways and are realized only unevenly, as trends, the labour of the realist is extraordinarily arduous, since it has both an artistic and an intellectual dimension. Firstly, he has to discover these relationships intellectually and give them artistic shape. Secondly, although in practice the two processes are indivisible, he must artistically conceal the relationships he has just discovered through the process of abstraction – i.e. he has to transcend the process of abstraction. This twofold labour creates a new immediacy, one that is artistically mediated; in it, even though the surface of life is sufficiently transparent to allow the underlying essence to shine through (something which is not true of immediate experience in real life), it nevertheless manifests itself as immediacy, as life as it actually appears. Moreover, in the works of such writers we observe the whole surface of life in all its essential determinants, and not just a subjectively perceived moment isolated from the totality in an abstract and over-intense manner.

This, then, is the artistic dialectic of appearance and essence. The richer, the more diverse, complex and 'cunning' (Lenin) this dialectic is, the more firmly it grasps hold of the living contradictions of life and society, then the greater and the more profound the realism will be.

In contrast to this, what does it mean to talk of an abstraction away from reality'? When the surface of life is only experienced immediately, it remains opaque, fragmentary, chaotic and uncomprehended. Since the objective mediations are more or less consciously ignored or passed over, what lies on the surface is frozen and any attempt to see it from a higher intellectual vantage-point has to be abandoned.

There is no state of inertia in reality. Intellectual and artistic activity must move either towards reality or away from it. It might seem paradoxical to claim that Naturalism has already provided us with an instance of the latter. The milieu theory, a view of inherited characteristics fetishized to the point of mythology, a mode of expression which abstractly pinpointed the immediate externals of life, along with a number of other factors, all those things thwarted any real artistic breakthrough to a living dialectic of appearance and essence. Or, more precisely, it was the absence of such a breakthrough that led to the Naturalist style. The two things were functions of each other.

This is why the photographically and phonographically exact imitations of life which we find in Naturalism could never come alive; this is why they remained static and devoid of inner tension. This is why the plays and novels of Naturalism seem to be almost interchangeable – for all their apparent diversity in externals. (This would be the place to discuss one of the major artistic tragedies of our time: the reasons why Gerhart

Hauptmann failed to become a great realist writer after such dazzling beginnings. But we have no space to explore this here. We would merely observe in passing that Naturalism inhibited rather than stimulated the development of the author of *The Weavers* and *The Beaver Coat*, and that even when he left Naturalism behind him he was still unable to discard its ideological assumptions.)

The artistic limitations of Naturalism quickly became obvious. But they were never subjected to fundamental criticism. Instead, the preferred method was always to confront one abstract form with another, apparently contrary, but no less abstract form. It is symptomatic of the entire process that each movement in the past confined its attention entirely to the movement immediately preceding it; thus Impressionism concerned itself exclusively with Naturalism, and so on. Hence neither theory nor practice ever advanced beyond the stage of abstract confrontation. This remains true right up to the present discussion. Rudolf Leonhard, for example, argues the historical inevitability of Expressionism in just this way: 'One of the foundations of Expressionism was the antagonism felt towards an Impressionism which had become unbearable, even impossible.' He develops this idea quite logically, but fails to say anything about the other foundations. It looks as if Expressionism were utterly opposed to, and incompatible with, the literary trends that preceded it. After all, what Expressionism emphasizes is its focus on essences; this is what Leonhard refers to as the 'non-nihilistic' feature of Expressionism.

But these essences are not the objective essence of reality, of the total process. They are purely subjective. I will refrain from quoting the old and now discredited theoreticians of Expressionism. But Ernst Bloch himself, when he comes to distinguish the true Expressionism from the false, puts the emphasis on subjectivity: 'In its original form Expressionism meant the shattering of images, it meant breaking up the surface from an original, i.e. subjective, perspective, one which wrenched things apart and dislocated them.'

This very definition made it inevitable that essences had to be torn from their context in a conscious, stylized and abstract way, and each essence taken in isolation. When followed through logically, Expressionism repudiated any connection with reality and declared a subjectivist war on reality and all its works. I would not wish to intervene here in the debate about whether, and to what extent, Gottfried Benn can be thought of as a typical Expressionist. But I find that the sense of life which Bloch describes so picturesquely and fascinatingly in his account of Expressionism and Surrealism, finds its most direct, candid and vivid expression in Benn's book *Kunst und Macht*: 'Between 1910 and 1925 the anti-naturalist style reigned supreme in Europe to the exclusion of almost everything else. For the fact is that there was no such thing as reality, at best there were only travesties of reality. Reality – that was a capitalist concept. . . . Mind [*Geist*] had no reality.' Wangenheim, too in his highly eclectic apologia for Expressionism, arrives at similar conclusions, although by a less analytical, more descriptive route: 'Successful works could not be expected in any quantity, since there was no reality corresponding to it [i.e. to Expressionism. – G.L.] . . . Many an Expressionist longed to discover a new world by abandoning terra firma, leaping into the air and clinging to the clouds.'

We can find a perfectly clear and unambiguous formulation of this situation and its implications in Heinrich Vogeler. His accurate assessment of abstraction in Expressionism leads him to the correct conclusion: 'It [i.e. Expressionism – G.L.] was the Dance of Death of bourgeois art . . . The Expressionists thought they were conveying the "essence of things" [*Wesen*], whereas in fact they revealed their decomposition [*Verwesung*].'

One inescapable consequence of an attitude alien or hostile to reality makes itself increasingly evident in the art of the 'avant-garde': a growing paucity of content, extended to a point where absence of content or hostility towards it is upheld on principle. Once again Gottfried Benn has put the situation in a nutshell: 'The very concept of content, too, has become problematic. Content – what's the point of it nowadays, it's all washed up, worn out, mere sham – self-indulgence of emotions, rigidity of feelings, clusters of discredited elements, lies, amorphous shapes. . . .'

As the reader can see for himself, this account closely parallels Bloch's own description of the world of Expressionism and Surrealism. Needless to say, their respective analyses lead Bloch and Benn to entirely opposite conclusions. At a number of points in his book, Bloch clearly sees the problematic nature of modern art as something arising from the attitude he himself describes: 'Hence major writers no longer make their home in their own subject-matter, for all substances crumble at their touch. The dominant world no longer presents them with a coherent image to depict, or to take as the starting-point for their imagination. All that remains is emptiness, shards for them to piece together.' Bloch goes on to explore the revolutionary period of the bourgeoisie down to Goethe. He then continues: 'Goethe was succeeded not by a further development of the novel of education, but by the French novel of disillusionment, so that today in the perfected non-world, anti-world or ruined world of the grand bourgeois vacuum, "reconciliation" is neither a danger nor an option for the writer. Only a dialectical approach [?! – G.L.] is possible here: either as material for a dialectical montage or as an experiment in it. In the hands of Joyce even the world of Odysseus became a kaleidoscopic gallery of the disintegrating and disintegrated world of today in microscopic cross-section – no more than a cross-section, because people today lack something, namely the most important thing of all . . .'

We have no desire to quibble with Bloch over trifles, such as his purely idiosyncratic use of the word 'dialectics', or the mistaken logic which allows him to suggest that the novel of disillusionment follows directly upon Goethe. (My early work, *The Theory of the Novel*, is partly to blame for Bloch's *non-sequitur* here.) We are concerned with more vital issues. In particular, with the fact that Bloch – although his evaluation is the reverse of ours – expresses the notion that the subject-matter and the composition of works of literature depend on man's relationship to objective reality. So far so good. But when Bloch comes to demonstrate the historical legitimacy of Expressionism and Surrealism, he ceases to concern himself with the objective relations between society and the active men of our time, relations which, as we can see from *Jean Christophe*,[6] even permit a novel of education to be written. Instead, taking the isolated state of mind of a specific class of intellectuals as his starting-point, he constructs a sort of home-made model of the contemporary world, which logically enough appears to him as a 'non-world' – a conception which, regrettably enough, turns out to be very similar to that of Benn. For writers who adopt this kind of stance towards reality there obviously cannot be any action, structure, content or composition in the 'traditional sense'. For people who experience the world like this it is in fact perfectly true that Expressionism and Surrealism are the only modes of self-expression still available. This philosophical justification of Expressionism and Surrealism suffers 'merely' from the fact that Bloch fails to make reality his touchstone and instead uncritically takes over the Expressionist and Surrealist attitude towards reality, and translates it into his own richly imaginative language.

Despite my sharp disagreement with all of Bloch's judgements, I find his formulation of certain facts both correct and valuable. In particular,

[6] The major work of Romain Rolland, a novel in 10 volumes whose theme is Franco-German relations as reflected in the life of a German musician.

he is the most consistent of all defenders of modernism in his demonstration that Expressionism necessarily leads to Surrealism. In this context he also deserves praise for having recognized that montage is the inevitable mode of expression in this phase of development. Moreover, his achievement here is all the greater because he shows that montage is important not only in modernist art, but also in the bourgeois philosophy of our time.

However, one consequence of this is that he brings out the anti-realistic one-dimensionality of the entire trend much more starkly than other theoreticians who think along these lines. This one-dimensionality – about which, incidentally, Bloch has nothing to say – was already a feature of Naturalism. In contrast to the Naturalist, the artistic 'refinement' introduced by Impressionism 'purifies' art even more completely of the complex mediations, the tortuous paths of objective reality, and the objective dialectics of Being and Consciousness. The symbolist movement is clearly and consciously one-dimensional from the outset, for the gulf between the sensuous incarnation of a symbol and its symbolic meaning arises from the narrow, single-tracked process of subjective association which yokes them together.

Montage represents the pinnacle of this movement and for this reason we are grateful to Bloch for his decision to set it so firmly in the centre of modernist literature and thought. In its original form, as photomontage, it is capable of striking effects, and on occasion it can even become a powerful political weapon. Such effects arise from its technique of juxtaposing heterogeneous, unrelated pieces of reality torn from their context. A good photomontage has the same sort of effect as a good joke. However, as soon as this one-dimensional technique – however legitimate and successful it may be in a joke – claims to give shape to reality (even when this reality is viewed as unreal), to a world of relationships (even when these relationships are held to be specious), or of totality (even when this totality is regarded as chaos), then the final effect must be one of profound monotony. The details may be dazzlingly colourful in their diversity, but the whole will never be more than an unrelieved grey on grey. After all, a puddle can never be more than dirty water, even though it may contain rainbow tints.

This monotony proceeds inexorably from the decision to abandon any attempt to mirror objective reality, to give up the artistic struggle to shape the highly complex mediations in all their unity and diversity and to synthesize them as characters in a work of literature. For this approach permits no creative composition, no rise and fall, no growth from within to emerge from the true nature of the subject-matter.

Whenever these artistic trends are dismissed as decadent, there is a cry of indignation against 'pedantic hectoring by eclectic academics'. Perhaps I shall be permitted, therefore, to appeal to Friedrich Nietzsche, an expert on decadence whom my opponents hold in high regard in other matters too: 'What is the mark of every form of literary decadence?' he enquires. He replies: 'It is that life no longer dwells in the totality. The word becomes sovereign and escapes from the confines of the sentence; the sentence encroaches on the page, obscuring its meaning; the page gains in vitality at the cost of the whole – the whole ceases to be a whole. But that is the equation of every decadent style: always the same anarchy of the atoms, disintegration of the will. . . . Life, the same vitality, the vibrance and exuberance of life is compressed into the most minute structures, while the rest is impoverished. Paralysis, misery, petrifaction or hostility and chaos everywhere: in either case the consequences are the more striking, the higher one rises in the hierarchy of organizations. The whole as such no longer lives at all; it is composite, artificial, a piece of cerebration, an artefact.'[7] This passage from Nietzsche is just as truthful an account of the artistic implications of these literary trends as that of Bloch or Benn. I would invite Herwarth Walden, who dismisses every critical interpretation of Expressionism as a vulgarization and who regards every example used to illustrate the theory and practice of Expressionism as an instance of 'vulgar-Expressionism' which proves nothing, to comment on the following adaptation of Nietzsche's theory of decadence to the theory of literary language in general: 'Why should only the sentence be comprehensible and not the word? . . . Since the poets like to dominate, they go ahead and make sentences, ignoring the rights of words. But it is the word that rules. The word shatters the sentence and the work of art is a mosaic. Only words can bind. Sentences are always just picked up out of nowhere.' This 'vulgar-Expressionist' theory of language comes in fact from Herwarth Walden himself.

It goes without saying that such principles are never applied with absolute consistency, even by Joyce. For 100 per cent chaos can only exist in the minds of the deranged, in the same way that Schopenhauer had already observed that a 100 per cent solipsism is only to be found in a lunatic asylum. But since chaos constitutes the intellectual cornerstone of modernist art, any cohesive principles it contains must stem from a

[7] The words significantly omitted by Lukács after 'disintegration of the will' are '. . . freedom of the individual, in moral terms – generalized into a political theory: "equal rights for all".' F. Nietzsche, *Der Fall Wagner*.

subject-matter alien to it. Hence the superimposed commentaries, the theory of simultaneity,[8] and so on. But none of this can be any more than a surrogate, it can only intensify the one-dimensionality, of this form of art.

5.

The emergence of all these literary schools can be explained in terms of the economy, the social structure and the class struggles of the age of imperialism. So Rudolf Leonhard is absolutely right when he claims that Expressionism is a necessary historical phenomenon. But it is at best a half-truth when he goes on to assert, echoing Hegel's celebrated dictum, that 'Expressionism was real; so if it was real it was rational.' Even in Hegel the 'rationality of history' was never as straightforward as this, although he occasionally contrived to smuggle an apologia for the actual into his concept of reason. For a Marxist, 'rationality' (historical necessity) is unquestionably a more complex business. For Marxism the acknowledgment of a historical necessity neither implies a justification of what actually exists (not even during the period when it exists), nor does it express a fatalistic belief in the necessity of historical events. Once again we can illustrate this best with an example from economics. There can be no doubt that primitive accumulation, the separation of the small producers from their means of production, the creation of the proletariat, was – with all its inhumanities – a historical necessity. Nevertheless, no Marxist would dream of glorifying the English bourgeoisie of the period as the embodiment of the principle of reason in Hegel's sense. Even less would it occur to a Marxist to see thereby any fatalistic necessity in the development from capitalism to socialism. Marx repeatedly protested against the way in which people fatalistically insisted that the only possible development for the Russia of his day was from primitive accumulation to capitalism. Today, in view of the fact that socialism has been established in the Soviet Union, the idea that undeveloped countries can only achieve socialism via the route of primitive accumulation and capitalism, is a recipe for counter-revolution. So if we concur with Leonhard, and agree that the emergence of Expressionism was historically necessary, this is not to say that we find it artistically valid, i.e. that it is a necessary constituent of the art of the future.

[8] Theory developed by Robert Delauney, who together with Kandinsky was one of the pioneers of abstraction in art. In his great series of 'Window' paintings starting in 1912, he sought to put it into practice. Taking the transparent interpenetrating colours of Cézanne's later period, he fused them with the forms of analytical Cubism, and claimed that the result, a simultaneous impact of two or more colours, gave the picture a dynamic force.

For this reason we must demur when Leonhard discerns in Expressionism 'the definition of man and the consolidation of things as a stepping-stone towards a new realism'. Bloch is absolutely in the right here when, unlike Leonhard, he looks to Surrealism and the dominance of montage as the necessary and logical heir to Expressionism. Our dear old Wangenheim inevitably arrives at completely eclectic conclusions when he tries to use the debate on Expressionism for his own purposes, i.e. to salvage and preserve the formalistic tendencies of his early work – tendencies which so often inhibited and even suppressed his native realism – by bringing them under the umbrella of a broad and undogmatic conception of realism. His aim in defending Expressionism is to rescue for socialist realism a priceless heritage of permanent value. He attempts to defend his position in this way: 'Fundamentally, the theatre of Expressionism, even when its effects were powerful, reflected a world in tatters. The theatre of socialist realism reflects uniformity amidst all the diversity of its forms.' Is this why Expressionism has to become an essential component of socialist realism? Wangenheim has not got a single aesthetic or logical argument in reply, merely a biographical one: a reluctance to jettison his own earlier formalism.

Taking as his starting-point the historical assessment of Expressionism clearly stated in my old essay, Bloch goes on to make the following criticism of me: 'The result is that there can be no such thing as an avant-garde within late capitalist society; anticipatory movements in the superstructure are disqualified from possessing any truth.' This accusation arises from the circumstance that Bloch regards the road that leads to Surrealism and montage as the only one open to modern art. If the role of the avant-garde is disputed, the inescapable conclusion in his eyes is that any ideological anticipation of social tendencies must be called in question.

But this is quite simply untrue. Marxism has always recognized the anticipatory function of ideology. To remain within the sphere of literature, we need only remind ourselves of what Paul Lafargue has to say about Marx's evaluation of Balzac: 'Balzac was not just the chronicler of his own society, he was also the creator of prophetic figures who were still embryonic under Louis Philippe and who only emerged fully grown after his death, under Napoleon III.' But is this Marxian view still valid in the present? Of course it is. Such 'prophetic figures', however, are to be found exclusively in the works of the important realists. In the novels, stories and plays of Maxim Gorky such figures abound. Anyone who has been following recent events in the Soviet Union attentively and dispassionately will have realized that in his *Karamora*, his *Klim Samgin* his *Dostigayev*, etc., Gorky has created a series of typical figures which have only now revealed their real nature and who were 'prophetic' anticipations in Marx's sense. We might point with equal justice to the earlier works of Heinrich Mann, novels such as *Der Untertan* and *Professor Unrat*.[9] Who could deny that a large number of the repellent, mean and bestial features of the German bourgeoisie, and of a petty bourgeoisie seduced by demagogues, were 'prophetically' portrayed here and that they only blossomed completely later under Fascism? Nor should we overlook the character of Henri IV in this context.[10] On the one hand, he is a historically authentic figure, true to life; on the other hand he anticipates those humanist qualities which will only emerge fully in the struggles leading to the defeat of Fascism, in the fighters of the anti-Fascist Front.

Let us consider a counter-illustration, likewise from our own time. The ideological struggle against war was one of the principal themes of the best expressionists. But what did they do or say to anticipate the new imperialist war raging all around us and threatening to engulf the whole civilized world? I hardly imagine that anyone today will deny that these works are completely obsolete and irrelevant to the problems of the present. On the other hand the realist writer Arnold Zweig anticipated a whole series of essential features of the new war in his novels *Sergeant Grischa* and *Education before Verdun*. What he did there was to depict the relationship between the war at the front and what went on behind the lines, and to show how the war represented the individual and social continuation and intensification of 'normal' capitalist barbarity.

There is nothing mysterious or paradoxical about any of this – it is the very essence of all authentic realism of any importance. Since such realism must be concerned with the creation of types (this has always been the case, from *Don Quixote* down to *Oblomov* and the realists of our own time), the realist must seek out the lasting features in people, in their relations with each other and in the situations in which they have to act; he must focus on those elements which endure over long periods and which constitute the objective human tendencies of society and indeed of mankind as a whole.

Such writers form the authentic ideological avant-garde since they depict the vital, but not immediately obvious forces at work in objective

[9] Translated into English as *Man of Straw* and *The Blue Angel* respectively.
[10] The eponymous hero of two novels Heinrich Mann published in the 1930s: *Die Jugend des Königs Henri Quatre* and *Die Vollenhung des Königs Henri Quatre*.

48

reality. They do so with such profundity and truth that the products of their imagination receive confirmation from subsequent events – not merely in the simple sense in which a successful photograph mirrors the original, but because they express the wealth and diversity of reality, reflecting forces as yet submerged beneath the surface, which only blossom forth visibly to all at a later stage. Great realism, therefore, does not portray an immediately obvious aspect of reality but one which is permanent and objectively more significant, namely man in the whole range of his relations to the real world, above all those which outlast mere fashion. Over and above that, it captures tendencies of development that only exist incipiently and so have not yet had the opportunity to unfold their entire human and social potential. To discern and give shape to such underground trends is the great historical mission of the true literary avant-garde. Whether a writer really belongs to the ranks of the avant-garde is something that only history can reveal, for only after the passage of time will it become apparent whether he has perceived significant qualities, trends, and the social functions of individual human types, and has given them effective and lasting form. After what has been said already, I hope that no further argument is required to prove that only the major realists are capable of forming a genuine avant-garde.

So what really matters is not the subjective belief, however sincere, that one belongs to the avant-garde and is eager to march in the forefront of literary developments. Nor is it essential to have been the first to discover some technical innovation, however dazzling. What counts is the social and human content of the avant-garde, the breadth, the profundity and the truth of the ideas that have been 'prophetically' anticipated.

In short, what is at issue here is not whether or not we deny the possibility of anticipatory movements in the superstructure. The vital questions are: *what* was anticipated, in what manner and by whom?

We have already given a number of illustrations, and we could easily multiply them, to show what the major realists of our time have anticipated in their art, by their creation of types. So let us now turn the question round and enquire what Expressionism anticipated? The only answer we can possibly receive, even from Bloch, is: Surrealism, i.e. yet another literary school whose fundamental failure to anticipate social trends in its art has emerged with crystal clarity, and nowhere more clearly than from the description of it given by its greatest admirers. Modernism has not, nor has it ever had, anything to do with the creation of 'prophetic figures' or with the genuine anticipation of future developments.

If we have been successful in clarifying the criterion by which the literary avant-garde is to be distinguished, then it is no great problem to answer certain concrete questions. Who in our literature belongs to the avant-garde? 'Prophetic' writers of the stamp of Gorky, or writers like the late Hermann Bahr who, like a drum-major, marched proudly at the head of every new movement from Naturalism to Surrealism, and then promptly dismissed each phase a year before it went out of fashion? Granted, Hermann Bahr is a caricature, and nothing could be further from my mind than to put him on the same footing as the sincere defenders of Expressionism. But he is the caricature of something real, namely of a formalist modernism, bereft of content, cut off from the mainstream of society.

It is an old truth of Marxism that every human activity should be judged according to its objective meaning in the total context, and not according to what the agent believes the importance of his activity to be. So, on the one hand, it is not essential to be a conscious 'modernist' at all costs (Balzac, we recall, was a royalist); and, on the other hand, even the most passionate determination, the most intense sense of conviction that one has revolutionized art and created something 'radically new', will not suffice to turn a writer into someone who can truly anticipate future trends, if determination and conviction are his sole qualifications.

6.

This ancient truth can also be expressed as a commonplace: the road to hell is paved with good intentions. The validity of this proverb may on occasion appear with the force of a home-truth to anyone who takes his own development seriously and is therefore prepared to criticize himself objectively and without pulling any punches. I am quite willing to start with myself. In the winter of 1914–15: subjectively, a passionate protest against the War, its futility and inhumanity, its destruction of culture and civilization. A general mood that was pessimistic to the point of despair. The contemporary world of capitalism appeared to be the consummation of Fichte's 'age of absolute sinfulness'. My subjective determination was a protest of a progressive sort. The objective product, *The Theory of the Novel*, was a reactionary work in every respect, full of idealistic mysticism and false in all its assessments of the historical process. Then 1922: a mood of excitement, full of revolutionary impatience. I can still hear the bullets of the Red War against the imperialists whistling around my head, the excitement of being an outlaw in Hungary still reverberates within me. Everything in me rebelled against the notion that the first great revolutionary wave was past and that the resolution of the Communist vanguard was insufficient to bring about the overthrow of capitalism. Thus the subjective foundation was revolutionary impatience. The objective product was *History and Class Consciousness* – which was reactionary because of its idealism, because of its faulty grasp of the theory of reflection and because of its denial of a dialectics in nature. It goes without saying that I am not alone in having had such experiences at this time. On the contrary, it also happened to countless others. The opinion expressed in my old essay on Expressionism which has aroused so many dissenting voices, namely the assertion that ideologically Expressionism was closely related to the Independent Socialists, is based on the aforementioned ancient truth.

In our debate on Expressionism, revolution (Expressionism) and Noske have been put in opposing camps – in the good old Expressionist manner. But could Noske have managed to emerge the victor without the Independent Socialists, without their vacillation and hesitation, which prevented the Workers' Councils from seizing power while tolerating the organization and arming of reactionary forces? The Independent Socialists were, in party terms, the organized expression of the fact that even those German workers who were radical at the level of their feelings, were not yet equipped ideologically for revolution. The Spartacus League was too slow in detaching itself from the Independent Socialists and it did not criticize them incisively enough; both failures are an important index of the weakness and backwardness of the subjective side of the German revolution, the very factors that Lenin singled out right from the start in his critique of the Spartacus League.

Of course, the whole situation was anything but straightforward. In my original essay, for instance, I drew a very sharp distinction between leaders and masses within the Independent Socialists. The masses were instinctively revolutionary. They showed that they were also objectively revolutionary by going on strike in munitions factories, by undermining efforts at the front and by a revolutionary enthusiasm which culminated in the January strike. For all that, they remained confused and hesitant; they let themselves be ensnared by the demagogy of their leaders. The latter were in part consciously counter-revolutionary (Kautsky, Bernstein and Hilferding) and worked objectively and expressly to preserve bourgeois rule, in collaboration with the old SPD leadership. Other leaders were subjectively sincere, but when it came to the crisis, they were unable to offer effective resistance to this sabotage of the revolution.

Notwithstanding their sincerity and their reluctance, they slipped into the wake of the right-wing leadership until their misgivings finally led to a split within the Independent Socialists and so to their destruction. The really revolutionary elements in the Independent Socialist Party were those who, after Halle,[11] pressed for the Party's dissolution and the repudiation of its ideology.

What then of the Expressionists? They were ideologues. They stood between leaders and masses. For the most part their convictions were sincerely held, though they were also mostly very immature and confused. They were deeply affected by the same uncertainties to which the immature revolutionary masses were also subject. In addition they were profoundly influenced by every conceivable reactionary prejudice of the age, and this made them more than susceptible to the widest possible range of anti-revolutionary slogans – abstract pacifism, ideology of non-violence, abstract critiques of the bourgeoisie, or all sorts of crazy anarchist notions. As ideologists, they stabilized both intellectually and artistically what was essentially a merely transitional ideological phase. From a revolutionary point of view, this phase was much more retrograde in many respects than the one in which the vacillating masses of Independent Socialists supporters found themselves. But the revolutionary significance of such phases of ideological transition lies precisely in their fluidity, in their forward movement, in the fact that they do not yield a crystallization. In this case stabilization meant that the Expressionists and those who were influenced by them were prevented from making further progress of a revolutionary kind. This negative effect, typical of every attempt to systematize ideological states of flux, received an especially reactionary colouring in the case of the Expressionists: firstly, because of the highflown pretensions to leadership, the sense of mission, which led them to proclaim eternal truths, particularly during the revolutionary years; secondly, because of the specifically anti-realist bias in Expressionism, which meant that they had no firm artistic hold on reality which might have corrected or neutralized their misconceptions. As we have seen, Expressionism insisted on the primacy of immediacy, and by conferring a pseudo-profundity and pseudo-perfection on immediate experience both in art and thought, it intensified the dangers which inevitably accompany all such attempts to stabilize an essentially transitional ideology.

Thus, to the extent that Expressionism really had any ideological

---

[11] At its Congress in Halle in 1920, the USPD voted by a majority to merge with the KPD.

influence, its effect was to discourage rather than to promote the process of revolutionary clarification among its followers. Here, too, there is a parallel with the ideology of the Independent Socialists. It is no coincidence that both came to grief on the same reality. It is an oversimplification for the Expressionists to claim that Expressionism was destroyed by Noske's victory. Expressionism collapsed, on the one hand, with the passing of the first wave of revolution, for the failure of which the ideology of the Independent Socialists must carry a heavy burden of responsibility. On the other hand, it suffered a loss of prestige from the growing clarity of the revolutionary consciousness of the masses who were beginning to advance with increasing confidence beyond the revolutionary catchwords from which they had started.

But Expressionism was not dethroned by the defeat of the first wave of revolution in Germany alone. The consolidation of the victory of the proletariat in the Soviet Union played an equally important role. As the proletariat gained a firmer control of the situation, as Socialism began to permeate more and more aspects of the Soviet economy, and as the cultural revolution gained wider and wider acceptance among the masses of the workers, so the art of the 'avant-garde' in the Soviet Union found itself gradually but inexorably forced back on to the defensive by an increasingly confident school of realism. So in the last analysis the defeat of Expressionism was a product of the maturity of the revolutionary masses. The careers of Soviet poets like Mayakovsky, or of Germans such as Becher, make it clear that this is where the true reasons for the demise of Expressionism have to be sought and found.

7.

Is our discussion purely literary? I think not. I do not believe that any conflict between literary trends and their theoretical justification would have had such reverberations or provoked such discussion were it not for the fact that, in its ultimate consequences, it was felt to involve a political problem that concerns us all and influences us all in equal measure: the problem of the Popular Front.

Bernhard Ziegler raised the issue of popular art in a very pointed manner. The excitement generated by this question is evident on all sides and such a vigorous interest is surely to be welcomed. Bloch, too, is concerned to salvage the popular element in Expressionism. He says: 'It is untrue that Expressionists were estranged from ordinary people by their overweening arrogance. Again, the opposite is the case. The *Blue Rider* imitated the stained glass at Murnau, and in fact was the first to open people's eyes to this moving and uncanny folk art. In the same way, it focused attention on the drawings of children and prisoners, on the disturbing works of the mentally sick, and on primitive art.' Such a view of popular art succeeds in confusing all the issues. Popular art does not imply an ideologically indiscriminate, 'arty' appreciation of 'primitive' products by connoisseurs. Truly popular art has nothing in common with any of that. For if it did, any swank who collects stained glass or negro sculpture, any snob who celebrates insanity as the emancipation of mankind from the fetters of the mechanistic mind, could claim to be a champion of popular art.

Today, of course, it is no easy matter to form a proper conception of popular art. The older ways of life of the people have been eroded economically by capitalism, and this has introduced a feeling of uncertainty into the world-view, the cultural aspirations, the taste and moral judgement of the people; it has created a situation in which people are exposed to the perversions of demagogy. Thus it is by no means always progressive simply to collect old folk products indiscriminately. Nor does such a rescue operation necessarily imply an appeal to the vital instincts of the people, which do remain progressive against all obstacles. Similarly, the fact that a literary work or a literary trend is greatly in vogue does not in itself guarantee that it is genuinely popular. Retrograde traditionalisms, such as regional art [*Heimatkunst*], and bad modern works, such as thrillers, have achieved mass circulation without being popular in any true sense of the word.

With all these reservations, however, it is still not unimportant to ask how much of the real literature of our time has reached the masses, and how deeply it has penetrated. But what 'modernist' writer of the last few decades can even begin to compare with Gorky, with Anatole France, Romain Rolland or Thomas Mann? That a work of such uncompromising artistic excellence as *Buddenbrooks* could be printed in millions of copies, must give all of us food for thought. The whole problem of popular art would, as old Briest in Fontane's novel used to say, 'lead us too far afield' for us to discuss it here. We shall confine ourselves therefore to two points, without pretending to an exhaustive treatment of either.

In the first place, there is the question of the cultural heritage. Wherever the cultural heritage has a living relationship to the real life of the people it is characterized by a dynamic, progressive movement in which the active creative forces of popular tradition, of the sufferings and joys of the people, of revolutionary legacies, are buoyed up, preserved, transcended and further developed. For a writer to possess a living relationship to the cultural heritage means being a son of the people, borne along by the current of the people's development. In this sense Maxim Gorky is a son of the Russian people, Romain Rolland a son of the French and Thomas Mann a son of the German people. For all their individuality and originality, for all their remoteness from an artiness which artificially collects and aestheticizes about the primitive, the tone and content of their writings grow out of the life and history of their people, they are an organic product of the development of their nation. That is why it is possible for them to create art of the highest quality while at the same time striking a chord which can and does evoke a response in the broad masses of the people.

The attitude of the modernists to the cultural heritage stands in sharp contrast to this. They regard the history of the people as a great jumble sale. If one leafs through the writings of Bloch, one will find him mentioning the topic only in expressions like 'useful legacies', 'plunder', and so on. Bloch is much too conscious a thinker and stylist for these to be mere slips of the pen. On the contrary, they are an index of his general attitude towards the cultural heritage. In his eyes it is a heap of lifeless objects in which one can rummage around at will, picking out whatever one happens to need at the moment. It is something to be taken apart and stuck together again in accordance with the exigencies of the moment.

Hanns Eisler has expressed the same attitude very clearly in an article he and Bloch wrote together. He was – rightly – highly enthusiastic about the *Don Carlos* demonstration in Berlin.[12] But instead of pondering what Schiller really represented, where his achievement and his limitations actually lay, what he has meant for the German people in the past and still means today, and what mountain of reactionary prejudices would have to be cleared away in order to forge the popular and progressive aspects of Schiller into a usable weapon for the Popular Front and for the emancipation of the German people – instead of all that, he merely puts forward the following programme for the benefit of writers in exile: 'What must our task be outside Germany? It is evident that it can only be for us all to help select and prepare classical material that is suitable for such a struggle.' Thus what Eisler proposes is to reduce the classics to an anthology and then to reassemble whatever 'material is suitable'. It would be impossible to conceive of a more alien, arrogant or negative attitude towards the glorious literary past of the German people.

[12] Hanns Eisler/Ernst Bloch: *Die Kunst zu erben*.

Objectively, however, the life of the people is a continuum. A theory like that of the modernists which sees revolutions only as ruptures and catastrophes that destroy all that is past and shatter all connection with the great and glorious past, is akin to the ideas of Cuvier,[13] not those of Marx and Lenin. It forms an anarchistic pendant to the evolutionary theories of reformism. The latter sees nothing but continuity, the former sees nothing but ruptures, fissures and catastrophes. History, however, is the living dialectical unity of continuity and discontinuity, of evolution and revolution.

Thus here, as everywhere, everything depends on a correct appreciation of content. Lenin puts the Marxist view of the cultural heritage in this way: 'Marxism attained its world-historical importance as the ideology of the revolutionary proletariat by virtue of its refusal to reject the most valuable achievements of the bourgeois era. Instead, it appropriated and assimilated all that was valuable in a tradition of human thought and human culture stretching back over 2000 years.' So everything depends on recognizing clearly where to look for what is truly of value.

If the question is correctly formulated, in the context of the life and the progressive tendencies of the people, then it will lead us organically to our second point: the question of realism. Modern theories of popular art, strongly influenced by avant-garde ideas, have pushed the sturdy realism of folk art very much into the background. On this issue, too, we cannot possibly discuss the entire problem in all its ramifications, so we shall confine our observations to one single, crucial point.

We are talking here to writers about literature. We must remind ourselves that owing to the tragic course of German history, the popular and realistic element in our literature is nothing like as powerful as in England, France or Russia. That very fact should spur us to attend all the more closely to the popular, realistic literature of the German past and to keep its vital, productive traditions alive. If we do so, we shall see that despite the whole 'German *misère*', popular, realistic literature produced such major masterpieces as the *Simplizissimus* of Grimmelshausen.[14] It may be left to the Eislers of this world to take the book to

---

[13] Georges Cuvier (1769–1832). According to his theory every geological era terminated in a catastrophe and every new one was brought about by an immigration and a re-creation. He rejected theories of evolution.

[14] H. J. Chr. von Grimmelshausen (*c*.1621–76). His picaresque novel, *The Adventures of a Simpleton* (1669) set in the Thirty Years' War is the major German literary work of the 17th century.

pieces and estimate their montage value; for the living tradition of German literature it will continue to survive intact in all its greatness, and with all its limitations.[15]

Only when the masterpieces of realism past and present are appreciated as *wholes*, will their topical, cultural and political value fully emerge. This value resides in their inexhaustible diversity, in contrast to the one-dimensionality of modernism. Cervantes and Shakespeare, Balzac and Tolstoy, Grimmelshausen and Gottfried Keller, Gorky, Thomas and Heinrich Mann – all these can appeal to readers drawn from a broad cross-section of the people because their works permit access from so many different angles. The large-scale, enduring resonance of the great works of realism is in fact due to this accessibility, to the infinite multitude of doors through which entry is possible. The wealth of the characterization, the profound and accurate grasp of constant and typical manifestations of human life is what produces the great progressive reverberation of these works. The process of appropriation enables readers to clarify their own experiences and understanding of life and to broaden their own horizons. A living form of humanism prepares them to endorse the political slogans of the Popular Front and to comprehend its political humanism. Through the mediation of realist literature the soul of the masses is made receptive for an understanding of the great, progressive and democratic epochs of human history. This will prepare it for the new type of revolutionary democracy that is represented by the

[15] The plural formulation 'It may be left to the Eislers . . .' provoked Brecht to write the following *Minor Correction:* 'In the debate on Expressionism in *Das Wort* something has happened in the heat of battle that stands in need of a minor correction. Lukács has been wiping the floor, so to speak, with my friend Eisler, who, incidentally, is hardly anyone's idea of a pale aesthete. It appears that Eisler has failed to exhibit the pious reverence towards the cultural heritage expected from the executors of a will. Instead he just rummaged around in it and declined to take everything into his possession. Well, it may be that, as an exile, he is not in a position to lug so much stuff around with him. However, perhaps I may be allowed a few comments on the formal aspects of the incident. Reference was made to "the Eislers", who were alleged to be doing, or not doing, something or other. In my opinion, the Lukácses ought to refrain from using such plurals when in fact there is only one Eisler among our musicians. The millions of white, yellow and black workers who have inherited the songs Eisler wrote for the masses will undoubtedly share my opinion here. But in addition there are all sorts of experts on music who think highly of Eisler's works, in which, so they tell me, he magnificently builds on and extends the cultural heritage of German music, and they would be very confused if the German émigrés should seek to outdo the seven cities of Greece, who quarrelled about which of them had produced a single Homer, by allowing themselves to start boasting that they had seven Eislers.' When the essay was revised for republication in book-form (Aufbau, Berlin 1948) Lukács rewrote the sentence to read 'It may be left to Eisler and Bloch . . .', while in vol. 4 *Probleme des Realismus*, Luchterhand 1971, we find: 'It may be left to Eisler . . .'.

Popular Front. The more deeply anti-Fascist literature is embedded in this soil, the better able it will be to create contrasting types of good and evil, models of what should be admired and what hated – and the greater will be its resonance among the people.

In contrast to this, it is but a very narrow doorway which leads to Joyce or the other representatives of avant-garde literature: one needs a certain 'knack' to see just what their game is. Whereas in the case of the major realists, easier access produces a richly complex yield in human terms, the broad mass of the people can learn nothing from avant-garde literature. Precisely because the latter is devoid of reality and life, it foists on to its readers a narrow and subjectivist attitude to life (analogous to a sectarian point of view in political terms). In realism, the wealth of created life provides answers to the questions put by the readers themselves – life supplies the answers to the questions put by life itself! The taxing struggle to understand the art of the 'avant-garde', on the other hand, yields such subjectivist distortions and travesties that ordinary people who try to translate these atmospheric echoes of reality back into the language of their own experience, find the task quite beyond them.

A vital relationship to the life of the people, a progressive development of the masses' own experiences – this is the great social mission of literature. In his early works Thomas Mann found much to criticize in the literature of Western Europe. It is no accident that his objections to the problematic nature and remoteness from life of many modern works were counter-balanced by his indication of an alternative creative ideal, in his description of the Russian literature of the nineteenth century as 'sacred'.[16] What he had in mind was this very same life-creating, popular progressiveness.

The Popular Front means a struggle for a genuine popular culture, a manifold relationship to every aspect of the life of one's own people as it has developed in its own individual way in the course of history. It means finding the guidelines and slogans which can emerge out of this life of the people and rouse progressive forces to new, politically effective activity. To understand the historical identity of the people does not of course, imply an uncritical attitude towards one's own history – on the contrary, such criticism is the necessary consequence of real insight into one's own history. For no people, and the Germans least of all, has succeeded in establishing progressive democratic forces in a perfect

---

[16] Lukács is evidently referring to the celebrated discussion on the value of literature in *Tonio Kröger*.

form and without any setbacks. Criticism must be based, however, on an accurate and profound understanding of the realities of history. Since it was the age of imperialism which created the most serious obstacles to progress and democracy in the spheres of both politics and culture, a trenchant analysis of the decadent manifestations of this period – political, cultural and artistic – is an essential prerequisite for any breakthrough to a genuinely popular culture. A campaign against realism, whether conscious or not, and a resultant impoverishment and isolation of literature and art is one of the crucial manifestations of decadence in the realm of art.

In the course of our remarks we have seen that we should not simply accept this decline fatalistically. Vital forces which combat this decadence not just politically and theoretically, but also with all the instruments at the disposal of art, have made and continue to make themselves felt. The task that faces us is to lend them our support. They are to be found in a realism which has true depth and significance.

Writers in exile, together with the struggles of the Popular Front in Germany and other countries, have inevitably strengthened these positive forces. It might be thought sufficient to point to Heinrich and Thomas Mann, who, starting from different assumptions, have steadily grown in stature in recent years both as writers and thinkers. But we are concerned here with a broad trend in anti-Fascist literature. We need only compare Feuchtwanger's *Sons* with his *History of the Jewish Wars* to see the strenuous efforts he is making to overcome the subjectivist tendencies which distanced him from the masses, and to assimilate and formulate the real problems of ordinary people. Just a short while ago Alfred Döblin gave a talk in the Paris SDS[17] in which he declared his commitment to the historical and political relevance of literature and in which he saw a realism of the kind practised by Gorky as exemplary – an event of no little importance for the future course of our literature. In the third number of *Das Wort*, Brecht published a one-act playlet (*The Informer*)[18] in which he turns to what is for him a novel, highly differen-

[17] SDS – *Der Schutzvergand deutscher Schriftsteller* (Association for the Protection of the Rights of German Authors) where Döblin gave an important lecture *Die deutsche Literatur (im Ausland seit 1933)* in January 1938.

[18] A scene from *Furcht und Elend des dritten Reichs*, trans. by Eric Bentley as *The Private Life of the Master Race*. Brecht's reaction to Lukács's praise has been recorded in his *Arbeitsjournal* (vol. I, p. 22): 'Lukács has welcomed *The Informer* as if I were a sinner returning to the bosom of the Salvation Army. At last something taken from life itself! He has overlooked the montage of 27 scenes and the fact that it is really no more than a catalogue of gestures, such as the gesture of falling silent, of looking over one's shoulder, of terror, etc.; in short, the gestures of life under a dictatorship'.

tiated and subtle form of realism as a weapon in the struggle against the inhumanity of Fascism. By depicting the fates of actual human beings, he provides a vivid image of the horrors of the Fascist reign of terror in Germany. He shows how Fascism destroys the entire foundations of the human community, how it destroys the trust between husbands, wives and children, and how in its inhumanity it actually undermines and annihilates the family, the very institution it claims to protect. Along with Feuchtwanger, Döblin and Brecht one could name a whole series of writers – the most important and the most talented we have – who have adopted a similar strategy, or are beginning to do so.

But this does not mean that the struggle to overcome the anti-realist traditions of the era of imperialism is over. Our present debate shows, on the contrary, that these traditions are still deeply rooted in important and loyal supporters of the Popular Front whose political views are unquestionably progressive. This is why such a forthright but comradely discussion was of such vital importance. For it is not just the masses who learn through their own experiences in the class-struggle; ideologists, writers and critics, have to learn too. It would be a grave error to overlook that growing trend towards realism which has emerged from the experiences of fighters in the Popular Front and which has even affected writers who favoured a very different approach before their emigration.

To make this very point, to reveal some of the intimate, varied and complex bonds which link the Popular Front, popular literature and authentic realism, is the task I have set out to accomplish in these pages.

Translated by Rodney Livingstone

Presentation II

The general literary canons of Georg Lukács are by now relatively well-known in the English-speaking world. Translations of his most important theoretical essays of the thirties have still, however, to be published. It was during this decade that Lukács, having abandoned political responsibilities in the Hungarian Communist Party, turned to aesthetic writings and gradually acquired a commanding position as a critic within the ranks of the German literary left. His debut in this role occurred in the Third Period phase of the Comintern, as a contributor to *Linkskurve*, the organ of the *Bund Proletarisch-Revolutionärer Schriftsteller* (BPRS) or Association of Proletarian Revolutionary Writers, created by the KPD in late 1928. Lukács first distinguished himself in *Linkskurve* by mordant attacks on novels by Willi Bredel, a worker-writer who had been a turner in the engineering industry, and Ernst Ottwalt, a close associate and collaborator of Brecht, for what he alleged was the substitution of journalistic 'reportage' for classical 'creation of characters' in their fiction.[1] Brecht himself, together with the Soviet writer Tretyakov, was expressly linked to the negative trend exemplified by these writers, and his conception of an objectivist 'anti-aristotelian' theatre repudiated. After the Nazi seizure of power in Germany, and the switch of the Third International to Popular Front policies against fascism, Lukács's literary views became increasingly influential in the official organs of the German Communist emigration, where they could be used as an aesthetic counterpoint to political attacks on 'leftism' within the intelligentsia and the workers' movement.[2] In exile, Lukács's next

[1] See 'Willi Bredels Romane' in *Linkskurve*, November 1931, and 'Reportage oder Gestaltung? Kritische Bemerkungen anlässlich eines Romans von Ottwalt' in *Linkskurve*, July–August 1932, followed by a reply by Ottwalt and a concluding rejoinder by Lukács in subsequent issues. Ottwalt co-scripted the film *Kuhle Wampe* with Brecht in the same year.

[2] Since the Second World War, it has often been alleged that Lukács's critical views can be seen essentially as a cultural justification or derivative of the Popular Front. While there is no doubt that they were to be politically instrumentalized as such, it is emphatically not

target was the legacy of expressionism in German literature, which he vigorously belaboured in the journal *Internationale Literatur* in January 1934, in an essay entitled '*Grosse und Verfall des Expressionismus*'. Brecht, like many other German writers of his generation, had of course started his career as a para-expressionist himself, in his plays of the early twenties. Lukács had thus assailed, in reverse order, both the two main phases of his own artistic development. Two years later, Lukács published his richest and most seminal essay of the period, *Erzählen oder Beschreiben?*. In this text, he set out the main categories and principles of the doctrine of literary realism that he was to maintain for the rest of his life: the reiterated antithesis between naturalism and realism, the notion of the typical character as a nexus of the social and individual, the rejection of both external reportage and internal psychologism, the distinction between passive description and active narrative, the extolment of Balzac and Tolstoy as classical models for the contemporary novel. Those modern artists who ignored or contravened these regulative norms of literary creation were insistently pilloried for 'formalism' by Lukács.

Brecht, the greatest German writer to have emerged in the Weimar epoch, and a fellow Marxist, evidently came to feel an increasing pressure and isolation as Lukács's precepts, ably articulated in the USSR itself (where Lukács had moved in 1933) and seconded by lesser associates like Kurella, acquired more and more official authority within the ambience of the Comintern. Benjamin, recording his conversations with Brecht in Denmark in 1938, noted: 'The publications of Lukács, Kurella *et al* are giving Brecht a good deal of trouble'.[3] Nominally, Brecht was

the case that they represented an *ex post facto* adaptation of his convictions on Lukács's part. On the contrary, having abandoned political for literary work in 1929 precisely because of his opposition to the sectarian policies of the Third Period, he anticipated Popular Front orientations in his new field by at least three years. This was paradoxically possible at the height of the KPD's rabid campaigns against 'social-fascism', because of the protection in 1931–2 of Heinz Neumann and Willi Munzenberg, who sought to use the cultural apparatus of the party more flexibly than its mainline political strategy warranted, and covered Lukács's literary flanks in *Linkskurve*. (For the complex history of this conjuncture in the BPRS, see Helga Gallas, *Marxistische Literatur-theorie*, Neuwied/Berlin 1971, esp. pp. 60, 68–9, 200). After the Nazi seizure of power, Lukács's attack on expressionism still predated the adoption of the Popular Front turn by some months. The advent of the new policy in mid-1934, which finally synchronized Lukács's evolution with that of the Comintern, at most affected the tactical trimmings of his pronouncements. The substance of his aesthetic positions had been arrived at by an original and independent route much earlier.

[3] See below, 'Conversations with Brecht', p. 95. It should be remembered, in assessing this episode, that Lukács had been an official and senior Communist militant in the International for nearly two decades, while Brecht's convergence with the KPD was relatively recent and had not led to formal party membership.

himself one of the three co-editors of the emigré front journal *Das Wort*, published in Moscow between 1936 and 1939; his two colleagues being Willi Bredel and Leon Feuchtwanger. In fact, his name was used for prestige reasons on the mast-head, and he had no say in its policy from his own exile in Svendborg. During 1938 however, besides giving vent to his feelings in violent objurgations in his private diaries, he wrote a series of trenchant and sardonic counter-attacks against Lukács, designed as public interventions in *Das Wort* – where a major debate was meanwhile still raging over the issue of expressionism, whose merits had been defended by, among others, Ernst Bloch and Hanns Eisler. The four most important of these texts written by Brecht, entitled respectively *Die Essays von Georg Lukács* (I), *Über den formalistischen Charakter der Realismustheorie* (II), *Bermerkungen zu einem Aufsatz* (III), and *Volkstümlichkeit und Realismus* (IV), are translated below. None of them were ever published in *Das Wort*, or anywhere else, in Brecht's life-time. Whether Brecht submitted them to *Das Wort* in Moscow and they were rejected, or whether his own characteristic tactical prudence dissuaded him from ever sending them, still remains unclear. Benjamin, to whom he read some of the texts, reports that: 'He asked my advice whether to publish them. As, at the same time, he told me that Lukács's position "over there" is at the moment very strong, I told him I could offer no advice. "There are questions of power involved. You ought to get the opinion of someone from over there. You've got friends there haven't you?" – Brecht: "Actually, no, I haven't. Neither have the Muscovites themselves – like the dead."'[4] At the height of the Great Terror, Brecht may well have himself decided against any release of these articles. In the event, they first came to light in 1967, with the posthumous publication of Suhrkamp Verlag's edition of his *Schriften zur Kunst und Literatur* in West Germany.

Brecht's polemic against Lukács, while avoiding overly frequent invocations of his name after the first text, was in no way defensive in tone. On the contrary, it was caustic and aggressive, mustering a wide range of arguments designed to demolish the whole tenor of Lukács's aesthetic. To start with, Brecht fastened on the manifest contradiction between Lukács's view of the great European realists of the 19th century as essentially bourgeois writers, and his claim that their literary achievements should serve as a guide to proletarian or socialist writers in the 20th century: for if the novels of Balzac or Tolstoy were determinate

[4] See below, pp. 97–8.

products of a particular phase of class history, now superseded, how could any Marxist argue that the principles of their fiction could be recreated in a subsequent phase of history, dominated by the struggles of another and antagonistic class? The social reality of capitalism had undergone radical modifications in the 20th century, and necessarily no longer produced historical forms of individuality of the Balzacian or Tolstoyan type – hence to refurbish such figures in new conditions would actually be a signal flight from realism. The position of women in the contemporary USA, for example, let alone the USSR, structurally precluded the peculiar pattern of conflicting passions typical of Balzac. Conversely, where Lukács charged 'modernist' writing with formalism because of its use of such fragmented techniques as interior monologue or montage, it was actually Lukács himself who had fallen into a deluded and timeless formalism, by attempting to deduce norms for prose purely from literary traditions, without regard for the historical reality that encompasses and transforms all literature in its own processes of change. True realism, of which Brecht considered himself to be a staunch champion and practitioner, was not merely an aesthetic optic: it was a political and philosophical vision of the world and the material struggles that divided it. At the same time, Brecht pointed out the extremely narrow range of literature in terms of which Lukács's theory was con- structed, even within the aesthetic field itself – its overwhelming pre- occupation with the novel, to the exclusion of poetry or drama. The omitted genres were, of course, those in which Brecht himself excelled. More generally, many of the most radical innovations within German culture after 1918 had been first developed in the theatre. Brecht stressed the indispensable need for experimentation in the arts, and the necessary freedom of the artist to be allowed to fail, or only partially to succeed, as the price of the invention of new aesthetic devices in any transitional epoch of history. Interior monologue, montage, or mixture of genres within a single work were all permissible and fruitful, so long as they were disciplined by a watchful truthfulness to social reality. Fertility of technique was not the mark of a 'mechanical' improverishment of art, but a sign of energy and liberty. The fear that technical novelties as such tended to render works of art alien or incomprehensible to the masses, moreover, was a fundamental error. Tartly reminding Lukács that working-class readers might often find notable *longueurs* in the leisurely narratives of Balzac or Tolstoy, Brecht invoked his own experience as a playwright as evidence that proletarian audiences and participants welcomed experimental audacity on the stage, and were generous rather than censorious towards artistic excesses, where these were committed. By contrast, any fixed or inherited concept of 'popular art' (*Volkstümlichkeit*) was contaminated by notoriously reactionary traditions, especially in Germany. To reach the exploited classes in the tempestuous era of their final struggle with their exploiters, art had to change together with their own revolutionary change of the world and of themselves.

The legitimacy and stringency of Brecht's riposte to Lukács in the oblique polemic between the two, are plain and tonic. Brecht's positions have, in fact, won very wide assent on the Marxist Left in West Germany since the recent publication of his texts, on the eve of the political rebirth of 1968. Few critiques of Lukács's aesthetic theory have been so tersely effective in their own terms. Brecht's diagnosis of the insurmountable anomalies and contradictions of his adversary's recommendations for contemporary art remains largely unanswerable. Moreover, perhaps no other Marxist writer has defended (and illustrated) so forcefully – because soberly – the basic necessity for constant freedom of artistic experiment in the socialist movement. The intensity of Brecht's feelings about the dangers to his own work latent in the generic strictures of Lukács and his colleagues in Moscow against formalism, can be judged from his outburst to Benjamin: 'They are, to put it bluntly, enemies of production. Production makes them uncomfortable. You never know where you are with production; production is the unforeseeable. You never know what's going to come out. And they themselves don't want to produce. They want to play the *apparatchik* and exercise control over other people. Every one of their criticisms contains a threat.'[5] This reaction of the artist to the critic, as practioner to spectator, confers much of its strength on Brecht's case. At the same time, it also indicates its limitations as a negative *fin de non recevoir*. For while Brecht was able to single out the weaknesses and paradoxes of Lukács's literary theory, he was not capable of advancing any positive alternative to it, on the same plane. For all its narrowness and rigidity, Lukács's work represented a real attempt to construct a systematic Marxist account of the historical development of European literature from the Enlightenment onwards. The precepts for 20th-century art with which it concluded were often nostalgic or retrograde; but analytically it was far more serious in its attention to the past, as the precondition of the present, than anything Brecht was to assay. Brechtian aesthetic maxims always remained pro-

[5] Below, p. 97.

gramme notes for his own productions. A remarkable achievement in its own way, even his doctrine of the theatre was essentially an expeditious apology for his particular practice, rather than a genuine explanatory typology of universal drama. Brecht's precepts were far more emancipated than those of Lukács, but his theoretical reach was much shallower. The great vices of Lukács's system were its consistent Europocentrism, and its arbitrary selectivity within the diverse strands of European literature itself – in other words, it suffered from too little history. Brecht was not in a position to correct these defects: his own attitude to the European past was at best empirical and eclectic (random borrowings, rather than repressive traditions), while his sporadic enthusiasm for Asian cultures was superficial and mythopoeic.[6] Tendencies to axe contemporary aesthetic debates within Marxism too centrally along the contrast between Brecht and Lukács, such as have currently developed in West Germany, overlook certain limits that in different ways they shared. In their own time, Lukács's aversion to Joyce, Brecht's to Mann, are suggestive of the divisions between them. But their common denunciation of Dostoevsky or Kafka is a reminder of the political and cultural bonds that made them interlocutors as well as antagonists in the thirties.

This degree of affinity can be seen most clearly by comparison with the two other outstanding German Marxists concerned with literature in the same period, Benjamin and Adorno.[7] Both the latter, of course, assigned pivotal importance to the work of Kafka, not to speak of Mallarmé or Proust. At the same time, there is a curious symmetry between the relationships of Benjamin to Adorno and Brecht to Lukács. With the Nazi consolidation of power, the German emigration had dispersed in opposite directions. By 1938, Lukács was institutionally installed in the USSR, Adorno was similarly established in the USA; Brecht remained solitary in Denmark, Benjamin in France. The personal, perhaps political, friendship between Brecht and Benjamin was much closer than their official relationships with Lukács or Adorno. Nevertheless, the main intellectual field of tension for both lay with their symbolically distributed correspondents in Moscow and New

[6] His uncritical cult of the Chinese philosophers Mo Ti (see his *Buch der Wendungen*) and Confucius (to whom he dedicated a projected play), as repositories of Oriental wisdom, are examples. The virulent campaigns recently orchestrated against Confucius in China cast an ironic light on Brecht's predilection for the latter. Needless to say, neither attitude towards Confucius has anything in common with historical materialism.

[7] See the important correspondence between Adorno and Benjamin, printed below, pp. 110–141.

York, respectively. From each of these capitals, theoretical challenges were made to the two men, which engaged the whole direction of their work. In both cases, the ideological interpellation was not exempt from institutional pressures, but was never reducible to the latter.[8] The organizational co-ordinates of the Communist movement created a common space between Lukács and Brecht, as the more impalpable ambience of the Institute of Social Research linked Benjamin to Adorno; but ultimately Adorno's criticisms of Benjamin and Lukács's of Brecht acquired their force because of their degree of cogency and proximity of concern to the work at which they were directed. It is noticeable that the 'Western' debate reproduced the same dual problematic as its 'Eastern' counterpart: a dispute over both the art of the historical past of the 19th century, and the present aims and conditions of aesthetic practice in the 20th century. Consonant with Brecht's desire to broaden Marxist literary theory beyond the novel, the prime object of the Adorno–Benjamin exchange was the poetry of Baudelaire. At the same time, whereas the clash between Lukács and Brecht over contemporary issues involved opposed conceptions of what socialist works of art should be within a framework of declared political militancy, the dispute between Benjamin and Adorno over modern cultural practice had different parameters: it was concerned with the relations between 'avant-garde' and 'commercial' art under the dominion of capital. The continuity and intractability of this problem has made it a central focus of aesthetic controversy on the left ever since, where the contradiction between 'high' and 'low' genres – the one subjectively progressive and objectively elitist, the other objectively popular and subjectively regressive – has never been durably overcome, despite a complex, crippled dialectic between the two. Against this history, Brecht's art retrospectively acquires a unique relief. For his theatre represents perhaps the only major body of art produced after the Russian Revolution to be uncompromisingly advanced in form, yet intransigently popular in intention. The most important of Brecht's claims in his polemic with Lukács was his assertion that his own plays found a vital resonance within the German working-class itself. The extent of the validity of this claim needs some scrutiny. Brecht's biggest successes in the Weimar period – above all,

[8] The coincidence of dates is striking. Brecht's remarks to Benjamin about the implications of Lukács's criticisms, cited above, were made in July 1938. Benjamin received the fateful comments from Adorno on his Baudelaire study on his return to Paris a few months later, in November. However, it should always be remembered that, although potential sanctions lay in the background of their interventions, neither Adorno nor Lukács were themselves at all secure in their own contrasted asylums.

The Threepenny Opera – enjoyed a large bourgeois audience, in ordinary commercial theatres. His fuller conversion to Marxism post-dated them. His greatest plays were then written during exile and war without any contact with a German audience of any kind (*Mother Courage*: 1939; *Galileo Galilei*: 1939; *Puntila*: 1941; *The Caucasian Chalk Circle*: 1944–5). When they were finally staged in East Germany after the War, their audiences were certainly in the main proletarian, but since alternative entertainments (to use a Brechtian term) were not widely available in the DDR, the spontaneity and reality of working-class responses to the Berliner Ensemble remain difficult to estimate. But that the overall structure of Brecht's dramaturgy was always potentially lucid and comprehensible to the spectators for whom it was designed, cannot be doubted. The magnitude of this achievement is suggested by its very isolation. After the Second World War, despite a plethora of socialist writers, no comparable work was produced anywhere in Europe; while in the West, the ascent of Beckett (critically consecrated by Adorno) as a new avatar of 'high' art, was actually to provoke Brecht to plan a play deliberately intended as an antidote to *Godot*. The fragility of Brecht's synthesis, already evidenced in this episode shortly before his death, has only been confirmed by aesthetic developments since. The collapse of the cinema of Jean-Luc Godard, in many ways the most brilliant and ambitious revolutionary artist of the last decade, when it attempted a political turn and ascesis not unlike that effected by Brecht's theatre in the thirties, is the most recent and eloquent testimony to the implacable antinomies of cultural innovation in the imperialist world. Brecht's example marks a frontier that has not been passed, or even reached again, by his successors.

Bertolt Brecht

Against Georg Lukács

I

[The Essays of Georg Lukács]

I have occasionally wondered why certain essays by Georg Lukács, although they contain so much valuable material, nevertheless have something unsatisfying about them. He starts from a sound principle, and yet one cannot help feeling that he is somewhat remote from reality. He investigates the decline of the bourgeois novel from the heights it occupied when the bourgeoisie was still a progressive class. However courteous he is in his treatment of contemporary novelists, in so far as they follow the example of the classic models of the bourgeois novel and write in at least a formally realistic manner, he cannot help seeing in them too a process of decline. He is quite unable to find in them a realism equal to that of the classical novelists in depth, breadth and attack. But how could they be expected to rise above their class in this respect? They inevitably testify, too, to a decay in the technique of the novel. There is plenty of technical skill; it is merely that technique has acquired a curious technicality – a kind of tyranny if you like. A formalistic quality insinuates itself even into realistic types of construction on the classical model.

Some of the details here are curious. Even those writers who are conscious of the fact that capitalism impoverishes, dehumanizes, mechanizes human beings, and who fight against it, seem to be part of the same process of impoverishment: for they too, in their writing, appear to be less concerned with elevating man, they rush him through events, treat his inner life as a *quantité négligeable* and so on. They too rationalize, as it were. They fall into line with the 'progress' of physics. They abandon strict causality and switch to statistical causality, by abandoning the individual man as a causal nexus and making statements only about large groups. They even – in their own way – adopt Schrödinger's uncertainty principle. They deprive the observer of his authority and credit and mobilize the reader against himself, advancing purely subjective propositions, which actually characterize only those who make them (Gide, Joyce, Döblin).[1] One can follow Lukács in all these observations and subscribe to his protests.

But then we come to the positive and constructive postulates of Lukács's conception. With a wave of his hand he sweeps away 'inhuman' technique. He turns back to our forefathers and implores their degenerate descendants to emulate them. Are writers confronted by a dehumanized man? Has his spiritual life been devastated? Is he driven through existence at an intolerable pace? Have his logical capacities been weakened? Is the connection between things no longer so visible? Writers just have to keep to the Old Masters, produce a rich life of the spirit, hold back the pace of events by a slow narrative, bring the individual back to the centre of the stage, and so on. Here specific instructions dwindle into an indistinct murmur. That his proposals are impracticable is obvious. No one who believes Lukács's basic principle to be correct, can be surprised at this. Is there no solution then? There is. The new ascendant class shows it. It is not a way back. It is not linked to the good old days but to the bad new ones. It does not involve undoing techniques but developing them. Man does not become man again by stepping out of the masses but by stepping back into them. The masses shed their dehumanization and thereby men become men again – but not the same men as before. This is the path that literature must take in outrage when the masses are beginning to attract to themselves everything that is valuable and human, when they are mobilizing people against the dehumanization produced by capitalism in its fascist phase. It is the element of capitulation, of withdrawal, of utopian idealism which still lurks in Lukács's essays and which he will undoubtedly overcome, that makes his work, which otherwise contains so much of value, unsatisfactory; for it gives the impression that what concerns him is enjoyment rather than struggle, a way of escape rather than an advance.

[1] Alfred Döblin (1878–1957): German novelist and exponent both of Expressionism and *Neue Sachlichkeit* (Neo-Objectivity). His major work was *Berlin Alexanderplatz* (1929), written under the influence of Joyce and Dos Passos.

II

On the Formalistic Character of the Theory of Realism

The formalistic nature of the theory of realism is demonstrated by the fact that not only is it exclusively based on the form of a few bourgeois novels of the previous century (more recent novels are merely cited in so far as they exemplify the same form), but also exclusively on the particular genre of the *novel*. But what about realism in lyric poetry, or in drama? These are two literary genres which – specially in Germany – have achieved a high standard.

I shall continue in a personal vein so as to provide concrete material for my argument. My activity is, as I see it myself, much more diverse than our theorists of realism believe. They give a totally one-sided picture of me. At the present time I am working on two novels, a play and a collection of poems. One of the novels is historical and requires extensive research in the field of Roman history. It is satirical. Now the novel is the chosen sphere of our theorists. But I am not being malicious if I say that I am unable to get the smallest tip from them for my work on this novel: *The Business Affairs of Herr Julius Caesar*. The procedure, taken over by 19th century novelists from the drama, of massing all manner of personal conflicts in long, expensive drawing-room scenes, is of no use to me. For large sections I use the diary form. It has proved necessary for me to change the point of view for other sections. The montage of the points of view of the two fictitious authors incorporates my point of view. I suppose that this sort of thing ought not to have proved necessary. Somehow it does not fit the intended pattern. But this technique has proved to be necessary for a firm grasp of reality, and I had purely realistic motives in adopting it. My play, on the other hand, is a cycle of scenes which deals with life under the Nazis. So far I have written 27 separate scenes. Some of them fit roughly into the 'realistic' pattern X, if one shuts one eye. Others don't – absurdly enough, because they are very short. The whole work doesn't fit into it at all. I consider it to be a realistic play. I learnt more for it from the paintings of the peasant Breughel than from treatises on realism.

I scarcely dare to speak about the second novel, on which I have been working for a long time, so complicated are the problems involved and so primitive is the vocabulary which the aesthetic of realism – in its present state – offers me. The formal difficulties are enormous; I have constantly to construct models. Anyone who saw me at work would think I was only interested in questions of form. I make these models because I wish to represent reality. As far as my lyric poetry goes, there too I take a realistic point of view. But I feel that one would have to proceed with extreme caution if one wished to write about it. On the other hand, there would be a great deal to be learnt about realism in the novel and drama.

While I am looking through a stack of historical tomes (they are written in four languages, in addition to translations from two ancient languages) and attempting, full of scepticism, to verify a particular fact, rubbing the sand from my eyes the whole time, so to speak, I have vague notions of colours at the back of my mind, impressions of particular seasons of the year; I hear inflections without words, see gestures without meaning, think of desirable groupings of unnamed figures, and so on. The images are extremely undefined, in no way exciting, rather superficial, or so it seems to me. But they are there. The 'formalist' in me is at work. As the significance of Clodius's Funeral-Benefit Associations slowly dawns on me and I experience a certain pleasure in the discovery, I think: 'If one could only write a very long, transparent, autumnal, crystal-clear chapter with an irregular curve, a kind of red wave-form running through it! The City puts its democrat Cicero into the consulate; he bans the armed democratic street clubs; they turn into peaceful Funeral-Benefit Associations; the leaves are golden in the autumn. An unemployed man's funeral costs ten dollars; you pay a subscription; if you are too long in dying, it is a bad bargain. But we have the wave-form; sometimes weapons suddenly appear in these Associations; Cicero is driven from the city; he has losses; his villa is burnt down; it costs millions; how many? Let us look it up – no – it's not relevant here. Where were the street clubs on 9 November 91 BC? 'Gentlemen, I cannot give any guarantees' (Caesar).

I am at an early stage of my work.

Since the artist is constantly occupied with formal matters, since he constantly forms, one must define what one means by *formalism* carefully and practically, otherwise one conveys nothing to the artist. If one wants to call everything that makes works of art unrealistic *formalism*, then – if there is to be any mutual understanding – one must not construct the concept of formalism in purely aesthetic terms. Formalism on the one side – contentism on the other. That is surely too primitive and metaphysical. Looked at purely in terms of aesthetics, the concept presents no special difficulties. For instance if someone makes a statement which is untrue – or irrelevant – merely because it rhymes, then he is a formalist. But we have innumerable works of an unrealistic kind which did not become so because they were based on an excessive sense of form.

We can remain entirely comprehensible and yet give the concept a further, more productive, more practical meaning. We have only to look aside from literature for a moment and descend into 'everyday life'. What is formalism there? Let us take the expression: *Formally he is right*. That means that actually he is not right, but he is right according to the form of things and only according to this form. Or: *Formally the task is solved* means that actually it is not solved. Or: *I did it to preserve the form*. That means that what I did is not very important; I do what I want to do, but I preserve outward forms and in this way I can best do what I want. When I read that the autarky of the Third Reich is perfect *on paper*, then I know that this is a case of political formalism. National Socialism is socialism in form – another case of political formalism. We are not dealing with an excessive sense of form.

If we define the concept in this way, it becomes both comprehensible and important. We are then in a position, if we return to literature (without this time abandoning everyday life altogether), to characterize and unmask as formalistic even works which do not elevate literary form over social content and yet do not correspond to reality. We can even unmask works which are realistic in form. There are a great many of them.

By giving the concept of formalism this meaning, we acquire a yardstick for dealing with such phenomena as the *avant-garde*. For a vanguard can lead the way along a retreat or into an abyss. It can march so far ahead that the main army cannot follow it, because it is lost from sight and so on. Thus its unrealistic character can become evident. If it splits off from the main body, we can determine why and by what means it can reunite with it. *Naturalism* and a certain type of *anarchistic montage* can be confronted with their social effects, by demonstrating that they merely reflect the symptoms of the surface of things and not the deeper causal complexes of society. Whole tracts of literature which seem, judging by their form, to be radical, can be shown to be purely reformist, merely formal efforts which supply solutions *on paper*.

Such a definition of formalism also helps the writing of novels, lyric poetry and drama, and – last but not least – it does away once and for all with a certain formalistic style of criticism which appears to be interested only in the formal, which is dedicated to particular forms of writing, confined to one period, and attempts to solve problems of literary creation, even when it 'builds in' occasional glances at the historical past, in purely literary terms.

In Joyce's great satirical novel, *Ulysses*, there is – besides the use of various styles of writing and other unusual features – the so-called interior monologue. A petty-bourgeois woman lies in bed in the morning and meditates. Her thoughts are reproduced disconnectedly, criss-crossing, flowing into each other. This chapter could hardly have been written but for Freud. The attacks which it drew upon its author were the same as Freud in his day suffered. They rained down: pornography, morbid pleasure in filth, overestimation of events below the navel, immorality and so on. Astonishingly, some Marxists associated themselves with this nonsense, adding in their revulsion the epithet of petty-bourgeois. As a technical method the interior monologue was equally rejected; it was said to be *formalistic*. I have never understood the reason. The fact that Tolstoy would have done it differently is no reason to reject Joyce's method. The criticisms were so superficially formulated that one gained the impression that if Joyce had only set his monologue in a session with a psycho-analyst, everything would have been all right. Now the interior monologue is a method which is very difficult to use, and it is very useful to stress this fact. Without very precise measures (again of a technical sort) the interior monologue by no means reproduces reality, that is to say the totality of thought or association, as it super-ficially appears to do. It becomes another case of *only formally*, of which we should take heed – a falsification of reality. This is not a mere formal problem that could be solved by the slogan 'Back to Tolstoy'. In purely formal terms we did once have an interior monologue, which we actually prized very highly. I am thinking of Tucholsky.[2]

For many people to recall expressionism is to be reminded of a creed of libertarian sentiments. I myself was also at that time against 'self-expression' as a vocation. (See the instructions for actors in my *Versuche*.) I was sceptical of those painful, disturbing accidents in which someone was found to be 'beside himself'. What does this position feel like? It was very soon evident that such people had merely freed themselves from grammar, not from capitalism. Hašek won the highest honours for *Schweik*. But I believe that acts of liberation should also always be taken seriously. Today many people are still reluctant to see wholesale assaults

[2] Kurt Tucholsky (1890–1938): radical publicist and novelist of the Weimar period, and editor of *Die Weltbühne*.

on expressionism because they are afraid that acts of liberation are being suppressed for their own sake – self-liberation from constricting rules, old regulations which have become fetters; that the aim of such attacks is to preserve methods of description which suited land-owners even after land-owners themselves have been swept aside. To take an example from politics; if you want to counter putsches, you must teach revolution, not evolution.

Literature, to be understood, must be considered in its development, by which I do not mean self-development. Experimental phases can then be noted, in which an often almost unbearable narrowing of perspective occurs, one-sided or rather few-sided products emerge, and the applicability of results becomes problematic. There are experiments which come to nothing and experiments which bear late fruits or paltry fruits. One sees artists who sink under the burden of their materials – conscientious people who see the magnitude of the task, do not shirk it, but are inadequate for it. They do not always perceive their own errors; sometimes others see the errors at the same time as the problems. Some of them become wholly absorbed in specific questions – but not all of these are busy trying to square the circle. The world has reason to be impatient with these people and it makes abundant use of this right. But it also has reason to show patience towards them.

In art there is the fact of failure, and the fact of partial success. Our metaphysicians must understand this. Works of art can fail so easily; it is so difficult for them to succeed. One man will fall silent because of lack of feeling; another, because his emotion chokes him. A third frees himself, not from the burden that weighs on him, but only from a feeling of unfreedom. A fourth breaks his tools because they have too long been used to exploit him. The world is not obliged to be sentimental. Defeats should be acknowledged; but one should not conclude from them that there should be no more struggles.

For me, expressionism is not merely an 'embarrassing business', not merely a deviation. Why? Because I do not by any means consider it to be merely a 'phenomenon' and stick a label on it. Realists who are willing to learn and look for the practical side of things could learn a great deal from it. For them, there was a lode to be exploited in Kaiser, Sternberg, Toller and Goering.[3] Frankly I myself learn more easily where problems similar to my own are tackled. Not to beat about the bush, I learn with more difficulty (less) from Tolstoy and Balzac. They had to master

[3] Georg Kaiser, Leo Sternberg, Ernst Toller and Reinhard Goering were all expressionist playwrights and authors of the immediate post-World War One period.

other problems. Besides – if I may be allowed to use the expression – much of them has become part of my flesh and blood. Naturally I admire these people and the way in which they dealt with their tasks. One can learn from them too. But it is advisable not to approach them singly, but alongside other authors with other tasks, such as Swift and Voltaire. The diversity of aims then becomes clear, and we can more easily make the necessary abstractions and approach them from the standpoint of our own problems.

The questions confronting our politically engaged literature have had the effect of making one particular problem very actual – the jump from one kind of style to another within the same work of art. This happened in a very practical way. Political and philosophical considerations failed to shape the whole structure, the message was mechanically fitted into the plot. The 'editorial' was usually 'inartistically' conceived – so patently that the inartistic nature of the plot in which it was embedded, was overlooked. (Plots were in any case regarded as more artistic than editorials.) There was a complete rift. In practice there were two possible solutions. The editorial could be dissolved in the plot or the plot in the editorial, lending the latter artistic form. But the plot could be shaped artistically and the editorial too (it then naturally lost its editorial quality), while keeping the jump from one idiom to another and giving it an artistic form. Such a solution seemed an innovation. But if one wishes, one can mention earlier models whose artistic quality is beyond dispute, such as the interruption of the action by choruses in the Attic theatre. The Chinese theatre contains similar forms.

The issue of how many allusions one needs in descriptions, of what is too plastic and what not plastic enough, can be dealt with practically from case to case. In certain works we can manage with fewer allusions than our ancestors. So far as psychology is concerned, the questions as to whether the results of newly established sciences should be employed, is not a matter of faith. It is in individual cases that one has to test whether the delineation of a character is improved by incorporating scientific insights or not, and whether the particular way in which they are utilized is good or not. Literature cannot be forbidden to employ skills newly acquired by contemporary man, such as the capacity for simultaneous registration, bold abstraction, or swift combination. If a scientific approach is to be involved, it is the tireless energy of science that is needed to investigate in each individual case how the artistic adoption of these skills has worked out. Artists like to take short cuts, to conjure things out of the air, to work their way through large sections of a continuous process more or less consciously. Criticism, at least Marxist criticism, must proceed methodically and concretely in each case, in short scientifically. Loose talk is of no help here, whatever its vocabulary. In no circumstances can the necessary guide-lines for a practical definition of realism be derived from literary works alone. (Be like Tolstoy – but without his weaknesses! Be like Balzac – only up-to-date!) Realism is an issue not only for literature: it is a major political, philosophical and practical issue and must be handled and explained as such – as a matter of general human interest.

III

[Remarks on an Essay]

One must not expect too much from people who use the word 'form' too fluently as signifying something other than content, or as connected with content, whatever, or who are suspicious of 'technique' as something 'mechanical'. One must not pay too much attention to the fact that they quote the classics (of Marxism) and that the word 'form' occurs there too; the classics did not teach the technique of writing novels. The word 'mechanical' need frighten no one, as long as it refers to technique; there is a kind of mechanics that has performed great services for mankind and still does so – namely technology. The 'right thinking' people among us, whom Stalin in another context distinguishes from creative people, have a habit of spell-binding our minds with certain words used in an extremely arbitrary sense.

Those who administer our cultural heritage decree that no enduring figures can be created without 'reciprocal human relationships in struggle', without 'the testing of human beings in real action', without 'close interaction between men in struggle'. But where in Hašek are the 'complicated' (!) methods with which old authors set their plots in motion. Yet his Schweik is certainly a figure who is hard to forget. I do not know whether it will 'endure'; nor do I know whether a figure created by Tolstoy or Balzac will endure; I know no more than the next man. To be frank, I do not set such an excessively high value on the concept of endurance. How can we foresee whether future generations will wish to preserve the memory of these figures? (Balzac and Tolstoy will scarcely be in a position to oblige them to do so, however ingenious the methods with which they set their plots in motion.) I suspect it will depend on whether it will be a socially relevant statement if someone says: 'That' (and 'that' will refer to a contemporary) 'is a Père Goriot character.' Perhaps such characters will not survive at all? Perhaps they arose in a web of contorted relationships of a type which will by then no longer exist.

Characters and Balzac

I have no reason to advocate the montage technique used by Dos Passos, against wind or tide. When I wrote a novel I myself tried to create something in the nature of 'close interactions between human beings in struggle'. (Whatever elements of the montage technique I used, lay elsewhere in this novel). But I should not like to allow this technique to be condemned purely in favour of the creation of durable characters. First of all, Dos Passos himself has given an excellent portrayal of 'close interactions between human beings in struggle', even if the struggles he depicts are not the kind Tolstoy created, or his complexities those of Balzac's plots. Secondly, the novel certainly does not stand or fall by its 'characters', let alone with characters of the type that existed in the 19th century. We must not conjure up a kind of Valhalla of the enduring figures of literature, a kind of Madame Tussaud's panopticon, filled with nothing but durable characters from Antigone to Nana and from Aeneas to Nekhlyudov (who is he, by the way?).[4] I see nothing disrespectful in laughing at such an idea. We know something about the bases on which the cult of the individual, as practised in class society, rested. They are historical bases. We are far from wishing to do away with the individual. But we nevertheless notice with a certain pensiveness how this (historical, particular, passing) cult has prevented a man like André Gide from discovering any individuals among Soviet youth.[5] Reading Gide, I was on the point of discarding Nekhlyudov (whoever he may be) as an enduring figure, if – as certainly seemed possible – this was the only way those figures among Soviet youth, whom I have seen myself, could endure. To come back to our basic question: it is absolutely false, that is to say, it leads nowhere, it is not worth the writer's while, to simplify his problems so much that the immense, complicated, actual life-process of human beings in the age of the final struggle between the bourgeois and the proletarian class, is reduced to a 'plot', setting, or background for the creation of great individuals. Individuals should not occupy much more space in books and above all not a different kind of space,

[4] Nekhlyudov: liberal aristocrat who is the central figure of Tolstoy's novel *Resurrection*.
[5] Reference to Gide's *Retour de l'URSS*, which had been translated into German the previous year (1937).

than in reality. To talk in purely practical terms; for us, individuals emerge from a depiction of the processes of human co-existence and they can be 'big' or 'small'. It is absolutely false to say that one should take a great figure and allow it to respond in manifold ways, making its relationships with other figures as significant and lasting as possible.

The drama (force of collision), the passion (degree of heat), the range of the characters – none of this can be separated from social functions, and portrayed or propagated apart from it. Those close interactions between human beings in struggle are the competitive struggles of developing capitalism, which produced individuals in a quite particular way. Socialist emulation produces individuals in a different way and shapes different individuals. Then there is the further question whether it is as individuating a process as the competitive struggle of capitalism. In a certain sense, we hear from our critics the fateful slogan, once addressed to individuals: 'Enrich yourselves'.

Balzac is the poet of monstrosities. The multiplex character of his heroes (the breadth of their sunlit side, the depth of their shadowy side) reflects the dialectic of the progress of production as the progress of misery. 'With him business became poetical' (Taine) but: 'Balzac was first of all a businessman, indeed a businessman in debt . . . he took to speculation . . . suspended payments and wrote novels to pay his debts.' So in his case poetry in its turn became a business. In the primeval forest of early capitalism individuals fought against individuals, and against groups of individuals; basically they fought against 'the whole of society'. This was precisely what determined their individuality. Now we are advised to go on creating individuals, to recreate them, or rather to create new ones, who will naturally be different but made in the same way. So? 'Balzac's passion for collecting things bordered on mono-mania.' We find this fetishism of objects in his novels, too, on hundreds and thousands of pages. Admittedly we are supposed to avoid such a thing. Lukács wags his finger at Tretyakov on this account. But this fetishism is what makes Balzac's characters individuals. It is ridiculous to see in them a simple exchange of the social passions and functions which constitute the individual. Does the production of consumer goods for a collective today construct individuals in the same way as 'collecting'? Naturally one can answer 'yes' here too. This process of production does take place and there are individuals. But they are such very different individuals that Balzac would not have recognized them as such (and Gide today does not do so). They lack the element of monstrosity, the combination in one person of the lofty and the base, of criminality and sanctity, and so on.

No, Balzac does not indulge in montage. But he writes vast genealogies, he marries off the creatures of his fantasy as Napoleon did his marshals and brothers; he follows possessions (fetishism of objects) through generations of families and their transference from one to the other. He deals with nothing but the 'organic': his families are organisms in which the individuals 'grow'. Should we therefore be reconstructing such cells, or the factory or the soviet – given that, with the abolition of private ownership of the means of production, the family is generally supposed to have ceased to shape individuals? But these new institutions which undoubtedly shape individuals today are precisely – compared to the family – the products of montage, quite literally 'assembled'. For example in contemporary New York, not to speak of Moscow, woman is less 'formed' by man than in Balzac's Paris; she is less dependent on him. So far this is quite simple. Certain struggles 'to a fever-pitch' therefore cease; other struggles which take their place (naturally others do take their place) are just as fierce but perhaps less individualistic. Not that they have no individual characteristics, for they are fought out by individuals. But allies play an immense part in them, such as they could not in Balzac's time.

IV

Popularity and Realism

Whoever looks for slogans to apply to contemporary German literature, must bear in mind that anything that aspires to be called literature is printed exclusively abroad and can almost exclusively be read only abroad. The term *popular* as applied to literature thus acquires a curious connotation. The writer in this case is supposed to write for a people among whom he does not live. Yet if one considers the matter more closely, the gap between the writer and the people is not as great as one might think. Today it is not quite as great as it seems, and formerly it was not as small as it seemed. The prevailing aesthetic, the price of books and the police have always ensured that there is a considerable distance between writer and people. Nevertheless it would be wrong, that is to say unrealistic, to view the widening of this distance as a purely 'external' one. Undoubtedly special efforts have to be made today in order to be able to write in a popular style. On the other hand, it has become easier; easier and more urgent. The people have split away more clearly from their upper layers; their oppressors and exploiters have stepped out and joined a bloody battle with them of vast dimensions. It has become easier to take sides. An open battle has so to speak broken out among the 'public'.

The demand for a realistic style of writing can also no longer be so easily dismissed today. It has acquired a certain inevitability. The ruling classes use lies oftener than before – and bigger ones. To tell the truth is clearly an ever more urgent task. Suffering has increased and with it the number of sufferers. In view of the immense suffering of the masses, concern with little difficulties or with difficulties of little groups has come to be felt as ridiculous, contemptible.

There is only one ally against growing barbarism – the people, who suffer so greatly from it. It is only from them that one can expect anything. Therefore it is obvious that one must turn to the people, and now more necessary than ever to speak their language. Thus the terms *popular art* and *realism* become natural allies. It is in the interest of the people, of the broad working masses, to receive a faithful image of life from literature, and faithful images of life are actually of service only to the people, the broad working masses, and must therefore be absolutely comprehensible and profitable to them – in other words, popular. Nevertheless these concepts must first be thoroughly cleansed before propositions are constructed in which they are employed and merged. It would be a mistake to think that these concepts are completely transparent, without history, uncompromised or unequivocal. ('We all know what they mean – don't let's split hairs.') The concept of *popularity* itself is not particularly popular. It is not realistic to believe that it is. There is a whole series of abstract nouns in 'ity' which must be viewed with caution. Think of *utility, sovereignty, sanctity*; and we know that the concept of *nationality* has a quite particular, sacramental, pompous and suspicious connotation, which we dare not overlook. We must not ignore this connotation, just because we so urgently need the concept *popular*.

It is precisely in the so-called poetical forms that 'the people' are represented in a superstitious fashion or, better, in a fashion that encourages supersitition. They endow the people with unchanging characteristics, hallowed traditions, art forms, habits and customs, religiosity, hereditary enemies, invincible power and so on. A remarkable unity appears between tormenters and tormented, exploiters and exploited, deceivers and deceived; it is by no means a question of the masses of 'little' working people in opposition to those above them.

The history of the many deceptions which have been practised with this concept of the people is a long and complicated one – a history of class struggles. We do not intend to go into it here – we only wish to keep the fact of the deception in sight, when we say that we need popular art and mean thereby art for the broad masses, for the many who are oppressed by the few, 'the people themselves', the mass of producers who was for so long the object of politics and must now become the subject of politics. Let us recall that the people were for long held back from any full development by powerful institutions, artificially and forcefully gagged by conventions, and that the concept *popular* was given an ahistorical, static, undevelopmental stamp. We are not concerned with the concept in this form – or rather, we have to combat it.

Our concept of what is popular refers to a people who not only play a full part in historical development but actively usurp it, force its pace, determine its direction. We have a people in mind who make history, change the world and themselves. We have in mind a fighting people and therefore an aggressive concept of what is *popular*.

Popular means: intelligible to the broad masses, adopting and enriching their forms of expression / assuming their standpoint, confirming and correcting it / representing the most progressive section of the people so that it can assume leadership, and therefore intelligible to other sections of the people as well / relating to traditions and developing them / communicating to that portion of the people which strives for leadership the achievements of the section that at present rules the nation.

Now we come to the concept of *realism*. This concept, too, must first be cleansed before use, for it is an old concept, much used by many people and for many ends. This is necessary because the people can only take over their cultural heritage by an act of expropriation. Literary works cannot be taken over like factories; literary forms of expression cannot be taken over like patents. Even the realistic mode of writing, of which literature provides many very different examples, bears the stamp of the way it was employed, when and by which class, down to its smallest details. With the people struggling and changing reality before our eyes, we must not cling to 'tried' rules of narrative, venerable literary models, eternal aesthetic laws. We must not derive realism as such from particular existing works, but we shall use every means, old and new, tried and untried, derived from art and derived from other sources, to render reality to men in a form they can master. We shall take care not to describe one particular, historical form of novel of a particular epoch as realistic – say that of Balzac or Tolstoy – and thereby erect merely formal, literary criteria for realism. We shall not speak of a realistic manner of writing only when, for example, we can smell, taste and feel everything, when there is 'atmosphere' and when plots are so contrived that they lead to psychological analysis of character. Our concept of realism must be wide and political, sovereign over all conventions.

Realistic means: discovering the causal complexes of society / unmasking the prevailing view of things as the view of those who are in power / writing from the standpoint of the class which offers the broadest solutions for the pressing difficulties in which human society is caught up / emphasizing the element of development / making possible the concrete, and making possible abstraction from it.

These are vast precepts and they can be extended. Moreover we shall allow the artist to employ his fantasy, his originality, his humour, his invention, in following them. We shall not stick to too detailed literary models; we shall not bind the artist to too rigidly defined modes of narrative.

We shall establish that the so-called sensuous mode of writing – where one can smell, taste and feel everything – is not automatically to be identified with a realistic mode of writing; we shall acknowledge that there are works which are sensuously written and which are not realistic, and realistic works which are not written in a sensuous style. We shall have to examine carefully the question whether we really develop a plot best when our ultimate objective is to reveal the spiritual life of the characters. Our readers will perhaps find that they have not been given the key to the meaning of the events if, led astray by various artistic devices, they experience only the spiritual agitation of the heroes. By adopting the forms of Balzac and Tolstoy without testing them thoroughly, we might weary our readers – the people – as much as these writers often do themselves. Realism is not a mere question of form. Were we to copy the style of these realists, we would no longer be realists.

For time flows on, and if it did not, it would be a bad prospect for those who do not sit at golden tables. Methods become exhausted; stimuli no longer work. New problems appear and demand new methods. Reality changes; in order to represent it, modes of representation must also change. Nothing comes from nothing; the new comes from the old, but that is why it is new.

The oppressors do not work in the same way in every epoch. They cannot be defined in the same fashion at all times. There are so many means for them to avoid being spotted. They call their military roads motor-ways; their tanks are painted so that they look like MacDuff's woods. Their agents show blisters on their hands, as if they were workers. No: to turn the hunter into the quarry is something that demands invention. What was popular yesterday is not today, for the people today are not what they were yesterday.

Anyone who is not a victim of formalistic prejudices knows that the truth can be suppressed in many ways and must be expressed in many ways. One can arouse a sense of outrage at inhuman conditions by many methods – by direct description (emotional or objective), by narrative and parable, by jokes, by over- and under-emphasis. In the theatre, reality can be represented both in objective and in imaginative forms. The actors may not use make-up – or hardly any – and claim to be 'absolutely natural' and yet the whole thing can be a swindle; and they can wear masks of a grotesque kind and present the truth. It is hardly open to debate that the means must be questioned about the ends they serve. The people understand this. Piscator's great theatrical experiments in which conventional forms were constantly destroyed, found their greatest support in the most advanced cadres of the working class; so have my own. The workers judged everything according to the truth of its content; they welcomed every innovation which helped the represen-tation of truth, of the real mechanism of society; they rejected everything that seemed theatrical, technical equipment that merely worked for its own sake – that is to say, that did not yet fulfil, or no longer fulfilled, its purpose. The workers' arguments were never literary or stated in terms of theatrical aesthetics. One never heard it said that one can't mix theatre and film. If the film was not inserted properly in the play, then the most that was said was: 'We don't need that film. It's distracting.' Workers' choirs spoke verse-parts with complicated rhythms ('If it was in rhyme it would go down like water and nothing would be left'), and sang difficult (unfamiliar) compositions by Eisler ('That's strong stuff').[6] But we had to change certain lines whose sense was not clear or which were wrong. In the case of marching-songs, which were rhymed so that they could be learnt more quickly, and had a simpler rhythm so that they sank in better, certain refinements were introduced (irregularities, com-plications). Then they said: 'There's a little twist there – that's fun.' Anything that was worn out, trivial, or so commonplace that it no longer

[6] Reference to Brecht's work *Die Massnahme* (1930), intended as a vindication of party discipline and Comintern policy in China. The play was sharply criticized by the KPD itself, for its exaltation of expedient sacrifice. Lukács dismissed it in 1932 for reducing strategic and tactical problems of class struggle to ethical issues.

made one think, they did not like at all ('You get nothing out of it'). If one needed an aesthetic, one could find it here. I shall never forget how a worker looked at me when I replied to his suggestion that I should add something to a chorus about the Soviet Union ('It has to go in – otherwise what's the point?'), that it would destroy the artistic form. He put his head on one side and smiled. A whole area of aesthetics collapsed because of this polite smile. The workers were not afraid to teach us and they were themselves not afraid to learn.

I am speaking from experience when I say that one need not be afraid to produce daring, unusual things for the proletariat so long as they deal with its real situation. There will always be people of culture, connoisseurs of art, who will interject: 'Ordinary people do not understand that.' But the people will push these persons impatiently aside and come to a direct understanding with artists. There is high-flown stuff, made for cliques, and intended to create new cliques – the two-thousandth reblocking of an old felt hat, the spicing of old, rotting meat: this the proletariat rejects ('What a state they must be in!') with an incredulous, yet tolerant shake of the head. It was not the pepper that was rejected, but the decaying meat: not the two-thousandth blocking, but the old felt. When they themselves wrote and produced for the stage they were wonderfully original. So-called agitprop art, at which people, not always the best people, turned up their noses, was a mine of new artistic methods and modes of expression. From it there emerged magnificent, long-forgotten elements from ages of genuine popular art, boldly modified for new social aims: breathtaking contractions and compressions, beautiful simplifications, in which there was often an astonishing elegance and power and a fearless eye for the complex. Much of it might be primitive, but not in that sense in which the spiritual landscapes of bourgeois art, apparently so subtle, are primitive. It is a mistake to reject a style of representation because of a few unsuccessful compositions – a style which strives, frequently with success, to dig down to the essentials and to make abstraction possible. The sharp eyes of the workers penetrated the surface of naturalistic representations of reality. When the workers in *Driver Henschel* said of spiritual analyses, 'We don't want to know all that', they were expressing a desire to receive a more accurate image of the real social forces at work under an immediately visible surface. To cite my own experience, they did not object to the fantastic costumes and the apparently unreal milieu of the *Threepenny Opera*. They were not narrow – they hated narrowness (their homes were narrow and cramped). They did things on a grand scale; the entrepreneurs were mean. They found some things superfluous which the artists declared to be necessary; but then they were generous and not against excess; on the contrary they were against those who were superfluous. They did not put on a muzzle on a willing horse but they saw that it pulled its weight. They did not believe in such things as 'the' method. They knew that many methods were necessary to attain their goal.

The criteria for popular art and realism must therefore be chosen both generously and carefully, and not drawn merely from existing realistic works and existing popular works, as often happens; by so doing, one would arrive at formalistic criteria, and at popular art and realism in form only.

Whether a work is realistic or not cannot be determined merely by checking whether or not it is like existing works which are said to be realistic, or were realistic in their time. In each case, one must compare the depiction of life in a work of art with the life itself that is being depicted, instead of comparing it with another depiction. Where popularity is concerned, there is one extremely formalistic procedure of which one must beware. The intelligibility of a literary work is not guaranteed merely if it is written exactly like other works which were understood in their time. These other works which were understood in their time were also not always written like the works before them. Steps had been taken to make them intelligible. In the same way, we must do something for the intelligibility of new works today. There is not only such a thing as *being popular*, there is also the process of *becoming popular*.

If we wish to have a living and combative literature, which is fully engaged with reality and fully grasps reality, a truly popular literature, we must keep step with the rapid development of reality. The great working masses are already on the move. The industry and brutality of their enemies is proof of it.

Translated by Stuart Hood

Walter Benjamin

Conversations with Brecht

1934

4 July. Yesterday, a long conversation in Brecht's sickroom about my essay 'The Author as Producer'. Brecht thought the theory I develop in the essay – that the attainment of technical progress in literature eventually changes the function of art forms (hence also of the intellectual means of production) and is therefore a criterion for judging the revolutionary function of literary works – applies to artists of only one type, the writers of the upper bourgeoisie, among whom he counts himself. 'For such a writer,' he said, 'there really exists a point of solidarity with the interests of the proletariat: it is the point at which he can develop his own means of production. Because he identifies with the proletariat at this point, he is proletarianized – completely so – at this same point, i.e. as a producer. And his complete proletarianization at this one point establishes his solidarity with the proletariat all along the line.' He thought my critique of proletarian writers of Becher's type too abstract, and tried to improve upon it by analysing a poem of Becher's which appeared in a recent issue of one of the proletarian literary reviews under the title '*Ich sage ganz offen*' ('I say quite openly'). Brecht compared this poem, first, with his own didactic poem about Carola Neher, the actress and secondly with Rimbaud's *Bateau Ivre*. 'I taught Carola Neher all kinds of things, you know,' he said, 'not just acting – for example, she learned from me how to wash herself. Before that she used to wash just so as not to be dirty. But that was no way to do things. So I taught her how to wash her face. She became so perfect at it that I wanted to film her doing it, but it never came to that because I didn't feel like doing any filming just then and she didn't feel like doing it in front of anybody else. That didactic poem was a model. Anyone who learned from it was supposed to put himself in place of the "I" of the poem. When Becher says "I", he considers himself – as president of the Union of German Proletarian-Revolutionary Writers – to be exemplary. The only trouble is that nobody feels like following his example. He gets nothing across except that he is rather pleased with himself.' In this connection Brecht said he had been meaning for a long time to write a series of such model poems for different trades – the engineer, the writer. Then he compared Becher's poem with Rimbaud's. He thinks that Marx and Engels themselves, had they read *Le Bateau Ivre*, would have sensed in it the great historical movement of which it is the expression. They would have clearly recognized that what it describes is not an eccentric poet going for a walk but the flight, the escape of a man who cannot bear to live any longer inside the barriers of a class which – with the Crimean War, with the Mexican adventure – was then beginning to open up even the more exotic continents to its mercantile interests. Brecht thinks it is impossible to turn Rimbaud's attitude – the attitude of the footloose vagabond who puts himself at the mercy of chance and turns his back upon society – into a model representation of a proletarian fighter.

6 July. Brecht, in the course of yesterday's conversations: 'I often imagine being interrogated by a tribunal. "Now tell us, Mr Brecht, are you really in earnest?" I would have to admit that no, I'm not completely in earnest. I think too much about artistic problems, you know, about what is good for the theatre, to be completely in earnest. But having said "no" to that important question, I would add something still more important: namely, that my attitude is *permissible*.' I must admit he said this after the conversation had been going on for some little time. He had started by expressing doubt, not as to whether his attitude was permissible, but whether it was effective. His first remark was in answer to something I had said about Gerhart Hauptmann. 'I sometimes ask myself,' he said, 'whether writers like Hauptmann aren't, after all, the only ones who really get anywhere: I mean the *substance writers [Substanz-Dichter]*.' By this he means those writers who really are completely in earnest. To explain this thought he proceeds from the hypothesis that Confucius might once have written a tragedy, or Lenin a novel. That, he thinks, would be felt as improper, unworthy behaviour. 'Suppose you read a very good historical novel and later you discover that it is by Lenin. You would change your opinion of both, to the detriment of both. Likewise, it would be wrong for Confucius to have written a tragedy, say one of Euripides's tragedies; it would be felt as unworthy. Yet his parables are not.' All this leads, in short, to a differentiation between two literary types: the visionary artist, who is in earnest, and the cool-headed thinking man, who is not completely in earnest. At this point I raised the question of Kafka. To which of the two groups does he belong? I know that the question cannot be answered. And it is precisely its unanswerability which Brecht regards as an indication of the fact that Kafka, whom he considers to be a great writer, is, like Kleist, Grabbe or Büchner, a failure. Kafka's starting point is really the parable, which is governed by reason and which, therefore, so far as its actual wording is concerned, cannot be entirely in earnest. But then this parable has, all the same, to be given form. It grows into a novel. And if you look closely, you see that it contained the germ of a novel from the start. It was never altogether transparent. I should add that Brecht is convinced that Kafka would not have found his own special form without Dostoyevsky's Grand Inquisitor or that other episode in *The Brothers Karamazov* where the holy *starets* begins to stink. In Kafka, then, the parabolic element is in conflict with the visionary element. But Kafka as a visionary, says Brecht, saw what was coming without seeing what *is*. He emphasizes once more (as earlier at Le Lavandou, but in terms which are clearer to me) the prophetic aspect of Kafka's work. Kafka had one problem and one only, he says, and that was the problem of organization. He was terrified by the thought of the empire of ants: the thought of men being alienated from themselves by the forms of their life in society. And he anticipated certain forms of this alienation, e.g. the methods of the GPU. But he never found a solution and never awoke from his nightmare. Brecht says of Kafka's precision that it is the precision of an imprecise man, a dreamer.

12 July. Yesterday, after playing chess, Brecht said: 'You know, when Korsch comes, we really ought to work out a new game with him. A game in which the moves do not always stay the same; where the function of a piece changes after it has stood on the same square for a while: it should either become stronger or weaker. As it is the game doesn't develop, it stays the same for too long.'

23 July. Yesterday a visit from Karin Michaelis, who has just returned from her trip to Russia and is full of enthusiasm. Brecht remembers how he was taken round Moscow by Tretyakov. Tretyakov showed him the city and was proud of everything, no matter what it was. 'That isn't a bad thing,' says Brecht, 'it shows that the place belongs to him. One isn't proud of other people's property.' After a while he added: 'Yes, but in the end I got a bit tired of it. I couldn't admire everything, nor did I want to. The point is, they were his soldiers, his lorries. But not, alas, mine.'

24 July. On a beam which supports the ceiling of Brecht's study are painted the words: 'Truth is concrete.' On a window-sill stands a small wooden donkey which can nod its head. Brecht has hung a little sign round its neck on which he has written: 'Even I must understand it.'

5 August. Three weeks ago I gave B. my essay on Kafka. I'm sure he read it, but he never alluded to it of his own accord, and on two occasions when I steered the conversation round to it, he replied evasively. In the end I took the manuscript away again without saying a word. Last night he suddenly began speaking of this essay. The rather abrupt transition took the form of a remark to the effect that I, too, could not be completely acquitted of a diaristic style of writing *á la* Nietzsche. My Kafka essay, for instance. It treated Kafka purely from the phenomenal point of view – the work as something that had grown separately, by itself – the man, too: it detached the work from all connections, even with its author. In the end everything I wrote always came down to the question of *essence*. Now what would be the correct way of tackling the problem of Kafka? The correct way would be to ask: what does he do? how does he behave? And, at the start, to consider the general rather than the particular. It would then transpire that Kafka lived in Prague, in an unhealthy milieu of journalists, of self-important literati; in that world, literature was the principal reality, if not the only one. Kafka's strengths and weaknesses were bound up with this way of seeing the world – his artistic value, but also his feebleness in many respects. He was a Jew-boy – one could just as well coin the term 'Aryan boy' – a sorry, dismal creature, a mere bubble on the glittering quagmire of Prague cultural life, nothing more. Yet there were also some very interesting sides to him. One could bring these out. One might imagine a conversation between Lao Tzu and his disciple Kafka. Lao Tzu says: 'And so, Disciple Kafka, you have conceived a horror of the organizations, property relations and economic forms within which you live?' – 'Yes.' – 'You can't find your way about them any more?' – 'No.' – 'A share certificate fills you with dread?' – 'Yes.' – 'And so now you're looking for a leader you can hold on to, Disciple Kafka.' 'Of course such an attitude won't do,' says Brecht. 'I don't accept Kafka, you know.' He went on to speak about a Chinese philosopher's parable of 'the tribulations of usefulness'. In a wood there are many different kinds of tree-trunk. From the thickest they make ship's timbers; from those which are less thick but still quite sturdy, they make boxes and coffin-lids; the thinnest of all are made into whipping-rods; but of the stunted ones they make nothing at all: these escape the tribulations of usefulness. 'You've got to look around in Kafka's writings as you might in such a wood. Then you'll find a whole lot of very useful things. The images are good, of course. But the rest is pure mystification. It's nonsense. You have to ignore it. Depth doesn't get you anywhere at all. Depth is a separate dimension, it's just depth – and there's nothing whatsoever to be seen in it.' To conclude the discussion I told B. that penetrating into depth is my way of travelling to the antipodes. In my essay on Kraus I actually got there. I know that the one on Kafka doesn't come off to the same degree: I can't dismiss the charge that it has landed me in a diaristic style of notation. It is true that the study of the frontier area defined by Kraus and, in another way, by Kafka preoccupies me a great deal. In Kafka's case I haven't yet, I said, completed my exploration of this area. I am aware that it contains a lot of rubbish and waste, a lot of pure mystification. But I can't help thinking that the important thing about Kafka is something else, and some of this I touched upon in my essay. B.'s approach should, I said, be checked against interpretations of specific works. I suggested *The Next Village*, and immediately saw that this suggestion worried B. He resolutely rejected Eisler's view that this very short story is 'worthless', but neither could he get anywhere nearer to defining its value. 'One ought to study it more closely,' he said. Then the conversation broke off, as it was ten o'clock and time to listen to the news from Vienna.

31 August. The night before last a long and heated debate about my Kafka. Its foundation: the charge that it promotes Jewish fascism. It increases and spreads the darkness surrounding Kafka instead of dispersing it. Yet it is necessary to clarify Kafka, that is to say, to formulate the practicable suggestions which can be extracted from his stories. It is to be supposed that such suggestions *can* be extracted from them, if only because of their tone of superior calm. But these suggestions should be sought in the direction of the great general evils which assail humanity today. Brecht looks for the reflexion of these evils in Kafka's work. He confines himself, in the main, to *The Trial*. What it conveys above all else, he thinks, is a dread of the unending and irresistible growth of great cities. He claims to know the nightmare of this idea from his own intimate experience. Such cities are an expression of the boundless maze of indirect relationships, complex mutual dependencies and compartmentations into which human beings are forced by modern forms of living. And these in turn find expression in the longing for a 'leader'. The petty bourgeois sees the leader as the only man whom, in a world where everyone can pass the buck to someone else, he can make responsible for all his ills. Brecht calls *The Trial* a prophetic book. 'By looking at the Gestapo you can see what the Cheka may become.' Kafka's outlook is that of a man caught under the wheels. Odradek is characteristic of this outlook: Brecht interprets the caretaker as personifying the worries of a father of a family. The petty bourgeois is bound to get it in the neck. His situation is Kafka's own. But whereas the type of petty bourgeois current today – that is, the fascist – has decided to set his indomitable iron will against this situation, Kafka hardly opposes it; he is wise. Where the fascist brings heroism into play, Kafka responds with questions. He asks for safeguards for his situation. But the nature of his situation is such that the safeguards he demands must be unreasonable. It is a Kafkaesque irony that the man who appears to be convinced of nothing so much as of the frailty of all safeguards should have been an insurance agent. Incidentally, his unlimited pessimism is free from any tragic sense of destiny. For not only is his expectation of misfortune founded on nothing but empiricism (although it must be said that this foundation is unshakable), but also, with incorrigible naivety, he seeks the criterion of final success in the most insignificant and trivial undertakings – a visit from a travelling salesman, an inquiry at a government office. From time to time our conversation centred on the story *The Next Village*. Brecht says it is a counterpart to the story of Achilles and the tortoise. One never gets to the next village if one breaks the journey down into its smallest parts, not counting the incidental occurrences. Then a whole life is too short for the journey. But the fallacy lies in the word 'one'. For if the journey is broken down into its parts, then the traveller is too. And if the unity of life is destroyed, then so is its shortness. Let life be as short as it may. That does not matter, for the one who arrives in the next village is not the one who set out on the journey, but another. – I for my part offer the following interpretation: the true measure of life is memory. Looking back, it traverses the whole of life like lightning. As fast as one can turn back a few pages, it has travelled from the next village to the place where the traveller took the decision to set out. Those for whom life has become transformed into writing – like the grandfather in the story – can only read the writing backwards. That is the only way in which they confront themselves, and only thus – by fleeing from the present – can they understand life.

27 September. Dragør. In a conversation a few evenings ago Brecht spoke of the curious indecision which at the moment prevents him from making any definite plans. As he is the first to point out, the main reason for this indecision is that his situation is so much more privileged than that of most other refugees. Therefore, since in general he scarcely admits that exile can be a proper basis for plans and projects, he refuses all the more radically to admit it as such in his own particular case. His plans reach out to the period beyond exile. There, he is faced with two possibilities. On the one hand there are some prose projects waiting to be done: the shorter one of the *Ui* – a satire on Hitler in the style of the Renaissance biographers – and the long one of the *Tui* novel. This is to be an encyclopedic survey of the follies of the Tellectual-Ins (intellectuals); it seems that it will be set, in part at least, in China. A small-scale model of this work is already completed. But besides these prose works he is also preoccupied with other plans, dating back to very old studies and ideas. Whereas he was able, at a pinch, to set down in his notes and introductions to the *Versuche* the thoughts which occurred to him concerning epic theatre, other thoughts, although originating in the same interests, have become combined with the study of Leninism and also of the scientific tendencies of the empiricists, and have therefore outgrown that rather limited framework. For several years past they have been subsumed, now under one key concept, now under another, so that non-Aristotelian logic, behaviourist theory, the new encyclopedia and the critique of ideas have, in turn, stood at the centre of his preoccupations. At present these various pursuits are converging upon the idea of a philosophical didactic poem. But he has doubts about the matter. He wonders, in the first instance, whether, in view of his output to date and especially of its satirical elements, particularly the *Threepenny Novel*, the public would accept such a work. This doubt is made up of two distinct strands of thought. Whilst becoming more closely concerned with the problems and methods of the proletarian class struggle, he has increasingly doubted the satirical, and especially the ironic, attitude as such. But to confuse these doubts, which are mostly of a practical nature, with other, more profound ones would be to misunderstand them. The doubts at a deeper level concern the artistic and playful element in art, and above all those elements which, partially and occasionally, make art refractory to reason. Brecht's heroic efforts to legitimize art *vis-à-vis* reason have again and again referred him to the parable in which artistic mastery is proved by the fact that, in the end, all the artistic elements of a work cancel each other out. It is precisely his efforts connected with this parable, which are at present becoming visible in a radical form in his conception of the didactic poem. In the course of the conversation I tried to explain to Brecht that such a poem would not have to seek approval from a bourgeois public but from a proletarian one, which, presumably, would find its criteria less in Brecht's earlier, partly bourgeois-oriented work than in the dogmatic and theoretical content of the didactic poem itself. 'If this didactic poem succeeds in enlisting the authority of Marxism on its behalf,' I told him, 'then your earlier work is not likely to weaken that authority.'

4 October. Yesterday Brecht left for London. Whether it is that my presence offers peculiar temptations in this respect, or whether Brecht is now generally more this way inclined than before, at all events his aggressiveness (which he himself calls 'baiting') is now much more pronounced in conversation than it used to be. Indeed, I am struck by a special vocabulary engendered by this aggressiveness. In particular, he is fond of using the term *Würstchen* (little sausage). In Dragør I was reading Dostoyevsky's *Crime and Punishment*. To start with he blamed this choice of reading for my being unwell. As confirmation he told how, in his youth, a prolonged illness (which had doubtless been latent for a long time) had begun when a schoolfellow had played Chopin to him on the piano and he had not had the strength to protest. Brecht thinks that Chopin and Dostoyevsky have a particularly adverse effect on people's health. In other ways, too, he missed no opportunity of needling me about my reading matter, and as he himself was reading *Schweyk* at the time, he insisted on making comparative value judgements of the two authors. It became evident that Dostoyevsky simply could not measure up to Hašek, and Brecht included him without further ado among the *Würstchen*; only a little more and he would have extended to Dostoyevsky the description he keeps on hand, these days, for any work which lacks, or is said by him to lack, an enlightening character. He calls such a work a *Klump* (lump, or clot).

1938

28 June. I was in a labyrinth of stairs. This labyrinth was not entirely roofed over. I climbed; other stairways led downwards. On a landing I realized that I had arrived at a summit. A wide view of many lands opened up before me. I saw other men standing on other peaks. One of these men was suddenly seized by dizziness and fell. The dizziness spread; others were now falling from other peaks into the depths below. When I too became dizzy, I woke up.

On 22 June I arrived at Brecht's.

Brecht speaks of the elegance and nonchalance of Virgil's and Dante's basic attitude, which, he says, forms the backdrop to Virgil's majestic *gestus*. He calls both Virgil and Dante '*promeneurs*'. Emphasizing the classic rank of the *Inferno*, he says: 'You can read it out of doors.'

He speaks of his deep-rooted hatred of priests, a hatred he inherited from his grandmother. He hints that those who have appropriated the theoretical doctrines of Marx and taken over their management will always form a clerical camarilla. Marxism lends itself all too easily to 'interpretation'. Today it is a hundred years old and what do we find? (At this point the conversation was interrupted.) '"The State must wither away." Who says that? The State.' (Here he can only mean the Soviet Union.) He assumes a cunning, furtive expression, stands in front of the chair in which I am sitting – he is impersonating 'the State' – and says, with a sly, sidelong glance at an imaginary interlocutor: 'I know I *ought* to wither away.'

A conversation about new Soviet novels. We no longer read them. The talk then turns to poetry and to the translations of poems from various languages in the USSR with which *Das Wort* is flooded. He says the poets over there are having a hard time. 'If Stalin's name doesn't occur in a poem, it's interpreted as intentional.'

29 June. Brecht talks about epic theatre, and mentions plays acted by children in which faults of performance, which produce alienation effects, impart epic characteristics to the production. Something similar may occur in third-rate provincial theatre. I mentioned the Geneva production of *Le Cid*, where the sight of the crown worn crookedly on the king's head gave me the first inkling of the ideas I eventually developed in the *Trauerspiel* book nine years later. Brecht in turn quoted the moment at which the idea of epic theatre first came into his head. It happened at a rehearsal for the Munich production of *Edward II*. The battle in the play is supposed to occupy the stage for three-quarters of an hour. Brecht couldn't stage-manage the soldiers, and neither could Asya [Lacis], his production assistant. Finally he turned in despair to Karl Valentin, at that time one of his closest friends, who was attending the rehearsal, and asked him: 'Well, what is it? What's the matter with these soldiers? What's wrong with them?' Valentin: 'They're pale, they're scared, that's what!' The remark settled the issue, Brecht adding: 'They're tired.' Whereupon the soldiers' faces were thickly made up with chalk. That was the day the style of the production was determined.

Later the old subject of 'logical positivism' came up. I adopted a somewhat intransigent attitude and the conversation threatened to take a disagreeable turn. This was avoided by Brecht admitting for the first time that his arguments were superficial. This he did with the delightful formula: 'A deep need makes for a superficial grasp.' Later, when we were walking to his house (the conversation had taken place in my room): 'It's a good thing when someone who has taken up an extreme position then goes into a period of reaction. That way he arrives at a half-way house.' That, he explained, was what had happened to him: he had become mellow.

In the evening: I should like to get somebody to take a small present – a pair of gloves – to Asya. Brecht thinks this might be tricky. It could happen that someone thought the gloves were Jahnn's[1] way of repaying Asya for her espionage services. 'The worst thing is when whole sets of directives[2] are withdrawn en bloc, but the instructions they contain are still supposed to remain in force.'

1 July. Whenever I refer to conditions in Russia, Brecht's comments are highly sceptical. When I inquired the other day whether Ottwald was still 'doing time' in gaol, the answer came: 'If he's still got time, he'll be doing it.' Yesterday Gretl Steffin expressed the opinion that Tretyakov was no longer alive.

4 July. Brecht in the course of a conversation on Baudelaire last night: 'I'm not against the asocial, you know; I'm against the non-social.'

21 July. The publications of Lukács, Kurella *et al* are giving Brecht a good deal of trouble. He thinks, however, that one ought not to oppose them at the theoretical level. I then put the question on the political level. He does not pull his punches. 'A socialist economy doesn't need war, and that is why it is opposed to war. The "peace-loving nature of the Russian people" is an expression of this and nothing else. There can't be a socialist economy in one country. Rearmament has inevitably set the Russian proletariat back a lot, back to stages of historical development which have long since been overtaken – among others, the monarchic stage. Russia is now under personal rule. Only blockheads can deny this, of course.' This was a short conversation which was soon interrupted. – I should add that in this context Brecht emphasized that

[1] The name, presumably that of the proposed intermediary, cannot be deciphered with absolute certainty; perhaps Hans Henny Jahn?

[2] Uncertain reading of the manuscript.

as a result of the dissolution of the First International, Marx and Engels lost active contact with the working-class movement and thereafter only gave advice – of a private nature, not intended for publication – to individual leaders. Nor was it an accident – although regrettable – that at the end of his life Engels turned to the natural sciences.

Béla Kun, he said, was his greatest admirer in Russia. Brecht and Heine were the only German poets Kun studied [*sic*]. (Occasionally Brecht hints at the existence of a certain person on the Central Committee who supports him.)

25 July. Yesterday morning Brecht came over to my place to read me his Stalin poem, which is entitled 'The Peasant to his Ox'. At first I did not get its point, and when a moment later the thought of Stalin passed through my head, I did not dare entertain it. This was more or less the effect Brecht intended, and he explained what he meant in the conversation which followed. In this conversation he emphasized, among other things, the positive aspects of the poem. It was indeed a poem in honour of Stalin, who in his opinion had achieved great things. But Stalin is not yet dead. Besides, a different, more enthusiastic manner of honouring Stalin is not incumbent upon Brecht, who is sitting in exile and waiting for the Red Army to march in. He is following developments in Russia and also the writings of Trotsky. These prove that there exists a suspicion – a justifiable one – demanding a sceptical appraisal of Russian affairs. Such scepticism is in the spirit of the Marxist classics. Should the suspicion prove correct one day, then it will become necessary to fight the regime, and *publicly*. But, 'unfortunately or God be praised, whichever you prefer', the suspicion is at present not yet a certainty. There is no justification for constructing upon it a policy such as Trotsky's. 'And then there's no doubt that certain criminal cliques really are at work in Russia itself. One can see it, from time to time, by the harm they do.' Finally Brecht pointed out that we Germans have been especially affected by the setbacks we have suffered in our own country. 'We have had to pay for the stand we took, we're covered with scars. It's only natural that we should be especially sensitive.'

Towards evening Brecht found me in the garden reading *Capital*. Brecht: 'I think it's very good that you're studying Marx just now, at a time when one comes across him less and less, especially among people like us.' I replied that I prefer studying the most talked-about authors when they were out of fashion. We went on to discuss Russian literary policy. I said, referring to Lukács, Gábot and Kurella: 'You can't put on an act with people like this.' Brecht: 'You might put on an Act but certainly not a whole play. They are, to put it bluntly, enemies of production. Production makes them uncomfortable. You never know where you are with production; production is the unforseeable. You never know what's going to come out. And they themselves don't want to produce. They want to play the *apparatchik* and exercise control over other people. Every one of their criticisms contains a threat.' We then got on to Goethe's novels, I don't remember how; Brecht knows only the *Elective Affinities*. He said that what he admired about it was the author's youthful elegance. When I told him Goethe wrote this novel at the age of sixty, he was very much surprised. The book, he said, had nothing philistine about it. That was a tremendous achievement. He knew a thing or two about philistinism; all German drama, including the most significant works, was stamped with it. I remarked that *Elective Affinities* had been very badly received when it came out. Brecht: 'I'm pleased to hear it. – The Germans are a lousy nation [*ein Scheissvolk*]. It isn't true that one must not draw conclusions from Hitler about Germans in general. In me, too, everything that is German is bad. The intolerable thing about us Germans is our narrow-minded independence. Nowhere else were there Imperial Free Cities, like that lousy Augsburg. Lyons was never a free city; the independent cities of the Renaissance were city states. – Lukács is a German by choice, and he's run completely out of steam.'

Speaking of *The Finest Legends of Woynok the Brigand* by Anna Seghers, Brecht praised the book because it shows that Seghers is no longer writing to order. 'Seghers can't produce to order, whereas without an order, I wouldn't even know how to start writing.' He also praised the stories for having a rebellious, solitary figure as their central character.

26 July. Brecht, last night: 'There can't be any doubt about it any longer: the struggle against ideology has become a new ideology.'

29 July. Brecht read to me some polemical texts he has written as part of his controversy with Lukács, studies for an essay which is to be published in *Das Wort*. He asked my advice whether to publish them. As, at the same time, he told me that Lukács's position 'over there' is at the moment very strong, I told him I could offer no advice. 'There are questions of power involved. You ought to get the opinion of somebody from over there. You've got friends there, haven't you?' – Brecht: 'Actually, no, I haven't. Neither have the Muscovites themselves – like the dead.'

3 August. On 29 July in the evening, while we were in the garden, the conversation came round to the question whether a part of the *Children's Songs* cycle should be included in the new volume of poems. I was not in favour, because I thought that the contrast between the political and the private poems made the experience of exile particularly explicit, and this contrast would be diminished by the inclusion of a disparate sequence. In saying this, I probably implied that the suggestion once again reflected the destructive aspect of Brecht's character, which challenges everything almost before it has been achieved. Brecht: 'I know; they'll say of me that I was manic. When the present is passed on to the future, the capacity to understand my mania will be passed on with it. The times we live in will make a backdrop to my mania. But what I should really like would be for people to say about me: he was a *moderate* manic.' – His discovery of moderation, Brecht said, should find expression in this volume of verse: the recognition that life goes on despite Hitler, that there will always be children. He was thinking of the 'epoch without history' of which he speaks in his poem addressed to artists. A few days later he told me he thought the coming of such an epoch more likely than victory over fascism. But then, with a vehemence he rarely shows, he added yet another argument in favour of including the *Children's Songs* in the *Poems from Exile*: 'We must neglect nothing in our struggle against that lot. What they're planning is nothing small, make no mistake about it. They're planning for thirty thousand years ahead. Colossal things. Colossal crimes. They stop at nothing. They're out to destroy everything. Every living cell shrinks under their blows. That is why we too must think of everything. They cripple the baby in the mother's womb. We must on no account leave out the children.' While he was speaking like this I felt a power being exercised over me which was equal in strength to the power of fascism, a power that sprang from depths of history no less deep than the power of the fascists. It was a very curious feeling, and new to me. Then Brecht's thoughts took another turn, which further intensified this feeling I had. 'They're planning devastations on a mind-chilling scale. That's why they can't reach agreement with the Church, which is also geared to thousands of years. And they've proletarianized me too. It isn't just that they've taken my house, my fish-pond and my car from me; they've also robbed me of my stage and my audience. From my own vantage-point I can't admit that Shakespeare's talent was categorically greater than mine. But

Shakespeare couldn't have written just for his desk drawer, any more than I can. Besides, he had his characters before his eyes. The people he depicted were running around in the streets. He just observed their behaviour and picked out a few traits; there were many others, just as important, that he left out.'

Early August. 'In Russia there is dictatorship *over* the proletariat. We should avoid dissociating ourselves from this dictatorship for as long as it still does useful work for the proletariat – i.e. so long as it contributes towards a reconciliation between the proletariat and the peasantry, giving prime recognition to proletarian interests.' A few days later Brecht spoke of a 'workers' monarchy', and I compared this creature with certain grotesque sports of nature dredged up from the depths of the sea in the form of horned fish or other monsters.

25 August. A Brechtian maxim: 'Don't start from the good old things but the bad new ones.'

Translated by Anya Bostock

Presentation III

The largely posthumous publication of his later writings has made Walter Benjamin perhaps the most influential Marxist critic in the German-speaking world, after the Second World War. The major works of his mature period have recently become available in English for the first time, with the translation of a collection of his essays in *Illuminations* (Cape-Fontana), the record of his relationship to the greatest German writer of his day in *Understanding Brecht* (NLB), and now the completed portions of what would clearly have been his masterpiece, *Charles Baudelaire – A Lyric Poet in the Era of High Capitalism* (NLB). The widespread acclaim that Benjamin has received both in his own country and abroad, has, however, with some exceptions not been accompanied by critical appraisal of any great acuity. The Left has been in general concerned to defend his legacy from mystical appropriation of it, the Right to establish its distance from any orthodox canon of historical materialism. It may thus be a surprise that probably the best critique of Benjamin's development in his last phase remains that of his younger friend and colleague Adorno, addressed to him in a number of private letters at the time. The correspondence between the two represents, in fact, one of the most important aesthetic exchanges of the thirties anywhere in Europe. Four of the most significant of these letters are printed below – three from Adorno, with one reply from Benjamin. They concern, respectively: 1. Benjamin's draft outline for his *Arcades* project, written in 1935 (entitled 'Paris – The Capital of the Nineteenth Century', now in *Charles Baudelaire*, pp. 155–70); 2. his famous essay 'The Work of Art in the Age of Mechanical Reproduction', published in 1936 (included in *Illuminations*, pp. 219–53); 3. and 4. his original study of Baudelaire, composed in 1938 (designated 'The Paris of the Second Empire in Baudelaire', in *Charles Baudelaire*, pp. 9–106).

Adorno first met Benjamin in Frankfurt in 1923, and their acquaintance deepened during the subsequent years. In 1928, Benjamin seems to have started work on his *Arcades* project, which he first discussed at length with Adorno the following year at Konigstein. It was also in 1929 that Benjamin formed his close friendship with Brecht. After the Nazi seizure of power in Germany in 1933, Benjamin went into exile in Paris, while Adorno was attached to Oxford, returning periodically to Germany, where his institutional record was relatively unmarked. It was from the Black Forest that Adorno wrote his first substantial criticism of Benjamin's new work in August 1935. By that time, Benjamin was already receiving a regular stipend from the Institute of Social Research, then headed by Horkheimer in New York, which became his main source of support for the rest of the decade. The following year, Adorno received and commented on the manuscript of Benjamin's essay on the technical reproducibility of art, which was subsequently published in the journal of the Institute, the *Zeitschrift für Sozialforschung*, in early 1936. At the turn of the year in 1937–8, the two men saw each other again at San Remo, where they had a series of prolonged discussions before Adorno's final departure to the United States, where he rejoined the Institute for Social Research in February 1938. Later that year, Benjamin sent the three finished chapters of his planned work on Baudelaire to New York, for publication in the *Zeitschrift für Sozialforschung*. Adorno's dissentient response to the text, answering for the Institute as a whole, prevented its inclusion in the *Zeitschrift*. To meet Adorno's criticisms, Benjamin rewrote a part of it, which was published in the Institute's journal as 'On Some Motifs in Baudelaire', in 1939 (now included in *Charles Baudelaire*, pp. 107–54). The only important text subsequently written by Benjamin was his 'Theses on the Philosophy of History', completed a few months before his death in September 1940 – whose influence on the later intellectual development of the Frankfurt School in general, and Adorno in particular, was to be pronounced.

After the Second World War, Adorno was responsible for editing the first two-volume edition of Benjamin's *Schriften*, and for co-editing the two published volumes of his *Briefe*, in the fifties. A decade later, the relationship between Adorno and Benjamin became the object of considerable polemic on the West German Left, after the growth of the student movement and the revival of German Marxism. In assessing the correspondence printed below, however, it is necessary to avoid the illusions of political retrospection, and to situate the actual exchange between the two men historically. Benjamin had been trained in Wilhelmine Berlin before the First World War, where he was influenced by the neo-Kantian philosopher Rickert; early drawn towards Judaic mysticism, he gravitated for a time towards Zionism; in the twenties he discovered Marxism, travelled to Russia (1926–27), and came close to the KPD; his primary focus of interest was always literature. Adorno was eleven years younger, a product of Weimar Germany, and had no religious background; his formation was primarily in music, which he studied under Schönberg in Vienna; his philosophical training was untouched by Wilhelmine *Lebensphilosophie*; on the other hand, his political associations were very tenuous, even his collaboration with the Institute for Social Research only becoming permanent on the eve of the Second World War. At the time of his first letter to Benjamin printed below, he was 32. Culturally, the two men shared certain dominant axes of reference, both temporal and spatial – Proust, Valéry and Kafka, among others. Benjamin, however, always maintained a close interest in surrealism, whose European centre was Paris, that was foreign to Adorno; while Adorno, who had spent many years in Vienna, possessed a much deeper appreciation of psychoanalysis and of the significance of Freud than Benjamin. If contact with Brecht tended to inflect Benjamin towards a more direct Marxism than he normally displayed, communication with Benjamin tended in turn to inflect Adorno towards a more revolutionary materialism than he otherwise revealed – in part, no doubt, precisely to counteract the influence of Brecht. The complexity of this triangular relationship confers on the correspondence of 1935–9 much of its fascination.

Thus, contrary to what might have been expected, Adorno's opening letter to Benjamin, discussing his draft essay 'Paris – Capital of the Nineteenth Century', focuses its criticism essentially on the psychologistic subjectivism and ahistorical romanticism which he believed he could see beneath the dense and lapidary brilliance of Benjamin's text. With remarkable insight, Adorno pointed out that Benjamin's use of Marx's category of commodity fetishism unwarrantably subjectivized it, by converting it from an objective structure of exchange-value into a delusion of individual consciousness. Its erroneous description as a subjective 'dream' was accompanied, moreover, by the misguided corrective of a 'collective' unconscious as the repository of archaic 'myths'. As Adorno commented, this addition compounded rather than tempered Benjamin's initial mistake, since the idea of a collective unconscious inhabited by myths was precisely the ideological notion with which Jung – whose reactionary proclivities were easily visible – had tried to desexualize and erase the scientific concepts of Freud. Failure to understand the true import of psychoanalysis, he incidentally noted, might be related to the dangerous overtones of Benjamin's depreciation of *Art Nouveau*, which Adorno defended for its fundamental impulse towards erotic emancipation. At the same time, implicit valorization of myth could lead both to romantic nostalgia for a primal unity with nature as the realm of lost social innocence, or to its obverse, utopian visions of classlessness that were more 'classless' (in the bad sense) than utopian. The result of the undue confidence accorded to myth was thus necessarily an uncritical nonchalance with history. Adorno, shrewdly underlining the frequency with which the archetypal phrases 'the first time' and 'the last time' occured in the *exposé*, proceeded to raise a whole series of concrete historical objections to the actual imprecision of Benjamin's apparent concreteness of reference. In particular, he stressed the obvious fact that commodity production as such preceded the age of Baudelaire by many centuries, and that it was necessary to distinguish carefully within the development of capitalism between the phase of manufactures and the phase of factory industry proper. In the Second Empire, he suggested, the role of the Parisian arcades as bazaars of exotica could be linked to the overseas adventures of the Bonapartist regime; while the working-class could not be said to have ceased forever to be politically passive after the 1830's. Adorno's numerous smaller criticisms of detail were in the same sense: for example, bricks had preceded iron as an artificial building material, and snobbery should not be confused as a social phenomenon with dandyism. His general recommendation to Benjamin, in conclusion, was to radicalize his method towards greater historical accuracy and material evidence, and more rigorous economic analysis of the objective bases underlying the cultural configurations with which he was concerned.

Benjamin subsequently decided to make a separate book on Baudelaire, out of the original wider *Arcades* project. This was to be divided into three parts: a study of Baudelaire as an allegorist, a study of the social world of Paris in which he wrote, and a study of the commodity as a poetic object which would synthesize the meaning of poet and capital alike.[1] It was the second section of this triptych that he completed in 1938 and sent to New York. In many ways, it seemed to comply with the urgings of Adorno towards greater historical precision and materialist objectivity; all traces of Jungian influence had disappeared, as had any

[1] See Benjamin's *Briefe*, II, p. 774.

oneiric version of commodity fetishism, while a great wealth of meticulous documentation from the epoch of the Second Empire was now superbly assembled and presented by Benjamin. Adorno's response to this manuscript, however, was more astringently critical than to the original *exposé*. The grounds for his reserve were necessarily now somewhat different. In effect, he taxed Benjamin with so restricting the scope of his investigation that the accumulation of period detail risked becoming an occult positivism. Deprived of any explicit Marxist theorization, the relationship between the Paris of the Second Empire and the work of Baudelaire remained arbitrary and opaque. At best, or worst, specific contents of Baudelaire's poetry were directly reduced to economic peripeteia of the time, where a global account of the social structure as a whole could alone mediate a genuinely Marxist decipherment of his literary achievement. Benjamin's 'ascetic' renunciation of theory for an artless catalogue of facts did a disservice both to his own gifts and to historical materialism. Benjamin, in his reply, legitimately protested that the section of his *Baudelaire* submitted to the Institute should not be judged in isolation. Theoretical interpretation of the poet and the city were expressly reserved for the third section that was to conclude the work: hence their intentional absence from the historical treatment of the Parisian themes themselves. Yet it is clear that Adorno was not mistaken in detecting a deeper aversion in Benjamin to systematic theoretical exposition as such, an innate reluctance to decant the mysterious elixir of the world into any translucent vessel of ordered discourse. Beneath, or across, Benjamin's inclination to economic empiricism lay, he commented, traces of religious superstition: a theological reverence for names strangely united with a positivist acquisition of facts, by the common impulse of obsessive 'enumeration' rather than analytic explanation.[2] Adorno's diagnosis of the intellectual blockage that was likely to result from the coadjutant strains of esoteric mysticism and exoteric materialism was a feat of great critical penetration.

At the same time, however, the practical handling by Adorno of the theoretical divergences between the two men plainly lacked wisdom. In both letters to Benjamin about his *Arcades* manuscripts, there is a disturbing note of willed insistence on certain of Adorno's own ideas (the notion of 'dialectical image', the theme of 'hell', or the quotations from

---

[2] Nor were all romantic hints of *Lebensphilosophie* entirely banished, in Adorno's view, as a lingering citation from Simmel indicated. Benjamin later reacted vigorously in defence of this early influence on him: 'You look askance at Simmel: might it not be time to respect him as one of the ancestors of cultural belshevism (*Kulturbolshevismus*)?' *Briefe* II, p. 808.

Jean Paul) at the expense of complete respect for the autonomy of
Benjamin's concerns, incompatible with the proper discretion of a critic.
Much more seriously, the refusal of the Institute of Social Research to
publish the *Baudelaire* texts, for which Adorno was inevitably in large
measure responsible, was a heavy and heedless blow to inflict on Benjamin. The correct course for the *Zeitschrift* was, surely, to publish the
manuscript and then proceed to a critical discussion of it in the journal.
It can only be regretted that a public debate, rather than informal
exchanges by correspondence, was not allowed to appear in its pages.
Benjamin's own response to Adorno's criticism, which had obviously
shaken him, was precisely to plead for the necessity of free discussion in
print of his work – a plea which his personal conditions of acute isolation
and distress in Paris rendered all the more poignant. In the event,
Benjamin was denied this chance, and re-wrote a section of the Baudelaire
study closer to the wishes of the Institute, which published his new
draft 'On Some Motifs in Baudelaire' a few months later.[3] It is striking
that in this text there was a notable loss of the strength of the original
'Paris of the Second Empire in Baudelaire' – its intense absorption and
mastery of cross-connected historical materials – without compensating
gains in theoretical perception. In the new version, Dilthey was dismissed; Jung and Klages – the two figures singled out for attack by
Adorno in his first letter – were now, with a somewhat ostentatious zeal,
consigned to the camp of fascism; while Freud was centrally introduced
through extensive adoption of his notion of 'shock' from *Beyond the
Pleasure Principle*. Unfortunately, this was to select one of the least
successful of Freud's later metapsychological works, and Benjamin's
use of it resulted only in a thinner and weaker variant of the original
manuscript. Thus, while Adorno's own criticisms of Benjamin's work
were profound and powerful as independent contributions to a debate
between the two, Benjamin's obligation to rework his own writing to
approximate it to Adorno's preoccupations produced the opposite of an
improvement. Moreover, the circumstances of this imposition were
aggravated by the fact that the Institute in New York was by 1938–9
under severe pressure from the rabidly counter-revolutionary climate of
American academic culture at the time, and had started to make a series of
tactical adaptations to it. The original *Baudelaire* manuscript opens with
a political discussion of Marx's assessment of professional revolutionary
conspirators in the 1840s, contains constant allusions throughout to

[3] For Adorno's enthusiastic response to the new version, see his letter of 29 February
1940, in *Uber Walter Benjamin*, pp. 157–61.

the proletarian struggles on the barricades of 19th-century France, and closes with a moving evocation of Blanqui. It is unlikely to be an accident that all such passages disappeared from the essay eventually published in the *Zeitschrift für Sozialforschung*. If Benjamin in Paris was a too credulous believer in the thaumaturgical virtue of 'calling things by their names', his colleagues in New York certainly did not suffer from any trusting literalism: they were becoming too adept practitioners of the diplomatic art of euphemism and periphrasis, that knowingly does not call things by their name.

This indirection had already been evident in the Institute's treatment of Benjamin's earlier essay, 'The Work of Art in the Age of Mechanical Reproduction', if on a lesser scale. The version printed in the *Zeitschrift* in 1936 was typically altered by such substitutions as 'totalitarian doctrine' for 'Fascism', 'constructive forces of mankind' for 'communism', and 'modern warfare' for 'imperialist warfare'; while its preface, which directly invoked Marx, was omitted altogether. These deletions, however, were the work of Horkheimer in New York. Adorno at this stage was still uninvolved in the administration of the Institute, and received a typescript of the essay privately in London, some two years before his departure for the United States.

Adorno's own reflections on it to Benjamin were free from any editorial steering, and thus represent perhaps the best example of his critical intelligence at grips with the ideas of his senior. Riposting against Benjamin's attack on aesthetic 'aura' as a vestige of bourgeois culture and his celebration of the progressive function of technical reproducibility in art as the pathway to a new appropriation of it by the masses – realized above all in the cinema, Adorno replied with a defence of avant-garde art and a counter-attack against over-confidence in commerial-popular art. On the other hand, he argued, the 'technicization' of art was no less evident in Viennese atonal music than in Hollywood comedies: the inner formal development of avant-garde art itself had led to the anti-magical exhibition of its mechanisms of 'production', regarded by Benjamin as the great merit of industrial cinema. On the other hand, the allegedly popular art exalted by Benjamin, far from being necessarily non-aural, was in fact typically mimetic and infantilist: the American film industry, in particular, was a vehicle of bourgeois ideology even in its apparently most 'progressive' expressions. Chaplin, cult director of the Left, merely nurtured an inverted brutalism; jazz, ostensibly advanced and collective as a musical form, in fact rested on mesmeric repetition. The idea developed by Benjamin that the 'distraction' of a movie-goer or the 'expertise' of a sports fan could in any way be taken as prototypes of aesthetic liberation was flagrant romanticism. Economically, this conception implied that communist society would not have abolished the work-fatigue that generates the need for distraction, rather than emancipating imaginative energy and sensibility for a new intensity of concentration, as Marx had always envisaged it would. Politically, it forgot Lenin's critique of spontaneism, which Adorno interpreted as precluding any merely optimistic attribution to the working class of an immediate capacity to master the progressive potential or latent meaning of new forms of art, without the assimilation of theoretical knowledge. The real crux of modern aesthetic debate, he concluded, necessarily lay in the problem of the relationship between workers and intellectuals within the revolutionary movement.

The force of many of these arguments remains pertinent today. It is clear that Benjamin, following Brecht, tended to hypostasize techniques in abstraction from relations of production, and to idealize diversions in ignorance of the social determinants of their reproduction. His theory of the positive significance of distraction was based on a specious generalization from architecture,[4] whose forms are always directly used as practical objects and hence necessarily command a distinct type of attention from those of drama, cinema, poetry or painting. Against this rhetoric, Adorno's insistence on traditional norms of aesthetic concentration retains all its validity (just as his brusque dismissal of Chaplin's confused miserabilism can only be ratified today). On the other hand, Adorno's own analysis of jazz – which he himself counterposed to Benjamin's discussion of film – was notoriously myopic and rearguard: focused exclusively on the swing phase of the thirties, it failed completely to perceive the dynamics of jazz as an aesthetic form, with a past and future stretching far beyond the anodyne riffs to which he confined it. Where Benjamin manifestly overestimated the progressive destiny of the commercial-popular art of his time, Adorno no less clearly over-estimated that of the avant-garde art of the period. In fact, signs of imminent conservatism can be seen on both sides of the exchange. Benjamin was already lamenting the advent of sound in the cinema, while Adorno was later unable to muster any enthusiasm for the emergence of electronic music. Both, too, reveal a considerable distance from the actual range of work in the media they discuss, which results in a pervasive vagueness about the precise nature of the 'technique' to whose sovereign power they

[4] See *Illuminations*, pp. 241–2.

both hasten to pay tribute. Adorno tended to equate this simply with the formal laws of any art, while Benjamin identified it essentially with mechanical reproduction. But since technical reproducibility as such had existed at least since the invention of printing during the Renaissance,[5] Benjamin was for the most part obliged in practice to confine the term arbitrarily to the cinema, on the grounds that it alone exemplified reproduction not only in distribution but in production itself, in order to maintain his claim that the principle was a revolutionary innovation of contemporary art.[6] In general, the absolute necessity for a *differential* historical analysis of separate aesthetic forms, and their respective technical elements, was overlooked by both men, who shared a certain proneness to casual conflations. The subsequent development of the main media with which they were concerned has not only been uneven and asymmetrical; it has also demonstrated an extremely complex and variegated set of dialectical relationships between 'high' and 'low', 'avant-garde' and 'popular' strands, that was never envisaged by either. The cinematic expertise in Hollywoodiana which Benjamin prophesied was to be realized by a sophisticated elite of the intelligentsia, which was to use it to transform avant-garde films: for all their erratic merits, it may be doubted whether Benjamin would have savoured the *Cahiers du Cinema* with much zest. Conversely, the immanent development of the jazz abhorred by Adorno eventually led it towards the atonality he had once championed in 'serious' music. Painting, in another operation altogether, was to incorporate comic-strip and advertising motifs, between parody and solemnity. Perhaps the only form to approximate to a fertile aesthetic distraction has been rock, because of its use-relationship to dance. Literature, on the other hand, perhaps the most class-divided of all art forms because of its racination in language, has proved more resistant than any other to the intertwining of popular and vanguard genres.

Neither the complaisance of a perpetually obsolete modernism nor the

---

[5] Actually, of course, technical reproducibility of art-works long predated even the Renaissance: its real inauguration occurred if anything in the Roman epoch, with the perfection of casting and copying techniques in sculpture whose introduction diffused classical forms and images on an enormous scale throughout the Mediterranean world. In general, Benjamin seems to have been strangely unaware of the innovations of Antiquity. Adorno, reproaching him with believing that iron was the first artificial building material, pointed out the priority of brick. Both seem to have forgotten the Roman invention of the first forms of concrete. Both sculptural reproduction and architectural concrete date from the 2nd–1st centuries BC, when Roman hegemony was established in the Hellenistic world.

[6] See *Illuminations*, p. 246, for the privilege Benjamin accorded the cinema.

shrillness of a beleaguered traditionalism can account for these discordant histories. No aesthetic field has been exempt from the rending pressures of the two recurrent poles of all culture still subject to capital, autistically advanced or collusively popular. Adorno's basic dictum in this respect still holds true: 'Both are torn halves of an integral freedom, to which however they do not add up.' The shifting cultural landscape of the seventies inevitably lay far beyond the horizons of the theorists of the thirties. But despite some sectoral breakthroughs in specific disciplines, the themes of the Adorno–Benjamin exchanges have yet to be truly surpassed by any general progress of Marxist aesthetic theory since that time. The correspondence printed below, a dialogue between two idiosyncratic masters of German prose, remains a document of the utmost intellectual and literary interest today.

Theodor Adorno

Letters to Walter Benjamin

I.

Hornberg, Black Forest, 2 August 1935

Dear Herr Benjamin:

Today let me try to say something to you at long last about your draft essay, which I have studied very thoroughly and discussed with Felizitas[1] again; she fully shares the views I express here. It seems to me to be in keeping with the importance of the subject – which, as you know, I rate extremely highly – if I speak with complete candour and proceed without preliminaries to the questions which I believe are equally central for both of us. But I shall preface my critical discussion by saying that even though your method of work means that a sketch and a 'line of thought' cannot convey an adequate representation, your draft seems to me full of the most important ideas. Of these I should like to emphasize only the magnificent passage about living as a leaving of traces, the conclusive sentences about the collector, and the liberation of things from the curse of being useful. The outline of the chapter on Baudelaire as an interpretation of the poet and the introduction of the category of *nouveauté* on p. 172 also seem to me entirely convincing.[2] You will therefore guess what in any case you would hardly have expected to be otherwise: that I am still concerned with the complex which may be designated by the rubrics – prehistory of the 19th century, dialectical image, and configuration of myth and modernism. If I refrain from making a distinction between the 'material' and the 'epistemological' questions, this will still be in keeping, if not with the external organization of your

---

[1] Felizitas was Gretel Adorno, the writer's wife.

[2] All page references are to the English translation, *Charles Baudelaire – A Lyric Poet in the Era of High Capitalism* (NLB, 1973).

draft, at all events with its philosophical core, whose movement is to make the antithesis between the two disappear (as in both the more recent traditional sketches of the dialectic).

Let me take as my point of departure the motto on p. 159, *Chaque époque rêve la suivante* [Every epoch dreams its successor]. This seems to me an important key in that all those motifs of the theory of the dialectical image which underlie my criticism, crystallize around it as an *undialectical* sentence whose elimination could lead to a clarification of the theory itself. For the sentence implies three things: a conception of the dialectical image as a content of consciousness, albeit a collective one; its direct – I would almost say: developmental – relatedness to the future as Utopia; and a notion of the 'epoch' as proper, and self-contained subject of this content of consciousness. It seems extremely significant to me that this version of the dialectical image, which can be called an immanent one, not only threatens the original force of the concept, which was theological in nature, introducing a simplification which attacks not so much its subjective nuance as its basic truth; it also fails to preserve that social movement within the contradiction, for the sake of which you sacrifice theology.

If you transpose the dialectical image into consciousness as a 'dream' you not only take the magic out of the concept and render it sociable, but you also deprive it of that objective liberating power which could legitimize it in materialistic terms. The fetish character of the commodity is not a fact of consciousness; rather, it is dialectical, in the eminent sense that it produces consciousness. This means, however, that consciousness or unconsciousness cannot simply depict it as a dream, but responds to it in equal measure with desire and fear. But it is precisely this dialectical power of the fetish character that is lost in the replica realism (*sit venia verbo*) of your present immanent version of the dialectical image. To return to the language of the glorious first draft of your *Arcades* project: if the dialectical image is nothing but the way in which the fetish character is perceived in a collective consciousness, the Saint Simonian conception of the commodity world may indeed reveal itself as Utopia, but not as its reverse – namely, a dialectical image of the 19th century as Hell. But only the latter could put the idea of a Golden Age into the right perspective, and precisely this dual sense could turn out to be highly appropriate for an interpretation of Offenbach – that is, the dual sense of Underworld and Arcadia; both are explicit categories of Offenbach and could be pursued down into details of his instrumentation. Thus the abandonment of the category of Hell in your draft, and particularly the elimination of the brilliant passage about the gambler (for which the passage about speculation and games of chance is no substitute), seems to me to be not only a loss of lustre but also of dialectical consistency. Now I am the last to be unaware of the relevance of the immanence of consciousness for the 19th century. But the concept of the dialectical image cannot be derived from it; rather, the immanence of consciousness itself is, as *Intérieur*, the dialectical image for the 19th century as alienation. There I shall also have to leave the stake of the second chapter of my Kierkegaard book in the new game.[3] Accordingly, the dialectical image should not be transferred into consciousness as a dream, but in its dialectical construction the dream should be externalized and the immanence of consciousness itself be understood as a constellation of reality – the astronomical phase, as it were, in which Hell wanders through mankind. It seems to me that only the map of such a journey through the stars could offer a clear view of history as prehistory.

Let me try to formulate the same objection again from the diametrically opposite standpoint. In keeping with an immanent version of the dialectical image (with which, to use a positive term, I would contrast your earlier conception of a *model*) you construe the relationship between the oldest and the newest, which was already central to your first draft, as one of Utopian reference to a 'classless society'. Thus the archaic becomes a complementary addition to the new, instead of being the 'newest' itself; it is de-dialecticized. However, at the same time, and equally undialectically, the image of classlessness is put back into mythology instead of becoming truly transparent as a phantasmagoria of Hell. Therefore the category in which the archaic coalesces into the modern seems to me far less a Golden Age than a catastrophe. I once noted that the recent past always presents itself as though it has been destroyed by catastrophes. *Hic et nunc* I would say that it thereby presents itself as prehistory. And at this point I know I am in agreement with the boldest passage in your book on tragedy [*Der Ursprung des deutschen Trauerspiels*].[4]

If the disenchantment of the dialectical image as a 'dream' psychologizes it, by the same token it falls under the spell of bourgeois psychology. For who is the subject of the dream? In the 19th century it was surely only the individual; but in the individual's dream no direct depiction of

---

[3] Adorno's reference is to his first major work, *Kierkegaard: Konstruktion des Aesthetischen*, Tübingen 1933. Written in 1929–30, it was a critique of Kierkegaard's subjective interiority and spiritualist immediacy.

[4] Benjamin had published *Der Ursprung des deutschen Trauerspiels* in 1928. For an English edition, see *The Origin of German Tragic Drama*, NLB 1977.

either the fetish character or its monuments may be found. Hence the collective consciousness is invoked, but I fear that in its present form it cannot be distinguished from Jung's conception. It is open to criticism on both sides; from the vantage point of the social process, in that it hypostasizes archaic images where dialectical images are in fact generated by the commodity character, not in an archaic collective ego, but in alienated bourgeois individuals; and from the vantage point of psychology in that, as Horkheimer puts it, a mass ego exists only in earthquakes and catastrophes, while otherwise objective surplus value prevails precisely through individual subjects and against them. The notion of collective consciousness was invented only to divert attention from true objectivity and its correlate, alienated subjectivity. It is up to us to polarize and dissolve this 'consciousness' dialectically between society and singularities, and not to galvanize it as an imagistic correlate of the commodity character. It should be a clear and sufficient warning that in a dreaming collective no differences remain between classes.

Lastly, moreover, the mythic-archaic category of the 'Golden Age' – and this is what seems socially decisive to me – has had fateful consequences for the commodity category itself. If the crucial 'ambiguity' of the Golden Age is suppressed (a concept which is itself greatly in need of a theory and should by no means be left unexamined), that is, its relationship to Hell, the commodity as the substance of the age becomes Hell pure and simple, yet negated in a way which would actually make the immediacy of the primal state appear as truth. Thus disenchantment of the dialectical image leads directly to purely mythical thinking, and here Klages appears as a danger,[5] as Jung did earlier. Nowhere does your draft contain more remedies than at this point. Here would be the central place for the doctrine of the collector who liberates things from the curse of being useful. If I understand you correctly, this is also where Haussmann belongs; his class consciousness, precisely by a perfection of the commodity character in a Hegelian self-consciousness, inaugurates the explosion of its phantasmagoria. To understand the commodity as a dialectical image is also to see the latter as a motif of the decline and 'supersession' of the commodity, rather than as its mere regression to an older stage. The commodity is, on the one hand, an alienated object in which use-value perishes, and on the other, an alien survivor that outlives its own immediacy. We receive the promise of immortality in

[5] Ludwig Klages (1872–1956) was a conservative and neo-romantic cultural philosopher and historian.

commodities and not for people. To develop the relationship between the *Arcades* project and the book on the Baroque, which you have rightly established, the fetish is a faithless final image, comparable only to a death's-head. It seems to me that this is where the basic epistemological character of Kafka lies, particularly in Odradek, as a commodity that has survived to no purpose.[6] In this fairy tale by Kafka surrealism may come to an end, as baroque drama did in *Hamlet*. But within society this means that the mere concept of use-value by no means suffices for a critique of the commodity character, but only leads back to a stage prior to the division of labour. This has always been my real reservation toward Brecht;[7] his 'collective' and his unmediated concept of function have always been suspect to me, as themselves a 'regression'. Perhaps you will see from these reflections, whose substance concerns precisely those categories in your draft which may conform to those of Brecht, that my opposition to them is not an insular attempt to rescue autonomous art or anything like that, but addresses itself solemnly to those motifs of our philosophical friendship which I regard as basic. If I were to close the circle of my critique with one bold grip, it would be bound to grasp the extremes. A restoration of theology, or better yet, a radicalization of the dialectic into the glowing centre of theology, would at the same time have to mean the utmost intensification of the social-dialectical, indeed economic, motifs. These, above all, must be viewed historically. The *specific* commodity character of the 19th century, in other words, the industrial production of commodities, would have to be worked out much more clearly and materially. After all, commodities and alienation have existed since the beginning of capitalism – i.e. the age of manufactures, which is also that of baroque art; while the 'unity' of the modern age has since then lain precisely in the commodity character. But the complete 'prehistory' and ontology of the 19th century could be established only by an exact definition of the industrial form of the commodity as one clearly distinguished historically from the older form. All references to the commodity form 'as such' give that prehistory a certain metaphorical character, which cannot be tolerated in this serious case. I would surmise that the greatest interpretative results will be achieved here if you unhesitatingly follow your own procedure, the blind processing of material. If, by contrast, my critique moves in a certain theoretical sphere of abstraction, that surely is a difficulty, but I

[6] See *The Cares of a Family Man.*

[7] Brecht is referred to as 'Berta' in the original, for reasons of censorship, since Adorno was writing from Germany.

know that you will not regard it as a mere problem of 'outlook' and thereby dismiss my reservations.

However, permit me to add a few specific remarks of a more concrete character, which will naturally be meaningful only against this theoretical background. As a title I should like to propose *Paris, Capital of the Nineteenth Century*, not *The Capital* – unless the *Arcades* title is revived along with Hell. The division into chapters according to men does not strike me as quite felicitous; it makes for a certain forced systemization which leaves me a little uneasy. Were there not once sections according to materials, like 'plush', 'dust', etc? The relationship between Fourier and the arcades is not very satisfactory either. Here I could imagine as a suitable pattern a constellation of the various urban and commodity materials, an arrangement later to be deciphered as both dialectical image and its theory.

In the motto on p. 157 the word *portique* very nicely supplies the motif of 'antiquity'; in connection with the newest as the oldest, perhaps a morphology of the Empire should be given elementary treatment here (such as melancholy receives in the Baroque book). On p. 158, at any rate, the conception of the State in the Empire as an end in itself should be clearly shown to have been a mere ideology, which your subsequent remarks indicate that you had in mind. You have left the concept of construction completely unilluminated; as both alienation *and* mastery of material it is already eminently dialectical and should, in my opinion, forthwith be expounded dialectically (with a clear differentiation from the present concept of construction; the term engineer, which is very characteristic of the 19th century, probably provides a starting-point!) Incidentally, the introduction and exposition of the concept of the collective unconscious, on which I have already made some basic remarks, are not quite clear here. Regarding p. 158, I should like to ask whether cast iron really was the first artificial building material (bricks!); in general, I sometimes do not feel quite comfortable with the notion of 'first' in the text. Perhaps this formulation could be added: every epoch dreams that it has been destroyed by catastrophes. P. 159: The phrase 'the new and the old are intermingled' is highly dubious to me, given my critique of the dialectical image as regression. There is no reversion to the old, rather, the newest, as semblance and phantasmagoria, is itself the old. Here I may perhaps remind you, without being obtrusive, of some formulations, including certain remarks on ambiguity, in the *Intérieur* section of my work on Kierkegaard. By way of supplementing these: dialectical images are as models not social products, but objective constellations in which 'the social' situation represents itself. Consequently, no ideological or social 'accomplishment' can ever be expected of a dialectical image. My objection to your merely negative account of reification – the critique of the element of 'Klages' in your draft – is based primarily on the passage about machines on p. 159. An over-valuation of machine technology and machines as such has always been peculiar to bourgeois theories of retrospection; the relations of production are concealed by an abstract reference to the means of production.

The very important Hegelian concept of the second nature, which has since been taken up by Georg Lukács[8] and others, belongs on p. 161f. Presumably the '*Diable à Paris*' could lead to Hell. On p. 162, I would very much doubt that the worker appeared as a stage–extra etc, 'for the last time' outside his class. Incidentally, the idea of an early history of the feuilleton, about which so much is contained in your essay on Kraus, is most fascinating; this would be the place for Heine, too. In this connection an old journalistic term occurs to me: *Schablonstil* [cliché style], whose origin ought to be investigated. The term *Lebensgefühl* [attitude to life], used in cultural or intellectual history, is highly objectionable. It seems to me that your uncritical acceptance of the first appearance of technology is connected with your over-valuation of the archaic as such. I noted down this formulation: myth is not the classless longing of a true society, but the objective character of the alienated commodity itself. P. 163: Your conception of the history of painting in the 19th century as a flight from photography (to which there is an exact correspondence in the flight of music from 'banality') is formidable but undialectical, for the share of the forces of production not incorporated in commodity form in our store of paintings cannot be grasped concretely in this way but only in the negative of its trace (Manet is probably the source of this dialectic). This seems to be related to the mythologizing or archaizing tendency of your draft. Belonging to the past, the stock of paintings becomes, so to speak, fixed starry images in the philosophy of history, drained of their quota of productive force. The subjective side of the dialectic vanishes under an undialectically mythical glance, the glance of Medusa.

The Golden Age on p. 164 is perhaps the true transition to Hell. – I cannot see the relationship of the World Fairs to the workers; it sounds like conjecture and surely should be asserted only with extreme caution. Of course, a great definition and theory of phantasmagoria belong on

[8] Referred to simply as 'Georg' in the original.

p. 165f. The next page was a *mene tekel* [warning] to me. Felizitas and I remember the overwhelming impression which the Saturn quotation once made on us; the quotation has not survived a more sober inspection of it. The Saturn ring should not become a cast-iron balcony, but the balcony should become the real Saturn ring. Here I am happy not to offer you any abstract objections but to confront you with your own success: the incomparable moon chapter in your *Kindheit* whose philosophical content belongs here.[9] At this point I remembered what you once said about your *Arcades* study: that it could be wrested away only from the realm of madness. That it has removed itself from this realm rather than subjugating it is proved by the interpretation of the Saturn quotation which bounced off it. This is the centre of my real objections . . . this is where I have to speak so brutally because of the enormous seriousness of the matter. As was probably your intention, the fetish conception of the commodity must be documented with the appropriate passages from the man who discovered it.

The concept of the organic, which also appears on p. 166 and points to a static anthropology, etc, is probably not tenable either, or only in the sense that it merely existed as such prior to the fetish and thus is itself historical, like the idea of 'landscape'. The dialectical commodity motif of Odradek probably belongs on p. 166. The workers' movement appears here somewhat like a *deus ex machina* again. To be sure, as with some other analogous forms, the abbreviated style of your draft may be to blame; this is a reservation that applies to many of my reservations.

A propos the passage about fashion, which seems to me very important, but in its construction should probably be detached from the concept of the organic and brought into relationship with the living, i.e. not to a superior 'nature': the idea of the *changeant* occurred to me – the shot fabric which seems to have had expressive significance for the 19th century and presumably was tied to industrial processes. Perhaps you will pursue this some day; Frau Hessel, whose [fashion] reports in the *Frankfurter Zeitung* we always read with great interest, will surely have some information on it. The passage where I have particular misgivings about the overly abstract use of the commodity category is to be found on p. 166; I doubt if it appeared as such 'for the first time' in the 19th century. (Incidentally, the same objection applies also to the *Intérieur* and the sociology of interiority in my Kierkegaard, and every criticism

---

[9] Benjamin wrote his *Berliner Kindheit um Neunzehnhundert* in the thirties; it was published posthumously in Frankfurt in 1950.

118

that I make of your draft also goes for my own earlier study.) I believe
that the commodity category could be greatly concretized by the specifically modern categories of world trade and imperialism. Related to this
is the arcade as a bazaar, also antique shops as world-trade markets for
the temporal. The significance of 'compressed distance' lies perhaps in
the problems of winning over aimless social strata and imperial conquest.
I am only giving you suggestions; of course, you will be able to unearth
incomparably more conclusive evidence from your material and define
the specific shape of the world of things in the 19th century, perhaps
viewing it from its seamy side – its refuse, remnants, debris.

   The passage about the office, too, probably lacks historical exactitude.
To me the office seems less a direct opposite of the home [*intérieur*] than
a relic of older forms of rooms, probably baroque ones (cf. globes,
maps on the walls, railings, and other kinds of material). Regarding the
theory of *Art Nouveau* on p. 168: if I agree with you that it meant a
decisive shattering of the interior, for me this excludes the idea that it
'mobilizes all the reserve forces of interiority'. Rather, it seems to save
and actualize them through 'externalization'. (The theory of symbolism
in particular belongs here, but above all Mallarmé's interiors, which
have exactly the opposite significance of Kierkegaard's.) In place of interiority *Art Nouveau* put sex. It had recourse to sex precisely because
only in sex could a private person encounter himself not as inward but
as corporeal. This is true of all *Art Nouveau* from Ibsen to Maeterlinck
and d'Annunzio. Its origin is Wagner and not the chamber music of
Brahms. Concrete seems uncharacteristic of *Art Nouveau*; it presumably belongs in the strange vacuum around 1910. Incidentally, I think it
is probable that the real *Art Nouveau* coincided with the great economic
crisis around 1900. Concrete belongs to the pre-war boom. P. 168: Let
me also draw your attention to the very remarkable interpretation of
[Ibsen's] *The Master Builder* in Wedekind's posthumous works. I am
not acquainted with any psychoanalytic literature about awakening, but
I shall look into this. However, is not the dream-interpreting, awakening
psychoanalysis which expressly and polemically dissociates itself from
hypnotism (documentation in Freud's lectures[10]) itself part of *Art
Nouveau*, with which it coincides in time? This is probably a question
of the first order and one that may be very far-reaching. As a corrective
to my basic critique I should like to add the following here: if I reject
the use of the notion of the collective consciousness, it is naturally not

[10] The reference is to Freud's *Introductory Lectures on Psychoanalysis* of 1916–17.

in order to leave the 'bourgeois individual' intact as the real *substratum*. The interior should be made transparent as a social function and its self-containedness should be revealed as an illusion – not *vis-à-vis* a hypostasized collective consciousness, but *vis-à-vis* the real social process itself. The 'individual' is a dialectical instrument of transition that must not be mythicized away, but can only be superseded. Once more I should like to emphasize most strongly the passage about the 'liberation of things from the bondage of being useful' as a brilliant turning-point for the dialectical salvation of the commodity. On p. 169 I should be pleased if the theory of the collector and of the interior as a casing were elaborated as fully as possible.

On p. 170 I should like to call your attention to Maupassant's *La Nuit*, which seems to me the dialectical capstone to Poe's *Man of the Crowd* as cornerstone. I find the passage about the crowd as a veil wonderful. P. 171 is the place for the critique of the dialectical image. You undoubtedly know better than I do that the theory given here does not yet do justice to the enormous demands of the subject. I should only like to say that ambiguity is not the translation of the dialectic into an image, but the 'trace' of that image which itself must first be dialecticized by theory. I seem to remember that there is a serviceable statement concerning this in the Interior chapter of my Kierkegaard book. Re p. 172, perhaps the last stanza of the great 'Femmes Damnées' from [Baudelaire's] *Pièces condamnées*. In my view, the concept of false consciousness must be treated with the greatest caution and should in no case be used any longer without reference to its Hegelian(!) origin. 'Snob' was originally not an aesthetic concept but a social one; it was given currency by Thackeray. A very clear distinction should be made between snob and dandy; the history of the snob should be investigated, and Proust furnishes you the most splendid material for this. Your thesis on p. 172 about *l'art pour l'art* and the total work of art seems untenable to me in its present form. The total work of art and aestheticism in the precise sense of the word are not identical, but diametrically opposed attempts to escape from the commodity character. Thus Baudelaire's relationship to Wagner is as dialectical as his association with a prostitute.

I am not at all satisfied with the theory of speculation on p. 174. For one thing, the theory of games of chance which was so magnificently included in the draft of the *Arcades* study is missing; another thing that is lacking is a real economic theory of the speculator. Speculation is the negative expression of the irrationality of capitalistic reason. Perhaps it would be possible to cope with this passage, too, by means of 'extrapolation to extremes'. An explicit theory of perspective would be indicated on p. 176; I believe there was something on that in the original draft. The stereoscope, which was invented between 1810 and 1820, is relevant here. The fine dialectical conception of the Haussmann chapter could perhaps be brought out more precisely in your study than it is in the draft, where one has to interpret it first.

I must ask you once more to excuse the carping form of these comments; but I believe I owe you at least a few specific examples of my basic criticism.

In true friendship, Yours

II.

London, 18 March 1936

Derr Herr Benjamin:

If today I prepare to convey to you some notes on your extraordinary study ['The Work of Art in the Age of Mechanical Reproduction'], I certainly have no intention of offering you criticism or even an adequate response. The terrible pressure of work on me – the big book on logic,[11] the completion of my contribution to the monograph on Berg,[12] which is ready except for two analyses, and the study on jazz[13] – makes any such endeavour hopeless. This is especially true of a work in the face of which I am very seriously aware of the inadequacy of written communication, for there is not a sentence which I would not wish to discuss with you in detail. I cling to the hope that this will be possible very soon, but on the other hand I do not want to wait so long before giving you some kind of response, however insufficient it may be.

Let me therefore confine myself to one main theme. My ardent interest and my complete approval attach to that aspect of your study which appears to me to carry out your original intention – the dialectical construction of the relationship between myth and history – within the intellectual field of the materialistic dialectic: namely, the dialectical self-dissolution of myth, which is here viewed as the disenchantment of art.

[11] This was the philosophical work, a critique of phenomenology, on which Adorno was engaged while at Oxford. It was eventually published in Stuttgart in 1956 as *Zur Metakritik der Erkenntnistheorie. Studien über Husserl und die phänomenologischen Antinomien.*

[12] Included in Willi Reich (ed), *Alban Berg*, Vienna 1937.

[13] Published as 'Über Jazz' in the *Zeitschrift für Sozialforschung*, 5, 1936, and later included in Adorno's volume *Moments Musicaux*, Frankfurt 1964. For Adorno's views on jazz, see also his essay 'Perennial Fashion – Jazz', *Prisms*, London 1967.

You know that the subject of the 'liquidation of art' has for many years underlain my aesthetic studies and that my emphatic espousal of the primacy of technology, especially in music, must be understood strictly in this sense and in that of your second technique. It does not surprise me if we find common ground here; it does not surprise me, because in your book on the Baroque you accomplished the differentiation of the allegory from the symbol (in the new terminology, the 'aural' symbol) and in your *Einbahnstrasse*[14] you differentiated the work of art from magical documentation. It is a splendid confirmation – I hope it does not sound immodest if I say: for both of us – that in an essay on Schönberg which appeared in a *Festschrift* two years ago[15] and with which you are not familiar, I proposed formulations about technology and dialectics as well as the alteration of relationships to technology, which are in perfect accord with your own.

It is this accord which for me constitutes the criterion for the differences that I must now state, with no other aim than to serve our 'general line', which is now so clearly discernible. In doing so, perhaps I can start out by following our old method of immanent criticism. In your earlier writings, of which your present essay is a continuation, you differentiated the idea of the work of art as a structure from the symbol of theology and from the taboo of magic. I now find it disquieting – and here I see a sublimated remnant of certain Brechtian motifs – that you now casually transfer the concept of magical aura to the 'autonomous work of art' and flatly assign to the latter a counter-revolutionary function. I need not assure you that I am fully aware of the magical element in the bourgeois work of art (particularly since I constantly attempt to expose the bourgeois philosophy of idealism, which is associated with the concept of aesthetic autonomy, as mythical in the fullest sense). However, it seems to me that the centre of the autonomous work of art does not itself belong on the side of myth – excuse my topic parlance – but is inherently dialectical; within itself it juxtaposes the magical and the mark of freedom. If I remember correctly, you once said something similar in connection with Mallarmé, and I cannot express to you my feeling about your entire essay more clearly than by telling you that I constantly found myself wishing for a study of Mallarmé as a counterpoint to your essay, a study which, in my estimation, you owe us as an important contribution to our knowledge. Dialectical though your essay may be, it is not so in the

[14] Benjamin's volume of aphorisms *Einbahnstrasse* was published in Berlin in 1928. and then later included in Adorno's collection *Impromptus*, Frankfurt 1968.
[15] This essay, 'Der dialektische Komponist', was originally published in Vienna in 1934.

case of the autonomous work of art itself; it disregards an elementary experience which becomes more evident to me every day in my own musical experience – that precisely the uttermost consistency in the pursuit of the technical laws of autonomous art changes this art and instead of rendering it into a taboo or fetish, brings it close to the state of freedom, of something that can be consciously produced and made. I know of no better materialistic programme than that statement by Mallarmé in which he defines works of literature as something not inspired but made out of words; and the greatest figures of reaction, such as Valéry and Borchardt (the latter with his essay about villas[16] which, despite an unspeakable comment about workers, could be taken over in a materialistic sense in its entirety), have this explosive power in their innermost cells. If you defend the *kitsch* film against the 'quality' film, no one can be more in agreement with you than I am; but *l'art pour l'art* is just as much in need of a defence, and the united front which exists against it and which to my knowledge extends from Brecht to the Youth Movement, would be encouragement enough to undertake a rescue.

[In your essay on *The Elective Affinities*][17] you speak of play and appearance as the elements of art; but I do not see why play should be dialectical, and appearance – the appearance which you have managed to preserve in Ottilie who, together with Mignon and Helena,[18] now does not come off so well – should not. And at this point, to be sure, the debate turns political quickly enough. For if you render rightly technicization and alienation dialectical, but not in equal measure the world of objectified subjectivity, the political effect is to credit the proletariat (as the cinema's subject) directly with an achievement which, according to Lenin, it can realize only through a theory introduced by intellectuals as dialectical subjects, who themselves belong to the sphere of works of art which you have consigned to Hell.

Understand me correctly. I would not want to claim the autonomy of the work of art as a prerogative, and I agree with you that the aural element of the work of art is declining – not only because of its technical reproducibility, incidentally, but above all because of the fulfilment of

---

[16] Rudolf Borchardt (1877–1945) was a prominent litterateur in Germany, whose essay on Tuscan villas is included in the edited volume of his writings, *Prosa III*, Stuttgart 1960, pp. 38–70.

[17] Benjamin's essay *Goethes Wahlverwandtschaften* was published in Hofmannsthal's journal *Neue Deutsche Beiträge* in 1924–5.

[18] Characters in Goethe's *Elective Affinities*, *Wilhelm Meister's Apprenticeship*, and *Faust II*, respectively.

its own 'autonomous' formal laws (this is the subject of the theory of musical reproduction which Kolisch and I have been planning for years). But the autonomy of the work of art, and therefore its material form, is not identical with the magical element in it. The reification of a great work of art is not just loss, any more than the reification of the cinema is all loss. It would be bourgeois reaction to negate the reification of the cinema in the name of the ego, and it would border on anarchism to revoke the reification of a great work of art in the spirit of immediate use-values. '*Les extrèmes me touchent*' [Gide], just as they touch you – but only if the dialectic of the lowest has the same value as the dialectic of the highest, rather than the latter simply decaying. Both bear the stigmata of capitalism, both contain elements of change (but never, of course, the middle-term between Schönberg and the American film). Both are torn halves of an integral freedom, to which however they do not add up. It would be romantic to sacrifice one to the other, either as the bourgeois romanticism of the conservation of personality and all that stuff, or as the anarchistic romanticism of blind confidence in the spontaneous power of the proletariat in the historical process – a proletariat which is itself a product of bourgeois society.

To a certain extent I must accuse your essay of this second romanticism. You have swept art out of the corners of its taboos – but it is as though you feared a consequent inrush of barbarism (who could share your fear more than I?) and protected yourself by raising what you fear to a kind of inverse taboo. The laughter of the audience at a cinema – I discussed this with Max, and he has probably told you about it already – is anything but good and revolutionary; instead, it is full of the worst bourgeois sadism. I very much doubt the expertise of the newspaper boys who discuss sports; and despite its shock-like seduction I do not find your theory of distraction convincing – if only for the simple reason that in a communist society work will be organized in such a way that people will no longer be so tired and so stultified that they need distraction. On the other hand, certain concepts of capitalist practice, like that of the test, seem to me almost ontologically congealed and taboo-like in function – whereas if anything does have an aural character, it is surely the film which possesses it to an extreme and highly suspect degree. To select only one more small item: the idea that a reactionary is turned into a member of the avant-garde by expert knowledge of Chaplin's films strikes me as out-and-out romanticization. For I cannot count Kracauer's[19]

---

[19] Siegfried Kracauer, long a friend of Adorno, was the author of *From Caligari to Hitler*, Princeton 1947, an attack on German expressionist cinema.

favourite director, even after *Modern Times*, as an avant-garde artist (the reason will be perfectly clear from my article on jazz), nor do I believe that any of the decent elements in this work will attract attention. One need only have heard the laughter of the audience at the film to know what is actually happening.

Your dig at Werfel gave me great pleasure. But if you take Mickey Mouse instead, things are far more complicated, and the serious question arises as to whether the reproduction of every person really constitutes that *a priori* of the film which you claim it to be, or whether instead this reproduction belongs precisely to that 'naïve realism' whose bourgeois nature we so thoroughly agreed upon in Paris. After all, it is hardly an accident if that modern art which you counterpose to technical art as aural, is of such inherently dubious quality as Vlaminck[20] and Rilke. The lower sphere, to be sure, can score an easy victory over this sort of art; but if instead there were the names of, let us say, Kafka and Schön-berg, the problem would be posed very differently. Certainly Schönberg's music is *not* aural.

Accordingly, what I would postulate is *more* dialectics. On the one hand, dialectical penetration of the 'autonomous' work of art which is transcended by its own technology into a planned work; on the other, an even stronger dialecticization of utilitarian art in its negativity, which you certainly do not fail to note but which you designate by relatively abstract categories like 'film capital', without tracking it down to its ultimate lair as immanent irrationality. When I spent a day in the studios of Neubabelsberg two years ago, what impressed me most was how *little* montage and all the advanced techniques that you emphasize are actually used; rather, reality is everywhere *constructed* with an infantile mimetism and then 'photographed'. You under-estimate the technicality of auto-nomous art and over-estimate that of dependent art; this, in plain terms, would be my main objection. But this objection could only be given effect as a dialectic between extremes which you tear apart. In my estima-tion, this would involve nothing less than the complete liquidation of the Brechtian motifs which have already undergone an extensive trans-formation in your study – above all, the liquidation of any appeal to the immediacy of interconnected aesthetic effects, however fashioned, and to the actual consciousness of actual workers who have absolutely no advantage over the bourgeois except their interest in the revolution, but otherwise bear all the marks of mutilation of the typical bourgeois

[20] Changed to Dérain in the published version of Benjamin's essay.

character. This prescribes our function for us clearly enough – which I certainly do not mean in the sense of an activist conception of 'intellectuals'. But it cannot mean either that we may only escape the old taboos by entering into new ones – 'tests', so to speak. The goal of the revolution is the abolition of fear. Therefore we need have no fear of it, nor need we ontologize our fear. It is not bourgeois idealism if, in full knowledge and without mental prohibitions, we maintain our solidarity with the proletariat instead of making of our own necessity a virtue of the proletariat, as we are always tempted to do – the proletariat which itself experiences the same necessity and needs us for knowledge as much as we need the proletariat to make the revolution. I am convinced that the further development of the aesthetic debate which you have so magnificently inaugurated, depends essentially on a true accounting of the relationship of the intellectuals to the working-class.

Excuse the haste of these notes. All this could be seriously settled only on the basis of the details in which the Good Lord – possibly not magical after all – dwells.* Only the shortage of time leads me to use the large categories which you have taught me strictly to avoid. In order at least to indicate to you the concrete passages to which I refer, I have left my spontaneous pencilled annotations on the manuscript, though some of them may be too spontaneous to be communicated. I beg your indulgence for this as well as for the sketchy nature of my letter.

I am going to Germany on Sunday. It is possible that I shall be able to complete my jazz study there, something that I unfortunately did not have time to do in London. In that case I would send it to you without a covering letter and ask you to send it on to Max immediately after reading it (it probably will amount to no more than 25 printed pages). This is not certain, because I do not know whether I shall find the time or, especially, whether the nature of this study will permit me to send it from Germany without considerable danger. Max has probably told you that the idea of the clown is its focal point. I would be very pleased if it appeared together with your study. Its subject is a very modest one, but it probably converges with yours in its decisive points, and will attempt to express positively some of the things that I have formulated negatively today. It arrives at a complete verdict on jazz, in particular by revealing its 'progressive' elements (semblance of montage, collective work, primacy of reproduction over production) as façades of something that is in truth quite reactionary. I believe that I have succeeded in really

* A reference to the programmatic dictum of the art historian Aby Warburg: *Der liebe Gott wohnt in Detail* (The Good Lord dwells in details).

decoding jazz and defining its social function. Max was quite taken with my study, and I could well imagine that you will be, too, Indeed I feel that our theoretical disagreement is not really a discord between us but rather, that it is my task to hold your arm steady until the sun of Brecht has once more sunk into exotic waters. Please understand my criticisms only in this spirit.

I cannot conclude, however, without telling you that your few sentences about the disintegration of the proletariat as 'masses' through revolution[21] are among the profoundest and most powerful statements of political theory that I have encountered since I read *State and Revolution*.

Your old friend,

Teddie Wiesengrund*

I should also like to express my special agreement with your theory of Dadaism. It fits into the essay as nicely as the 'bombast' and the 'horrors' fit into your Baroque book.

III.

New York, 10 November 1938

Dear Walter:

The tardiness of this letter levels a menacing charge against me and all of us. But perhaps this accusation already contains a grain of defence. For it is almost self-evident that a full month's delay in my response to your Baudelaire cannot be due to negligence.

The reasons are entirely objective in nature. They involve the attitude of all of us to the manuscript, and, considering my special interest in the question of the *Arcades* study, I can probably say without immodesty, my attitude in particular. I had been looking forward to the arrival of the Baudelaire with the greatest eagerness and literally devoured it. I am full of admiration for the fact that you were able to complete it by the appointed time, and it is this admiration which makes it particularly hard for me to speak of what has come between my passionate expectation and the text itself.

Your idea of providing in the *Baudelaire* a model for the *Arcades* study was something I took very seriously, and I approached the satanic scene much as Faust approached the phantasmagoria of the Brocken mountain

---

[21] This passage does not appear in any of the published versions of Benjamin's essay.

* Wiesengrund was Adorno's paternal name.

when he thought that many a riddle would now be solved. May I be excused for having had to give myself Mephistopheles' reply that many a riddle poses itself anew? Can you understand that reading your treatise, one of whose chapters is entitled *The Flâneur* and another *Modernism*, produced a certain disappointment in me?

The basic reason for this disappointment is that those parts of the study with which I am familiar do not constitute a model for the *Arcades* project so much as a prelude to it. Motifs are assembled but not elaborated. In your covering letter to Max [Horkheimer] you represented this as your express intention, and I am aware of the ascetic discipline which you impose on yourself to omit everywhere the conclusive theoretical answers to questions, and even make the questions themselves apparent only to initiates. But I wonder whether such an asceticism can be sustained in the face of such a subject and in a context which makes such powerful inner demands. As a faithful reader of your writings I know very well that in your work there is no lack of precedents for your procedure. I remember, for example, your essays on Proust and on Surrealism which appeared in *Die literarische Welt*. But can this method be applied to the complex of the *Arcades*? Panorama and 'traces', *flâneur* and arcades, modernism and the unchanging, *without* a theoretical interpretation – is this a 'material' which can patiently await interpretation without being consumed by its own aura? Rather, if the pragmatic content of these topics is isolated, does it not conspire in almost demonic fashion against the possibility of its own interpretation? In one of our unforgettable conversations in Königstein, you said that each idea in the *Arcades* had to be wrested away from a realm in which madness reigns. I wonder whether such ideas need to be as immured behind impenetrable layers of material as your ascetic discipline demands. In your present study the arcades are introduced with a reference to the narrowness of the pavements which impede the *flâneur* on the streets.[22] This pragmatic introduction, it seems to me, prejudices the objectivity of phantasmagoria – something that I so stubbornly insisted upon even at the time of our Hornberg correspondence – as much as does the disposition of the first chapter to reduce phantasmagoria to types of behaviour of the literary *bohème*. You need not fear that I shall suggest that in your study phantasmagoria should survive unmediated or that the study itself should assume a phantasmagoric character. But the liquidation of phantasmagoria can only be accomplished with true

[22] See *Charles Baudelaire*, p. 36.

profundity if they are treated as an objective historico-philosophical category and not as a 'vision' of social characters. It is precisely at this point that your conception differs from all other approaches to the 19th century. But the redemption of your postulate cannot be postponed for ever, or 'prepared' by a more harmless presentation of the matters in question. This is my objection. If in the third part, to use the old formulation, prehistory *in* the 19th century takes the place of the prehistory *of* the 19th century – most clearly in Péguy's statement about Victor Hugo[23] – this is only another way of stating the same point.

But it seems to me that my objection by no means concerns only the questionable procedure of 'abstention' in a subject which is transported by ascetic refusal of interpretation towards a realm to which asceticism is opposed: the realm where history and magic oscillate. Rather, I see a close connection between the points at which your essay falls behind its own *a priori*, and its relationship to dialectical materialism – and here in particular I speak not only for myself but equally for Max, with whom I have had an exhaustive discussion of this question. Let me express myself in as simple and Hegelian a manner as possible. Unless I am very much mistaken, your dialectic lacks one thing: mediation. Throughout your text there is a tendency to relate the pragmatic contents of Baudelaire's work directly to adjacent features in the social history of his time, preferably economic features. I have in mind the passage about the duty on wine, certain statements about the barricades,[24] or the above-mentioned passage about the arcades,[25] which I find particularly problematic, for this is where the transition from a general theoretical discussion of physiologies to the 'concrete' representation of the *flâneur* is especially precarious.

I feel this artificiality wherever you put things in metaphorical rather than categorical terms. A case in point is the passage about the transformation of the city into an *intérieur* for the *flâneur*;[26] there one of the most powerful ideas in your study seems to me to be presented as a mere as-if. There is a very close connection between such materialistic excursions, in which one never quite loses the apprehension that one feels for a swimmer who, covered with goose pimples, plunges into cold water, and the appeal to concrete modes of behaviour like that of the *flâneur*, or the subsequent passage about the relationship between seeing

[23] *Charles Baudelaire*, p. 84.
[24] *Charles Baudelaire*, p. 17ff, pp. 15–16.
[25] *Charles Baudelaire*, p. 36.
[26] *Charles Baudelaire*, p. 37.

and hearing in the city, which not entirely by accident uses a quotation from Simmel.[27] I am not entirely happy with all this. You need not fear that I shall take this opportunity to mount my hobby-horse. I shall content myself with serving it, in passing, a lump of sugar, and for the rest I shall try to give you the theoretical grounds for my aversion to that particular type of concreteness and its behaviouristic overtones. The reason is that I regard it as methodologically unfortunate to give conspicuous individual features from the realm of the superstructure a 'materialistic' turn by relating them immediately and perhaps even causally to corresponding features of the infrastructure. Materialist determination of cultural traits is only possible if it is mediated through the *total social process*.

Even though Baudelaire's wine poems may have been motivated by the wine duty and the town gates, the recurrence of these motifs in his work can only be explained by the overall social and economic tendency of the age – that is, in keeping with your formulation of the problem *sensu strictissimo*, by analysis of the commodity form in Baudelaire's epoch. No one is more familiar with the difficulties this involves than I am; the phantasmagoria chapter in my Wagner[28] certainly has not settled these problems as yet. Your *Arcades* study in its definitive form will not be able to shirk the same obligation. The direct inference from the duty on wine to *L'Ame du Vin* imputes to phenomena precisely that kind of spontaneity, palpability and density which they have lost in capitalism. In this sort of immediate – I would almost say again, anthropological – materialism, there is a profoundly romantic element, and the more crassly and roughly you confront the Baudelairean world of forms with the necessities of life, the more clearly I detect it. The 'mediation' which I miss and find obscured by materialistic-historiographic invocation, is nothing other than the theory which your study omits. The omission of the theory affects your empirical evidence itself. On the one hand, it lends it a deceptively epic character, and on the other it deprives the phenomena, which are experienced only subjectively, of their real historico-philosophical weight. To express it another way: the theological motif of calling things by their names tends to turn into a wide-eyed presentation of mere facts. If one wished to put it very drastically, one could say that your study is located at the crossroads of magic and positivism. That spot is bewitched. Only theory could break the spell –

---

[27] *Charles Baudelaire*, pp. 37–8.
[28] See Adorno's study, *Versuch über Wagner*, Frankfurt 1952, p. 90ff.

your own resolute, salutarily speculative theory. It is the claim of this theory alone that I am bringing against you.

Forgive me if this brings me to a subject which is bound to be of particular concern to me since my experiences with the Wagner study. I am referring to the ragpicker. It seems to me that his destiny as the figure of the lower limits of poverty is certainly not brought out by the way the word ragpicker appears in your study.[29] It contains none of the dog-like cringing, nothing of the sack on his back or the voice which, for instance, in Charpentier's *Louise* provides, as it were, the source of black light for an entire opera. There is nothing in it of the comet's tail of jeering children behind the old man. If I may venture into the region of the arcades once more: in the figure of the ragpicker the retreat of cloaca and catacomb should have been decoded theoretically. But I wonder whether I exaggerate in assuming that your failure to do so is related to the fact that the capitalist function of the ragpicker – namely, to subject even rubbish to exchange value – is not articulated. At this point the asceticism of your study takes on features which would be worthy of Savonarola. For the return of the ragpicker in the Baudelaire quotation in the third section comes very close to this question.[30] What it must have cost you not to close the gap completely!

This, I think, brings me to the centre of my criticism. The impression which your entire study conveys – and not only on me and my arcades orthodoxy – is that you have done violence to yourself. Your solidarity with the Institute [of Social Research], which pleases no one more than myself, has induced you to pay tributes to Marxism which are not really suited either to Marxism or to yourself. They are not suited to Marxism because the mediation through the total social process is missing, and you superstitiously attribute to material enumeration a power of illumination which is never kept for a pragmatic reference but only for theoretical construction. They do not suit your own individual nature because you have denied yourself your boldest and most fruitful ideas in a kind of pre-censorship according to materialist categories (which by no means coincide with the Marxist categories), even though it may be merely in the form of the above-mentioned postponement. I speak not only for myself, who am not qualified, but equally for Horkheimer and the others when I tell you that all of us are convinced that it would not only be beneficial to 'your' production if you elaborated your ideas without such considerations (in San Remo you raised counter-objections

[29] *Charles Baudelaire*, pp. 19–20.
[30] *Charles Baudelaire*, p. 79–80.

to this objection, and I am taking these very seriously), but that it would also be most helpful to the cause of dialectical materialism and the theoretical interests represented by the Institute, if you surrendered to your specific insights and conclusions without adding to them ingredients which you obviously find so distasteful to swallow that I cannot really regard them as beneficial. God knows, there is only one truth, and if your intelligence lays hold of this one truth in categories which on the basis of your idea of materialism may seem apocryphal to you, you will capture more of this one truth than if you use intellectual tools whose movements your hand resists at every turn. After all, there is more about this truth in Nietzsche's *Genealogy of Morals* than in Bukharin's *ABC of Communism*. I am confident that the thesis I am arguing cannot be suspected of laxity and eclecticism. Your study of Goethe's *Elective Affinities* and your Baroque book are better Marxism than the wine duty and the deduction of phantasmagoria from the behaviour of the feuilletonists. You may be confident that we are ready to make the most extreme experiments of your theory our own. But we are equally confident that you will actually make these experiments. Gretel once said in jest that you are an inhabitant of the cave-like depths of your Arcades and that you shrink from finishing your study because you are afraid of having to leave what you have built. Let us encourage you to give us access to the holy of holies. I believe you need not be concerned with either the stability of the structure or its profanation.

As regards the fate of your study, a rather strange situation has developed, in which I have had to act much like the singer of the song 'It is done to the sound of a muffled drum'.* Publication in the current issues of our periodical proved impossible because the weeks of discussion of your study would have caused an intolerable delay in our printing schedule. There was a plan to print the second chapter *in extenso* and the third in part; Leo Löwenthal urged that this be done. I myself am definitely opposed to it – not for editorial reasons, but for your own sake and for the sake of Baudelaire. This study does not represent you as it, of all your writings, must represent you. But since I am of the firm and unalterable conviction that it will be possible for you to produce a Baudelaire manuscript of full impact, I should like to entreat you to forgo the publication of the present version and to write that other version. Whether the latter would have to possess a

* 'Es geht bei gedämpfter Trommel Klang' – the opening line of 'Der Soldat' by Hans Christian Andersen, translated by Adelbert von Chamisso and set to music by Robert Schumann.

new formal structure or could be essentially identical with the still un-
written final part of your *book* on Baudelaire, I cannot surmise. You
alone can decide this. I should like to make it plain that this is a request
on my part and not an editorial decision or a rejection.

. . .

Let me close with some *epilegomena* to the Baudelaire. First a stanza
from the second Mazeppa poem of Victor Hugo (the man who is supposed to see all these things is Mazeppa, tied to the back of the horse):

> *Les six lunes d'Herschel, l'anneau du vieux Saturne,*
> *Le pôle, arrondissant une aurore nocturne*
>   *Sur son front boréal,*
> *Il voit tout ; et pour lui ton vol, que rien ne lasse,*
> *De ce monde sans borne à chaque instant déplace*
>   *L'horizon idéal.*

Also, the tendency toward 'unqualified statements' which you observe,
citing Balzac and the description of the employees in 'The Man of the
Crowd',[31] applies, astonishingly enough, to Sade as well. One of the
first tormentors of Justine, a banker, is described as follows: 'Monsieur
Dubourg, gros, court, et insolent comme tous les financiers'. The motif
of the unknown beloved appears in rudimentary form in Hebbel's poem
about an unknown woman which contains these memorable lines:
*Und kann ich Form Dir und Gestalt nicht geben, So reisst auch keine Form
Dich in die Gruft* [And even if I cannot give you form and shape, no form
will thrust you into the grave].

    Finally, a few sentences from the *Herbst-Blumine* of Jean Paul which
is a real *trouvaille* [find]: 'The day received one single sun, but the night
received a thousand suns, and the endless blue sea of the ether seems to
be sinking down to us in a drizzle of light. How many street lamps shim-
mer up and down the whole long Milky Way! These are lit, too, even
though it is summer or the moon is shining. Meanwhile, the night does
not merely adorn itself with the cloak full of stars which the ancients
depicted it as wearing and which I shall more tastefully call its *religious*
vestments rather than its ducal robe; it carries its beautification much
farther and imitates the ladies of Spain. They replace the jewels in their
head-dress with glow-worms in the darkness, and like them the night
studs the lower part of its cloak, where there are no glittering stars,

[31] *Charles Baudelaire*, pp. 39.

with such little animals, and often the children take them off.' The follow-ing sentences from a quite different piece in the same collection seem to me to belong in the same context:

'And more of the same; for I noticed not only that Italy was a moonlit Eden to us poor drift-ice people, because daily or nightly we encountered there the living fulfilment of the universal adolescent dream of nights spent wandering and singing, but I also asked why people merely walked around and sang in the streets at night like peevish nightwatch-men, instead of whole evening-star and morning-star parties assembling and in a colourful procession (for every soul was in love) roaming through the most magnificent leafy woods and the brightly moonlit flowery meadows, and adding two more phrases on the flute to the joyful harmony – namely, the double-ended extension of the brief night by a sunrise and a sunset plus the added dawn and dusk.' The idea that the longing which draws one to Italy is a longing for a country where one does not need to sleep is profoundly related to the later image of the roofed-over city. But the light which rests equally on the two images is, I think, none other than the light of the gas lamp, with which Jean Paul was not acquainted.

   Tout entier Yours

Walter Benjamin

Reply

Paris, 9 December 1938

Dear Teddie:

It will not have surprised you to notice that it took me some time to draft my reply to your letter of 10 November. Even though the long delay in your letter made me suspect what it would say, it still came as a jolt to me. Also, I wanted to await the arrival of the galleys which you had promised me, and they did not come until 6 December. The time thus gained gave me a chance to weigh your critique as prudently as I could. I am far from considering it unfruitful, let alone incomprehensible. I will try to react to it in basic terms.

I shall be guided by a sentence on the first page of your letter. You write: 'Panorama and traces, *flâneur* and arcades, modernism and the unchanging, without a theoretical interpretation – is this a "substance" which can patiently await interpretation?'. The understandable impatience with which you searched the manuscript for a definite *signalement* [characterization] has, in my opinion, led you astray in some important respects. In particular you were bound to arrive at what was to you a disappointing view of the third section, once it had escaped your attention that nowhere is modernism cited as the unchanging; actually, this important key concept is not used at all in the completed portion of my study.

Since the sentence quoted above offers, as it were, a compendium of your criticisms, I should like to go over it word by word. First you mention the panorama. In my text I refer to it in passing. In point of fact, in the context of Baudelaire's work the panoramic view is not appropriate. Since that passage is not destined to have correspondences in either the first or the third part, it would perhaps be best to omit it. The second item you mention is the 'trace'. In my covering letter I

134

wrote that the philosophical foundations of the book cannot be perceived from the vantage point of the second part. If a concept like the trace was to be given a convincing interpretation, it had to be introduced with complete naturalness at the empirical level. This could have been done still more convincingly. Actually, my first act after my return was to find a very important passage in Poe bearing on my construction of the detective story out of the obliteration or fixation of the traces of the individual in the big-city crowd. But the treatment of traces in the second part must remain on this level, precisely in order later to receive in the decisive contexts its sudden illumination. This illumination is intended. The concept of the trace finds its philosophical determination in opposition to the concept of aura.

The next item in the sentence which I shall examine is the *flâneur*. Even though I am well aware of the profound inner concern on which both your material and your personal objections are based, your erroneous estimate here makes me feel as if the ground were giving way under my feet. Thank God there is a branch that I can cling to which seems to be firm. It is your reference elsewhere to the fruitful tension between your theory about the consumption of exchange value and my theory about empathy with the soul of the commodity. I too believe that this is a theory in the strictest sense of the word, and my discussion of the *flâneur* culminates in it. This is the place, and to be sure the only one in this section, where the theory comes into its own in *unobstructed* form. It breaks like a single ray of light into an artificially darkened chamber. But this ray, broken down prismatically, suffices to give an idea of the nature of the light whose focus lies in the third part of the book. That is why this theory of the *flâneur*, the improvability of which at certain points I shall discuss below, is an adequate realization of the representation of the *flâneur* which I have had in mind for many years.

I go on to the next term, arcades. I feel so much the less inclined to say anything about it, as the bottomless bonhomie of its use cannot have escaped you. Why question this term? Unless I am very much mistaken, the arcade is really not destined to enter the context of the Baudelaire in any but this playful form. It occurs like the picture of a rocky spring on a drinking cup. That is why the invaluable passage from Jean Paul to which you referred me does not belong in the Baudelaire. Finally, in regard to modernism: as my text makes clear, this is Baudelaire's own term. The section with this title could not go beyond the limits imposed upon the word by Baudelaire's usage. But you will remember from San Remo that these limits are by no means definitive. The philosophical reconnaissance of modernism is assigned to the third part, where it is initiated with the concept of *Art Nouveau* and concluded with the dialectics of the new and the unchanging.

Remembering our conversations in San Remo, I should like to proceed to the passage in your letter where you refer to them yourself. If I refused there, in the name of my own productive interests, to adopt an esoteric intellectual development for myself and, disregarding the interests of dialectical materialism, . . . to get down to business, this involved, in the final analysis, not . . . mere loyalty to dialectical materialism, but solidarity with the experiences which all of us have shared in the past 15 years. Here too, then, it is a matter of very personal productive interests of mine; I cannot deny that they may occasionally tend to do violence to my original interests. Between them lies an antagonism of which I would not even in my dreams wish to be relieved. The overcoming of this antagonism constitutes the problem of my study, and the problem is one of construction. I believe that speculation can start its necessarily bold flight with some prospect of success only if, instead of putting on the waxen wings of the esoteric, it seeks its source of strength in construction alone. It is because of the needs of construction that the second part of my book consists primarily of philological material. What is involved there is less an 'ascetic discipline' than a methodological precaution. Incidentally, this philological part was the only one that could be completed independently – a circumstance which I had to bear in mind.

When you speak of a 'wide-eyed presentation of mere facts', you characterize the true philological attitude. This attitude was necessary not only for its results, but had to be built into the construction for its own sake. It is true that the indifference between magic and positivism, as you so aptly formulate it, should be liquidated. In other words, the philological interpretation of the author ought to be preserved and surpassed in the Hegelian manner by dialectical materialists. Philology is the examination of a text which proceeds by details and so magically fixates the reader on it. That which Faust took home in black and white,[1] and Grimm's devotion to little things, are closely related. They have in common that magical element whose exorcism is reserved for philosophy, here for the final part.

Astonishment, so you write in your *Kierkegaard*, indicates 'the pro-

[1] In the *Studierzimmer* scene of Goethe's *Faust*, Part I, the student says: 'Was man schwarz auf weiss besitzt, kann man getrost nach Hause tragen.' (What one possesses in black and white one can safely take home.)

foundest insight into the relationship between dialectics, myth, and image'. It might be tempting for me to invoke this passage. But instead I propose to emend it (as I am planning to do on another occasion with a subsequent definition of the dialectical image). I believe it should say that astonishment is an outstanding *object* of such an insight. The appearance of closed facticity which attaches to a philological investigation and places the investigator under its spell, fades to the extent that the object is construed in an historical perspective. The base lines of this construction converge in our own historical experience. Thus the object constitutes itself as a monad. In the monad everything that used to lie in mythical rigidity as a textual reference comes alive. Therefore it seems a misjudgment of the matter to me if you find in my study a 'direct inference from the wine duty to *L'Ame du Vin*'. Rather, the juncture was established legitimately in the philological context – just as it would have been done in the interpretation of a classical writer. It gives to the poem the specific gravity which it assumes when it is properly read – something that has so far not been practised widely in the case of Baudelaire. Only when this poem has thus come into its own can the work be touched, or perhaps even shaken, by interpretation. For the poem in question, an interpretation would focus not on matters of taxation but on the significance of intoxication for Baudelaire.

If you think of other writings of mine, you will find that a critique of the attitude of the philologist is an old concern of mine, and it is basically identical with my critique of myth. Yet in each case it is this critique that provokes the philological effort itself. To use the language of *Elective Affinities*, it presses for the exhibition of the material content in which the truth content can be historically revealed. I can understand that this aspect of the matter was less to the fore in your mind. But so, therefore, were a number of important interpretations. I am thinking not only of interpretations of poems – *A une passante* – or of prose pieces – *The Man of the Crowd* – but above all of the unlocking of the concept of modernity, which it was my particular concern to keep within philological bounds.

Let me note in passing that the Péguy quotation to which you object as an evocation of prehistory in the 19th century had its proper place in preparing the insight that the interpretation of Baudelaire should not be based on any chthonian elements. (In my draft of the *Arcades* project I had still attempted that sort of thing). For that reason I believe that neither the catacomb not the cloaca belonged in this interpretation. On the other hand, Charpentier's opera is very promising; I will follow up

your suggestion when there is an opportunity. The figure of the ragpicker is infernal in origin. It will reappear in the third part, set off
against the chthonian figure of Hugo's beggar.

. . .

Permit me to add some frank words. It would be rather prejudicial to
the *Baudelaire* if no part of this study, the product of a creative tension
not easily comparable with any of my earlier literary works, appeared
in your periodical. For one thing, the printed form gives an author
detachment from his work – something that is of incomparable value.
Then, too, in such form the text could become the subject of discussion, and no matter how inadequate the people available to me here
may be, such a discussion could compensate me somewhat for the isolation in which I am working. To my mind, the focal point of such a
publication would be the theory of the *flâneur*, which I regard as an
integral part of the Baudelaire study. I am certainly not speaking of an
unaltered text. The critique of the concept of the masses, as the modern
metropolis throws it into relief, should be given a more central position
than it occupies in the present version. This critique, which I initiate in
my passages on Hugo, should be elaborated by means of an interpretation of important literary documents. As a model I have in mind the
section about the man in the crowd. The euphemistic interpretation of
the masses – the physiognomic view of them – should be illustrated by
an analysis of the E. T. A. Hoffmann story that is mentioned in my
study. For Hugo a more detailed clarification needs to be developed. The
decisive point is the theoretical progress registered in these successive
views of the masses; the climax of it is indicated in the text, but this is
not brought out sufficiently. Hugo rather than Baudelaire lies at its end.
Hugo anticipated more than any other writer the present experiences of
the masses. The demagogue in him is a component of his genius.

You see that certain points of your critique appear convincing to me.
But I am afraid that an *outright* correction in the spirit indicated above
would be very questionable. The missing theoretical transparency to
which you rightly refer is by no means a *necessary* consequence of the
philological procedure prevailing in this section. I am more inclined to
see it as the result of the fact that this procedure has not been designated
as such. This deficiency may be traced in part to the daring attempt to
write the second part of the book before the first. Only in this way could
the appearance have arisen that phantasmagoria are described rather
than integrated into the construction. The above-mentioned emenda-

tions will benefit the second part only when it becomes firmly anchored in the overall context. Accordingly, my first step will be to re-examine the overall construction.

As regards the sadness I referred to above, there were, apart from my presentiment, sufficient reasons for it. For one thing, it is the situation of the Jews in Germany, from which none of us can disassociate himself. Added to this is the serious illness of my sister, who was found to be suffering from hereditary arteriosclerosis at the age of 37. She is almost immobile and thus also almost incapable of gainful employment. (At present she probably still has modest funds). The prognosis at her age is almost hopeless. Apart from all this, it is not always possible to live here without oppressive anxiety. It is understandable that I am making every effort to expedite my naturalization. Unfortunately the necessary steps cost not only a great deal of time but some money as well. Thus at present my horizon is somewhat blocked in this direction too.

The enclosed fragment of a letter to Max dated 17 November 1938, and the accompanying message from [Hans] Brill[2] concern a matter which may wreck my naturalization. You can thus appreciate its importance. May I ask you to take this matter in hand and request Max to give Brill permission immediately, preferably by telegram, to use the pseudonym Hans Fellner rather than my real name for my review in the next issue of your journal.

This brings me to your new work[3] and thus the sunnier portion of this letter. The subject matter of your study concerns me in two respects, both of which you have indicated. First, in those parts which relate certain characteristics of the contemporary acoustic perception of jazz to the optical characteristics of film, which I have described. *Ex improviso* I cannot decide whether the different distribution of the areas of light and shadow in our respective essays is due to theoretical divergencies. Possibly it is only a case of apparent differences between our points of view; it may really be a matter of viewing different objects from apparently different but equally acceptable angles. For it is not to be assumed that acoustic and optic perceptions are equally capable of being revolutionized. This may explain the fact that the prospect of a variant hearing which concludes your essay is not quite clear to a person, like me, for whom Mahler is not a fully illuminated experience.

---

[2] Brill was the secretary of the Paris office of the Institute for Social Research.
[3] Benjamin is referring to Adorno's essay 'Uber den Fetischcharakter in der Musik und die Regression des Hörens', published in the *Zeitschrift für Sozialforschung* 7, 1938, and later included in his volume *Dissonanzen*, Göttingen 1963.

In my essay ['The Work of Art in the Age of Mechanical Reproduction'] I tried to articulate positive moments as clearly as you managed to articulate negative ones. Consequently, I see strengths in your study at points where mine was weak. Your analysis of the psychological types produced by industry and your representation of their mode of production are most felicitous. If I had devoted more attention to this aspect of the matter, my study would have gained in historical plasticity. I see more and more clearly that the launching of the sound film must be regarded as an operation of the cinema industry designed to break the revolutionary primacy of the silent film, which generated reactions that were hard to control and hence politically dangerous. An analysis of the sound film would constitute a critique of contemporary art which would provide a dialectical mediation between your views and mine.

What I liked most about the conclusion of your essay is the reservation about the idea of progress which is indicated there. For the time being you motivate this reservation only casually and by reference to the history of the term. I should like to get at its roots and its origins. But I am well aware of the difficulties.

Finally I come to your question about the relationship between the views developed in your essay and those presented in my section on the *flâneur*. Empathy with the commodity presents itself to self-observation or inner experience as empathy with inorganic matter; next to Baudelaire, my chief witness here is Flaubert with his *Tentation [de Saint-Antoine]*. Basically, however, empathy with the commodity is probably empathy with exchange value itself. Actually, one could hardly imagine 'consumption' of exchange value as anything else but empathy with it. You write: 'The consumer really worships the money which he has spent on a ticket for a Toscanini concert.' Empathy with their exchange value turns even cannons into articles of consumption more pleasing than butter. If in popular parlance it is said of someone that 'he is loaded; he has five million marks', the 'racial community'[4] itself likewise feels that it is 'loaded' with a few billion; it empathizes with those billions. If I formulate it thus, I may get at the canon that underlies this mode of behaviour. I am thinking of that which underlies games of chance. A gambler directly empathizes with the sums which he bets against the bank or an opponent. Games of chance, in the form of stock-exchange speculation, paved the way for empathy with exchange value much as

---

[4] 'Racial community'= *Volksgemeinschaft*, a specifically Nazi term to which Benjamin alludes here.

World Fairs did. (The latter were the training schools in which the masses, forced away from consumption, learned to empathize with exchange value.)

One particularly important question I should like to reserve for a subsequent letter, or possibly for a conversation. What is the meaning of the fact that music and lyric poetry become comic? I can hardly imagine that this is a completely negative phenomenon. Or do you see any positive elements in the 'decline of sacred reconciliation'? I confess that I do not quite follow this. Perhaps you will have an opportunity to return to this question.

In any case I ask you to let me hear from you soon. Please ask Felizitas to send me, when she gets a chance, the fairy tales of [Wilhelm] Hauff, which I treasure because of Sonderland's illustrations. I shall write to her in the near future, but I would also like to hear from her.

As ever, cordially yours,

Walter

Translated by Harry Zohn

Presentation IV

After the end of the Second World War, the German emigration gradually reassembled in Central Europe. Benjamin was dead, a victim of fascism. Bloch and Brecht, after some hesitation, chose to go back to Leipzig and Berlin in East Germany. Adorno, also after some delay, returned to Frankfurt in West Germany. Lukács moved immediately back to Budapest. With the onset of the Cold War, Europe divided into two mobilized camps. In Hungary, Lukács's writings – for all their ostensible compliance with Stalinist etiquette – were soon (1949) violently assailed for 'revisionism', and his books ceased to appear. In East Germany, Bloch was published and honoured, while Brecht was granted every material privilege for the creation of his own theatre. Although their freedom of expression was circumscribed, neither was felt to represent a threat in the same way as Lukács. In West Germany, Horkheimer recreated the Frankfurt Institute of Social Research with the benevolent approval of the Adenauer regime. Adorno became its deputy director.

The end of Stalin's rule in 1953 unleashed a general political crisis in Eastern Europe. The first country to experience its impact was the DDR. In July 1953, there was a workers' rising, with a wave of strikes and street clashes against the apparatus of East German state – suppressed with the aid of Soviet troops. Brecht, bewildered and unnerved, reacted to this revolt of the masses with a mixture of truculent bluff and sentimental pathos in his private diaries.[1] He was to play no role in the

---

[1] Summary condemnation of the actual insurgency of the working-class was combined with ouvrierist exaltation of its in-dwelling virtues in the *Diary*. The demonstrations of 17 June, with 'their aimlessness and miserable helplessness' revealed the working-class to be 'once again the captive of the class enemy, the recrudescent capitalism of the fascist epoch (sic)' – yet even in this 'most depraved condition', it still exhibited the strength of 'the rising class' that was 'alone capable of ending capitalism': *Arbeitsjournal II, (1942–1955)*, Frankfurt 1973, p. 1009.

process of destalinization, dying shortly after the 20th Party Congress of the CPSU in 1956. Lukács, on the other hand, took an active part in cultural and political debates in Eastern Europe during the Thaw. Lecturing widely in Berlin, Warsaw, Budapest and Vienna in 1955, he restated his central aesthetic ideas, until recently harried and censored, and aggressively counter-attacked the Zhdanovite canon of 'revolutionary romanticism'. The written result of this activity was a book, *The Meaning of Contemporary Realism*, completed shortly after the 20th Party Congress. When the Hungarian Revolt erupted in October 1956, Lukács – while lucidly assessing the probable chances of success of an essentially spontaneous social explosion – did not hesitate to cast his lot with the cause of the insurgent workers and students. Participating in the Nagy government, in which he presciently warned against withdrawal from the Warsaw Pact, he was seized by Russian troops during the Soviet intervention, and confined in Rumania. Released in March 1957, he completed his preface to the book he had been writing, and sent it abroad. *The Meaning of Contemporary Realism* was published in West Germany in 1958. When it appeared, Hungary was held fast in the grip of repression, and Lukács was silenced in his own country, subject to attacks of increasing vehemence.[2] It was this book that Adorno was to review, in the major essay on Lukács printed below.

Adorno had become, in the same year, Director of the Institute of Social Research in Frankfurt. No two situations could have been more contrasted. Adorno, at the summit of his career, was free to write wherever he chose in the Federal Republic. In the event, his essay was published in *Die Monat*, a journal created by the US Army in West Germany and financed by the Central Intelligence Agency. Adorno's strictures on Lukács's mental 'chains' thus had their own irony: when he was writing, it was Lukács who was literally resisting police culture, while Adorno was unwittingly yielding to it. These circumstances should be remembered when reading Adorno's appraisal of Lukács; they are not an insulation against it. The substance of the critical positions represented by the two antagonists remains to be assessed today in its own right.

The theoretical premises of *The Meaning of Contemporary Realism* were essentially those which Lukács had defended from the late 1920s

[2] His department at the University of Budapest was closed, while in 1960 a volume of essays was published in East Berlin which renewed the attacks of 1949 and developed some further ones – although, as the editor remarked apologetically, these 'could of course only be a selection of the large number of critical commentaries and utterances to have been levelled against Lukács's theories in recent years by Marxist scholars in Hungary, the Soviet Union, the DDR and elsewhere.'

144

onwards. The distinctive emphases of the book were, however, shaped by the period in which it was written – between Stalin's death and the Twentieth Congress of the CPSU – and by the political perspectives then forming in the Eastern bloc. Lukács's allegiance to the policy of 'peaceful coexistence', with its reliance on 'progressive' currents in bourgeois politics and culture, and to a partial and rightist critique of Stalinism,[3] were registered in his literary criticism in the form of a twofold critical intervention, against the reactionary tendency that he believed to dominate the literature of the West, and the 'voluntarist' excesses that he discerned in that of the East. He opened with a stinging polemic against the major literary representatives of European modernism. These authors, he maintained, were united in their affiliation to a philosophical 'ontologism' whose aesthetic effects were subjectivism and formalism, with a corresponding attenuation of historical reality – into 'background', as with Musil, if not virtual nothingness, as in the work of Samuel Beckett. Indeed the finest – because most lucid and critical – theorist of modernism, Walter Benjamin, had obliquely predicted an immolation of art in consequence of its cancellation of history.[4] However, decadence was not the inescapable lot of the mid-century Western artist. Against the irrational stylisms and allegories of the tradition epitomized in Kafka stood another tradition, only superficially less 'modern', whose exemplar was Thomas Mann. The works of this alternative tradition represented, in effect, a renewal of the classical realist novel of the previous century, in a form appropriate to the epoch of socialist revolution; and the 'perspective' that guided this paradoxical achievement – the successful practice of a classical bourgeois form in the period of capitalist decline – was the admission of a 'reasonable question': the 'non-rejection' of socialism as an historic possibility. Lukács insisted that this 'critical realism' was the sole means to artistic excellence in the contemporary West. In his own way, Brecht had rallied to it in his later plays, for all his professions to the contrary, to become 'the greatest realistic playwright of the age.'[5] Lukács was also concerned to defend the titles of realism in the post-capitalist societies of the East. In contrast with its 'classical' and 'critical' siblings, 'socialist realism' was grounded in a 'concrete socialist perspective' and written 'from the

[3] For Lukács's political evolution from the 20s to the 60s, see the authoritative essay by Michael Löwy, 'Lukács and Stalinism', in *Western Marxism – A Critical Reader*. London NLB, 1977.

[4] *The Meaning of Contemporary Realism*, London 1962, pp. 41–3.

[5] *The Meaning of Contemporary Realism*, pp. 87–9.

inside', socially and ideologically. But for that reason, its development as a literary mode would inevitably be shaped by the ideological and material stresses of the period of transition. Thus, the main emphasis of Lukács's argument fell on the two deformations to which 'socialist realism' had shown itself prone: on the one hand, a 'naturalist' transcription of the actual state of society; on the other, a compensatory 'romanticism', aggravated by political errors, that occluded the real contradictions of socialist development. For the duration of the transitional period, Lukács concluded, 'critical realism' would remain a legitimate and valuable element in the culture of the workers' states.

It is necessary to recall the dual character of Lukács's intervention now, if only to draw attention to the political character of Adorno's assessment of it. His opening thrust – against the apologetic strain in the book – is not easily countered. Its tone and manner, by turns hectoring and affable, bespeak the same bureaucratic presumption that Brecht had protested at, years before. He was also quite right to insist on the social-darwinist affinities and philistine, conformist undertones of Lukács's notion of 'decadence', and to put the eminently historical question: where was the implied alternative – healthy, vigorous and normal – to be found in the present? On the other hand, Adorno's recourse to tendentious terms such as 'the people's community' (*Volksgemeinschaft*) for the Eastern countries, in a text published in the West at the height of the Cold War, displayed a seemingly calculated neglect of fundamental political discriminations, which can only have appeared to endorse the liberal ideology of 'totalitarianism' so prevalent at the time. His evident distaste for Lukács's aesthetic positions may help to explain this procedure, but it cannot fully excuse it.

Adorno's principle aesthetic charge was that Lukács variously misapprehended, underestimated or ignored the constitutive *formality* of the work of art. His obdurate defence of 'reflection' – theory and of realism – the 'imitation of empirical reality' – led him to read the 'images' of modernism as grossly distorted transcripts, unconscionable travesties of objective reality. At the same time, Lukács denied the 'autonomous' historical development of aesthetic technique and misconceived its role in artistic production. Thus, he was blind both to the unrealistic elements in his own chosen masters – Balzac, for example – and to the real nature of the 'images' or 'essences' that modernism distils from experience. For Adorno, the production of the work of art entails the appropriation of the objective world by the subject, in accordance with the 'laws' of aesthetic form. The 'image' so produced then stands in contradiction to the real, and as a critique of it – 'art is the negative knowledge of the actual world.' The outstanding merit of the works of Beckett, Kafka and Schönberg, in Adorno's view, was precisely their intransigent refusal of any form of reconciliation. As he wrote on another occasion, 'a successful work . . . is not one which resolves objective contradictions in a spurious harmony, but one which expresses the idea of harmony negatively by embodying the contradictions, pure and uncompromised, in its innermost structure.'[6]

Adorno was right to point to the epistemological aporia of realist aesthetic theory, to reaffirm the relative autonomy of the literary 'series' and to stress the productive function of literary form. These issues are central to any examination of Lukács's aesthetics, and were raised with special force by *The Meaning of Contemporary Realism*. It is all the more unfortunate, therefore, that these themes were not developed much beyond the point of emphasis or assertion. The fundamental categories of Adorno's aesthetics remain opaque: 'autonomous art', the 'laws' and 'logic' of artistic form, 'essences' that are not congeneric with the essences of philosophical idealism – none of these crucial terms is assigned a clearly delimited meaning. Dialectical tropes and epigrams that do not so much explain modernist art as re-create its moods and tempers served here for the kind of conceptual clarity that Lukács, for all his errors and evasions, rightly took to be the task of theoretical exposition. In the same way, while he can pass devastating judgment on the incompetence of Lukács's readings of individual texts (the lyric by Benn, or Mann's *Magic Mountain*), Adorno's own counter-arguments are scarcely more specific in their use of textual illustration. To dwell on these shared deficiencies of theory and concrete analysis is, in the first place, to be reminded of the need for equity in assessing this exchange between Lukács and Adorno. It is possible, however, that they are in fact the echoing symptoms of a fundamental theoretical community, in which both men participate equally.

In 1962, two years after the critique of Lukács, a German translation of Sartre's *What is Literature?* appeared. Adorno took the occasion to write an extended essay on 'Commitment'. Published in *Die Neue Rundschau*, the essay was essentially focussed on the work of Brecht, after some acute introductory remarks on Sartre. The two essays, on Lukács and on Brecht, are in an obvious sense complementary. The first was designed to combat the politically and aesthetically illegitimate

[6] *Prisms*, London 1967, p. 32.

prescriptions of Lukács's literary criticism, the second to resist a parallel intrusion into the practice of literature itself; in both cases, the 'autonomous' productions of modernism are affirmed as a politically valid alternative. The logical and empirical stresses of the first are still more clearly marked in the second, as the critique of Sartre makes plain. Adorno's strictures on Sartre's 'literature of ideas' have an undeniable force, but their validity is ultimately conditional on the *quid pro quo* which, elsewhere in the essay, he himself imposes on the Brechtian theatre. It is true that a professedly revolutionary art must, in elementary consistency, submit itself at some point to the criterion of political correctness. But the same must then be true of any professedly Marxist criticism. Adorno's dismissal of Sartre's literary attempt to incite individual subjects to free and active choice was based on the premiss that late capitalism had devised an all-inclusive 'administered universe', a political order purged of contradiction and therefore of the objective possibility of choice. Today, respecting Adorno's own injunction, few will fail to judge that the political assumptions of 'Critical Theory' have weathered rather less well than those of Sartre's 'libertarian existentialism'. It should be added here that the notion of a residual transcendental subject was structurally essential to Adorno's thought, furnishing the only point of leverage in a putatively totalitarian social order (and founding the possibility of a thought that could indict it as such).[7] No assessment of his aesthetics can overlook this semi-miraculous persistence of the subject in a conceptual schema that posits its complete reification. Sartre's belief in the efficacy of individual engagement seems much less questionable than a theory in which the production of 'autonomous' works of art is little less than magical.

Adorno's criticisms of Brecht are obviously subject to the same general *caveat*. But here, interestingly enough, his political idiom becomes more nuanced and concrete, in keeping perhaps with the avowedly Marxist purposes of the art now under discussion, and his aesthetic judgments are often very penetrating. Much of what Adorno has to say about Brecht's plays is incontrovertible. The 'trivialization' of fascism effected by *Arturo Ui*, the wilfully crude 'analyses' of plays like *Saint Joan* and *Mother Courage*, the constant recourse to archaism of different kinds – these are so many instances of a definite populist strain in Brecht's work. The *Threepenny Novel*, which Adorno does not mention here, is very striking in this respect. Confined mainly to the sphere of circulation and

[7] See *Minima Moralia*, London NLB, 1974, pp. 15–18.

set in a lumpen, semi-criminal milieu, the narrative is actually an exposé of capitalist relations of *corruption*. No one factor can adequately account for this aesthetic displacement towards populism. A theoretical slippage into a kind of left-utilitarianism is a familiar failing of Brecht's writings. His political weaknesses also took their toll – *The Measures Taken*, criticized here by Adorno, is a notorious case in point.[8] Further, unresolved difficulties of a specifically aesthetic character may have been partly responsible for some of the contradictions of the Brechtian theatre.

Nevertheless, Adorno was wrong to suggest that these contradictions were inherent in Brecht's artistic project. The film *Kuhle Wampe*, made by Slatan Dudow, Ernst Ottwald and himself in 1931, demonstrates that they were not – a demonstration corroborated *a contrario* by the misrepresentations to which Adorno was drawn in making a general case against him. His remarks on *Saint Joan* confine themselves to a 'content analysis' as brusque as any to be found in Lukács's writings. He does not consider the play in relation to Brecht's 'epic' dramaturgy – with which he was well acquainted – or pay any attention, even in his own terms, to its unusual formal characteristics. *The Good Woman of Szechuan* is mentioned only as 'a variation . . . in reverse' on *Saint Joan*; and yet here is a work that 'jolts signification' in the approved Adornian manner. The action of the play effects a gradual subversion of moralism, showing how the 'good' Shen Te can only remain so with the aid of her 'evil' alter ego, Shiu Ta. No resolution of this contradiction is enacted. or prescribed by the play, which thus ends in crisis, posing a question that it does not answer. It was disingenuous, therefore, to assimilate Brecht's theatrical practice to 'didacticism' *tout court*. His constant effort (it is another question how far or how consistently he succeeded) was not to dispense truths to a passive audience, in the manner of a George Bernard Shaw, but to provide structured possibilities for reflection on the nature of capitalist (and socialist) relations and the place of the spectator within them.

Neither Lukács nor Adorno was able to respond with much enthusiasm to Brecht, essentially because the relationship between politics and aesthetics as he conceived it was quite distinct from the conception held in common by them. All three were agreed that art could and should be a means of understanding historical reality. But Lukács and Adorno went on to accredit an intrinsic cognitive capacity to art – more precisely,

[8] Among more damaging examples, not cited by Adorno but vindicating his remarks on the dangers of Brecht's diction, may be noted his anthem to Lysenkoism 'The Cultivation of the Millet', written in 1951.

to specific forms of art. In so doing, they were led to elaborate Marxist versions of pre-existing ideologies of art. For Lukács, as for Aristotle and the subsequent tradition of realist aesthetic thought, art was properly 'the imitation of an action'; 'action' was to be interpreted in the light of historical materialism, but 'imitation' remained the unchallengeable purpose of all valid art. Adorno's essays were not so much a Marxist defence of modernism as the expression of a distinctively modernist Marxism: his positions were, *mutatis mutandis*, those of modernist ideology itself. The complementary oversights of the two critics were conditioned by their underlying aesthetic-ideological commitments. Lukács inveighed against the irrationalist element in modernism, but was wholly insensitive to its positive disruptive moment; Adorno was justly contemptuous of the 'optimism' prescribed by Soviet orthodoxy, but was unable or unwilling to acknowledge the equally reactionary 'pessimism' of Western liberal orthodoxy. Sardonically noting that a 'journalistically minded Westerner' could praise *The Caucasian Chalk Circle* as a 'hymn to motherhood', he forgot that the same stereotypical figures are never done extolling Kafka as the analyst of 'totalitarianism' and Beckett as the only undeluded poet of 'the human condition'.

Brecht's choices were the product of a different conception of the role of politics in aesthetics. 'Realism', as he defined it, was a political and ideological *end* whose formal *means* were variable, according to the dictates of time and place. His use of the term 'realism' no more signified an aesthetic allegiance to Balzac than his 'alienation effects' bespoke the activities of a 'modernist'. The techniques of classical narrative, popular song and expressionist theatre were among the elements of an artistic instrumentarium, to be drawn upon in whatever combinations the given circumstances seemed to suggest. The result was an aesthetic which, in conception at least, was much more alive to the shifting valencies of form than either Lukács's studies of the traditional literary past or Adorno's claims for the high avant-garde. Adorno was undoubtedly right to emphasize the problems of Brecht's political theatre. His critique of Brecht cannot be dismissed by any socialist: it remains of greater intellectual power than any of the numerous conventional homages to him. But to question, as he did, the very possibility of a successful political art was to confine Marxist aesthetics to more or less contemplative assessments of the available forms of bourgeois art. The respective limits of the two men are suggested by their final discomfiture at the publics for which they wrote. Brecht's disorientation before the revolt of a proletariat that belied (realized) his politics was to have its precise counterpart, fifteen years later, in Adorno's disarray at the rebellion of an intelligentsia that confounded (appropriated) his philosophy, in the great student demonstrations of the sixties. The quest for a revolutionary art has revived in the West with a new intensity since then.

Theodor Adorno

Reconciliation under Duress

The nimbus which still surrounds the name of Georg Lukács today, even outside the Soviet bloc, is something he owes to the writings of his youth – the volume of essays *Soul and Form*, *The Theory of the Novel* and the studies collected in *History and Class Consciousness*, in which he became the first dialectical materialist to apply the category of reification systematically to philosophy. Inspired originally by people like Simmel and Kassner, his ideas were then further developed by the South-Western school.[1] He soon began to reject psychological subjectivism in favour of an objectivistic philosophy of history, which became highly influential. *The Theory of the Novel* in particular had a brilliance and profundity of conception which was quite extraordinary at the time, so much so that it set a standard for philosophical aesthetics which has been retained ever since. As early as the beginning of the twenties his objectivism started to adjust itself, albeit not without some initial resistance, to the official communist doctrine. He acquiesced in the communist custom and disavowed his earlier writings. He took the crudest criticisms from the Party hierarchy to heart, twisting Hegelian motifs and turning them against himself; and for decades on end he laboured in a series of books and essays to adapt his obviously unimpaired talents to the un-relieved sterility of Soviet claptrap, which in the meantime had degraded the philosophy it proclaimed to the level of a mere instrument in the service of its rule. Only for the sake of the early writings, which were disparaged by his Party and which he had himself abjured, has anyone outside the Eastern bloc taken any notice at all of the works he has published over the last thirty years, among them a thick volume on the young Hegel. This remains true today, even though his former talent can still be discerned in one or two of his studies on German realist

[1] I.e. the neo-Kantians in Heidelberg such as Windelband, Rickert, Emil Lask, but also Max Weber.

152

literature in the 19th century, in particular those on Keller and Raabe. It was doubtless his book *The Destruction of Reason* which revealed most clearly the destruction of Lukács's own. In a highly undialectical manner, the officially licensed dialectician sweeps all the irrationalist strands of modern philosophy into the camp of reaction and Fascism. He blithely ignores the fact that, unlike academic idealism, these schools were struggling against the very same reification in both thought and life of which Lukács too was a dedicated opponent. Nietzsche and Freud are simply labelled Fascists, and he could even bring himself to refer to Nietzsche, in the condescending tones of a provincial Wilhelminian school inspector, as a man 'of above-average abilities'. Under the mantle of an ostensibly radical critique of society he surreptitiously reintroduced the most threadbare clichés of the very conformism which that social criticism had once attacked.

As for the book under consideration, *The Meaning of Contemporary Realism*,[2] published in the West by Claassen Verlag in 1958, we can detect in it traces of a change of attitude on the part of the 75-year-old writer. These presumably have to do with the conflict he became involved in through his active role in the Nagy government. Not only does he talk about the crimes of the Stalin era, but he even speaks up on behalf of 'a general commitment to the freedom to write', a formulation that would earlier have been unthinkable. Lukács posthumously discovers some merit in Brecht, his adversary of many years' standing, and praises as a work of genius his *Ballad of the Dead Soldier*, a poem which must strike the East German rulers as a cultural-Bolshevist atrocity. Like Brecht, he would like to widen the concept of socialist realism, which has been used for decades to stifle any spontaneous impulse, any product incomprehensible or suspect to the apparatchiks, so as to make room for works that rise above the level of despicable trash. He ventures a timid opposition in gestures which show him to be paralysed from the outset by the consciousness of his own impotence. His timidity is no mere tactic. Lukács's personal integrity is above all suspicion. But the conceptual structure to which he has sacrificed his intellect is so restricted that it suffocates anything which might have breathed more freely; the *sacrifizio dell'intelletto* does not let the intellect off scot-free. This casts a melancholy light on Lukács's unconcealed nostalgia for his own early writings. The notion of 'the immanent meaning of life' from *The Theory*

[2] The English edition was published by Merlin Press, London 1962. Page-numbers henceforward refer to the latter. Translations have sometimes been modified, however.

of the Novel recurs here, but it is reduced to the dictum that life in a
society building up socialism is in fact full of meaning – a dogma just
good enough to provide a plausible philosophical justification of the rosy
positive attitude expected of art in the peoples' republics. The book is
like a parfait or a sundae – halfway between a so-called thaw on the one
hand and a renewed freeze on the other.

Operating reductively, imperiously distributing labels such as critical
or socialist realism, Lukács still behaves like a Cultural Commissar, for
all his dynamic assurances to the contrary. Hegel's criticism of Kantian
formalism in aesthetics is reduced to the simplified assertion that in
modern art the emphasis on style, form and technique is grossly exaggerated (see esp. p. 19) – even though Lukács must be perfectly well
aware that these are the features that distinguish art as knowledge from
science, and that works of art which ignored their own form, would destroy
themselves as art. What looks like formalism to him, really means the
structuring of the elements of a work in accordance with laws appropriate to them, and is relevant to that 'immanent meaning' for which
Lukács yearns, as opposed to a meaning arbitrarily superimposed from
outside, something he objectively defends while asserting its impossibility.
Instead of recognizing the objective function of formal elements in
determining the aesthetic content of modern art, he wilfully misinterprets
them as arbitrary ingredients added by an over-inflated subjectivism.
The objectivity he misses in modern art and which he expects from the
subject-matter when placed in 'perspective', is in fact achieved by the
procedures and techniques which dissolve the subject-matter and
reorganize it in a way which does create a perspective – but these are the
very procedures and techniques he wishes to sweep away. He remains
indifferent to the philosophical question of whether the concrete meaning
of a work of art is in fact identical with the mere 'reflection of objective
reality' (p. 101), a vulgar-materialist shibboleth to which he doggedly
clings.

At all events, his own text disregards all the norms of the responsible
criticism which his own early writings had helped to establish. No
bearded Privy Councillor could pontificate about art in a manner more
alien to it. He speaks with the voice of the dogmatic professor who
knows he cannot be interrupted, who does not shrink from any digression,
however lengthy, and who has evidently dispensed with those reactions
which he castigates as aestheticist, formalistic and decadent, but which
alone permit any real relationship with art. Even though the Hegelian
concept of 'the concrete' still stands at a premium with him – especially

when he is concerned to restrict literature to the imitation of empirical reality – his own arguments remain largely abstract. His text hardly ever submits to the discipline imposed by a specific work of art and the problems implicit in it. Instead he issues decrees. The pedantry of his general manner is matched by his slovenliness in matters of detail. Lukács does not recoil from seedy truisms such as 'lecturing and writing are very different activities'; repeatedly uses the expression 'top-grade performance' [*Spitzenleistung*], whose origins lie in the world of commerce and record-breaking (p. 11); he calls the obliteration of the distinction between abstract and concrete potentiality 'appalling' [*verheerend*] and recalls how 'from Giotto on a new secularity triumphs more and more over the allegorizing of an earlier period'. (p. 40). We who figure as decadents in Lukács's vocabulary may seriously overvalue form and style, but at least it has preserved us hitherto from formulations such as 'from Giotto on', as well as from the temptation to praise Kafka because he is a 'marvellous observer' (p. 45). Nor will modernists have had very much to say about 'the series of extraordinarily numerous emotions which together combine to structure the inner life of man'. Confronted with such top-grade performances, which follow each other as rapidly as at the Olympic Games, one might well wonder whether a man who can write like this, in such obvious ignorance of the craft of the literature which he treats in such a cavalier manner, has any right at all to an opinion on literary matters. But in the stylistic amalgam of pedantry and irresponsibility to be found in Lukács, who was once able to write well, one senses a certain malice aforethought, a truculent determination to write badly, evidently in the belief that this sacrifice on his part will demonstrate by some magic trick that anyone who does otherwise and who takes pains with his work is a good-for-nothing. Indifference to style, we may remark in passing, is almost always symptomatic of the dogmatic sclerosis of content. The false modesty implicit in a style which believes itself to be dispassionate, as long as it abstains from self-reflection, only succeeds in concealing the fact that it has purified the dialectical process of its objective, as well as its subjective, value. Dialectics are paid lip-service, but for such a thinker all has been decided in advance. The writing becomes undialectical.

The core of his theory remains dogmatic. The whole of modern literature is dismissed except where it can be classified as either critical or socialist realism, and the odium of decadence is heaped on it without a qualm, even though such abuse brings with it all the horrors of persecution and extermination, and not only in Russia. The term 'decadence' belongs to the vocabulary of conservatism. Its use by Lukács, as well as his superiors, is designed to claim for the community the authority of a doctrine with which it is in fact incompatible. The idea of decadence can scarcely be entertained in the absence of its positive counterpart: the image of nature in all its vigour and abundance. The categories of nature are smuggled illicitly into the mediations of society, the very practice against which the tenor of Marx's and Engels' critique of ideology was directed. Not even the echoes of Feuerbach's doctrine of healthy sensuous existence were influential enough to procure entry for the terminology of Social Darwinism into their texts. As late as 1857–58, i.e. during the period when *Capital* was underway, we find the following statement in the rough draft of the *Grundrisse*: 'As much, then, as the whole of this movement appears as a social process, and as much as the individual moments of this movement arise from the conscious will and particular purposes of individuals, so much does the totality of the process appear as an objective interrelation, which arises spontaneously from nature; arising, it is true, from the mutual influence of conscious individuals on one another, but neither located in their consciousness, nor subsumed under them as a whole. Their own collisions with one another produce an *alien* social power standing above them, produce their mutual interaction as a process and power independent of them. . . . The social relation of individuals to one another as a power over the individuals which has become autonomous, whether conceived as a natural force, as chance or in whatever other form, is a necessary result of the fact that the point of departure is not the free social individual.'[3]

Such criticism does not even call a halt at that highly sensitive realm in which the appearance of the organic offers the most stubborn resistance to the social, and in which all indignation about decadence has its home: the sphere of sexuality. Somewhat earlier, in a review of C. F. Daumer's *The Religion of the New Age*, Marx had pilloried the following passage: 'Nature and womanhood are the truly Divine in contrast to humanity and manhood . . . The devotion of the human to the natural, of man to woman, is the authentic, the only true humility and selflessness; it is the most exalted, indeed the only virtue and piety that exists.' To which Marx appends the following commentary: 'We see here how the superficiality and ignorance of this speculative spokesman of religiosity are transformed into a pronounced form of cowardice. Herr Daumer flees

---

[3] Karl Marx, *Grundrisse*, Harmondsworth 1973, pp. 196–7, trans. by Martin Nicolaus.

from the tragedies of history which threaten to come too close to him for comfort and seeks refuge in so-called nature, i.e. the cretinous rustic idyll, and he preaches the cult of womanhood in order to cloak his own effeminate resignation.'[4]

Wherever people inveigh against decadence, this flight is re-enacted. Lukács is forced into it by a situation in which social injustice persists even though officially it has been abolished. Responsibility is shifted away from conditions for which men are responsible and back on to nature, or alternatively, on to a decadence which is conceived as its opposite. Lukács has of course made the attempt to conjure away the contradiction between Marxist theory and official Marxism by twisting the ideas of sick and healthy art back into social concepts: 'The relations between men change in the course of history, and the intellectual and emotional values placed on those relations change accordingly. But to realize this is not to embrace relativism. At any specific time one human relation-ship may be progressive and another reactionary. We can therefore make use of the concept of social health and establish it as the foundation of all really great art, for what is socially healthy becomes an integral part of the historical consciousness of mankind'.[5]

But the futility of this attempt is obvious. In any discussion of historical problems, the terms 'sick' and 'healthy' are best avoided altogether. They have no connection with the dimension represented by progress/reaction; they are simply dragged in for the sake of their demagogic appeal. Furthermore, the dichotomy of healthy/sick is as undialectical as that of the rise and fall of the bourgeoisie, which itself derives its norms from a bourgeois consciousness that has failed to keep pace with its own development.

I will not deign to dwell on the point that, in invoking the concepts of decadence and modernism – the two signify the same thing in his eyes – Lukács yokes together things and people who have absolutely nothing in common – not just Proust, Kafka, Joyce and Beckett, but also Benn, Jünger and perhaps even Heidegger; and in the realm of theory, Benjamin and myself. The facile tactic so popular nowadays of suggesting that an object of attack does not really exist as such, but disintegrates into a series of incompatible parts, is all too readily available to soften up attack and evade hostile argument with the gesture 'that doesn't apply to me'. At the risk therefore of being led to over-simplify by my own opposition

[4] Karl Marx: Review of C. F. Daumer's *The Religion of the New Age*, in the *Neue Rheinische Zeitung*, Hamburg 1850.

[5] Georg Lukács: *Healthy Art, or Sick* in *G.L. zum 70. Geburtstag*, Berlin 1955, p. 243.

to over-simplification, I shall keep hold of the central thread of Lukács's argument and not differentiate between the objects of his attack much more than he does himself, except where he travesties them to excess.

His efforts to bolster up the naive Soviet verdict on modern art, i.e. on any literature which shocks the naively realistic normal mind, by providing it with a philosophical good conscience, are carried out with a very limited range of tools, all of them Hegelian in origin. In the first place, in order to press home his point that modernist literature is a deviation from reality, he drags in the distinction between 'abstract' and 'real' potentiality: 'These two categories, their affinities, differences and opposition are rooted in life itself. Viewed abstractly, i.e. subjectively, potentiality is always richer than actual life. Countless possibilities seem open to the human mind, of which only a negligibly minute percentage can ever be realized. Modern subjectivism, discerning in this apparent plenitude the authentic abundance of the human soil, contemplates it with a melancholy tinged with admiration and sympathy. However, when reality declines to realize such possibilities, these feelings become transformed into a no less melancholy contempt' (p. 21–2). This point cannot simply be shrugged off, despite the percentage. When Brecht, to take an example, devised a kind of childish shorthand to try and crystallize out the essence of Fascism in terms of a sort of gangsterism, he made his 'resistible' dictator, Arturo Ui, the head of an imaginary and apocryphal Cauliflower Trust, instead of the most powerful economic organizations. This unrealistic device proved to be a mixed blessing. By thinking of Fascism as an enterprise belonging to a band of criminals who have no real place in the social system and who can therefore be 'resisted' at will, you strip it of its horror and diminish its social significance. This invalidates the caricature and makes it seem idiotic even in its own terms: the despotic rise of the minor criminal loses its plausibility in the course of the play itself. Satire which fails to stay on the level of its subject lacks spice.

But the demand for pragmatic fidelity to life can only refer to a writer's basic experience of reality and the *membra disjecta* of the subject-matter from which he fashions his work. In Brecht's case, this can only mean the actual bonds connecting politics and the economy as well as the need for the initial situation to fit the facts. It does not apply to what happens to these facts in the course of the work. Proust provides the most striking illustration of the unity of pragmatic fidelity and – in Lukácsian terms – unrealistic manner, for in his work we find the most intimate fusion of an extremely 'realistic' observation of detail with an aesthetic form based on the principle of involuntary recollection. If any of the intimacy of this synthesis is lost, if 'concrete potentiality' is interpreted in terms of an unreflecting overall realism, rigidly partitioned off from the object it observes, while any element of art antithetical to the subject-matter is permitted only as a 'perspective', i.e. in the sense that a meaning is allowed to become visible without reaching the centre of the work, the real objects at its core, then what results is an abuse of Hegel's distinction in the interests of a traditionalism whose aesthetic backwardness provides an index of its historical falsity.

Lukács's central line of attack, however, is the charge of 'ontologism', which, if sustained, would enable him to pin the whole of modernist literature on to the archaic existential notions of Heidegger. Of course, Lukács himself follows the fashion and insists that the question 'What is Man?' has to be put (p. 19), and that we must not be deterred by the prospect of where it might lead. However, he does at least modify it by reverting to Aristotle's familiar definition of man as a social animal. From this he deduces the scarcely contentious proposition that 'the human significance, the specific individual and typical quality' of the characters in great literature, 'their sensuous, artistic reality, cannot be separated from the context in which they were created' (Ibid.). 'Quite opposed to this', he goes on, is 'the ontological view governing the image of man in the work of leading modernist writers. To put it briefly: in their eyes "man" means the individual who has always existed, who is essentially solitary, asocial and – ontologically – incapable of entering into relationships with other human beings.' (Ibid.). This is supported by reference to a somewhat foolish utterance by Thomas Wolfe, which clearly has no relevance to literary works, to the effect that solitariness is the inescapable fact of man's existence. But as someone who claims to think in radically historical terms, Lukács of all people ought to know that in an individualistic society loneliness is socially mediated and so possesses a significant historical content.

All such categories as decadence, formalism and aestheticism can be traced back to Baudelaire, and Baudelaire shows no interest in an unchanging essence of man, his loneliness or his derelict existence [*Geworfenheit*], but rather in the essence of modernity. 'Essence' itself in this poetry is no abstract thing in itself; it is a social phenomenon. The objectively dominant idea in Baudelaire's work is that the new, the products of historical progress, are what has to be conjured up in his verse. To use Benjamin's expression, we find not an archaic, but a 'dialectical' image in his work. Hence the *Tableaux Parisiens*. Even in

Joyce's case we do not find the timeless image of man which Lukács would like to foist on to him, but man as the product of history. For all his Irish folklore, Joyce does not invoke a mythology beyond the world he depicts, but instead strives to mythologize it, i.e. to create its essence, whether benign or maleficent, by applying the technique of stylization so despised by the Lukács of today. One is almost tempted to measure the achievements of modernist writing by inquiring whether historical moments are given substance as such within their works, or whether they are diluted into some sort of timelessness.

Lukács would doubtless deprecate as idealistic the use of terms like 'image' and 'essence' in aesthetics. But their application in the realm of art is fundamentally different from what it is in philosophies of essence or of primitive images, especially refurbished versions of the Platonic Ideas. The most fundamental weakness of Lukács's position is probably his inability to maintain this distinction, a failure which leads him to transfer to the realm of art categories which refer to the relationship of consciousness to the actual world, as if there were no difference between them. Art exists in the real world and has a function in it, and the two are connected by a large number of mediating links. Nevertheless, as art it remains the antithesis of that which is the case. Philosophy has acknowledged this situation by defining art as 'aesthetic appearance'. Even Lukács will find it impossible to get away from the fact that the content of works of art is not real in the same sense as social reality. If this distinction is lost, then all attempts to provide a real foundation for aesthetics must be doomed to failure. But artistic appearance, the fact that art has set itself apart in qualitative terms from the immediate actuality in which it magically came into being, is neither its ideological Fall, nor does it make art an arbitrary system of signs, as if it merely reproduced the world without claiming to possess the same immediate reality. Any view as reductive as this would be a sheer mockery of dialectics.

More to the point is the assertion that the difference between art and empirical reality touches on the former's innermost being. It is no idealistic crime for art to provide essences, 'images'; the fact that many artists have inclined towards an idealist philosophy says nothing about the content of their works. The truth of the matter is that except where art goes against its own nature and simply duplicates existence, its task vis-à-vis that which merely exists, is to be its essence and image. This alone constitutes the aesthetic; art does not become knowledge with reference to mere immediate reality, i.e. by doing justice to a reality which veils its own essence and suppresses its truth in favour of a merely classificatory order. Art and reality can only converge if art crystallizes out its own formal laws, not by passively accepting objects as they come. In art knowledge is aesthetically mediated through and through. Even alleged cases of solipsism, which signify for Lukács the regression to an illusory immediacy on the part of the individual, do not imply the denial of the object, as they would in bad theories of knowledge, but instead aim at a dialectical reconciliation of subject and object. In the form of an image the object is absorbed into the subject instead of following the bidding of the alienated world and persisting obdurately in a state of reification. The contradiction between the object reconciled in the subject, i.e. spontaneously absorbed into the subject, and the actual unreconciled object in the outside world, confers on the work of art a vantage-point from which it can criticize actuality. Art is the negative knowledge of the actual world. In analogy to a current philosophical phrase we might speak of the 'aesthetic distance' from existence: only by virtue of this distance, and not by denying its existence, can the work of art become both work of art and valid consciousness. A theory of art which ignores this is at once philistine and ideological.

Lukács contents himself with Schopenhauer's aperçu that the principle of solipsism is 'only really viable with complete consistency in the most abstract form of philosophy' and 'even there only with a measure of sophistry' (p. 21). But his argument is self-defeating: if solipsism cannot be sustained, if it only succeeds in reproducing what it has begun by 'bracketing out', to use the phenomenological term, then we need have no fear of it as a stylistic principle. Objectively, then, in their works, the modernists have moved beyond the position Lukács ascribes to them. Proust decomposes the unity of the subjective mind by dint of its own introspection: the mind ends by transforming itself into a stage on which objective realities are made visible. His individualistic work becomes the opposite of that for which Lukács derides it: it becomes anti-individualistic. The *monologue intérieur*, the worldlessness of modern art which makes Lukács so indignant, is both the truth and the appearance of a free-floating subjectivity – it is truth, because in the universal atomistic state of the world, alienation rules over men, turning them into mere shadows of themselves – a point we may undoubtedly concede to Lukács. The free-floating subject is appearance, however, inasmuch as, objectively, the social totality has precedence over the individual, a totality which is created and reproduces itself through alienation and through the contradictions of society. The great works of modernist literature shatter this appearance of subjectivity by setting the individual in his frailty into context, and by grasping that totality in him of which the individual is but a moment and of which he must needs remain ignorant. Lukács evidently believes that when the Habsburg monarchy in Kafka and Musil, or Dublin in Joyce make themselves felt as a sort of 'atmospheric backcloth for the action' (p. 21), it somehow goes against the programme but nevertheless remains of secondary importance. But in arguing thus for the sake of his thesis, he clearly reduces something very substantial, a growing epic plenitude with all its negative potential, to the status of a mere accessory. The concept of atmosphere is in any event highly inappropriate as applied to Kafka. It goes back to an Impressionism which Kafka supersedes by his objectivist concern with historical essence. Even in Beckett – and perhaps in him above all – where seemingly all concrete historical components have been eliminated, and only primitive situations and forms of behaviour are tolerated, the unhistorical façade is the provocative opposite of the absolute Being idolized by reactionary philosophies. The primitivism with which his works begin so abruptly represents the final phase of a regression, especially obvious in *Fin de Partie*, in which, as from the far-distant realm of the self-evident, a terrestrial catastrophe is presupposed. His primitive men are the last men. One theme we discover in his works is something which Horkheimer and I have already discussed in *Dialectic of Enlightenment*: the fact that a society wholly in the grip of the Culture Industry displays all the reactions of an amphibian. The substantive content of a work of art can survive in the precise, wordless polemic which depicts the dawn of a nonsensical world; and it can vanish again as soon as it is positively asserted, as soon as existence is claimed for it, a fate similar to the one that befalls the didactic antithesis between a right and a wrong mode of life to be found in Tolstoy after *Anna Karenina*.

Lukács's favourite old idea of an 'immanent meaning' points towards that same dubious faith in the face value of things which his own theory sets out to destroy. Conceptions like Beckett's, however, have an objective, polemical thrust. Lukács twists them into 'the straightforward portrayal of the pathological, of the perverse, of idiocy, all of which are seen as types of the "condition humaine"' (p. 32) – and in this he follows the example of the film censor who regards the content as a defect of the treatment. Above all, Lukács's confusion of Beckett with the cult of Being and even with the inferior version of vitalism to be found in Montherlant (ibid.) exposes his inability to see what is in front of him. This blindness arises from his stubborn refusal to acknowledge the central claims of literary technique. He sticks imperturbably to what is narrated. But in literature the point of the subject matter can only be made effective by the use of techniques – something which Lukács himself hopes for from the more than suspect concept of 'perspective'. One would like to ask what would be left of Greek drama, which Lukács, like Hegel, has duly canonized, if the criterion of its value were the story which could be picked up in the street. The same holds good for the traditional novel and even for writers such as Flaubert who come into Lukács's category of the 'realist' novel: here too composition and style are fundamental.

Today, when empirical veracity has sunk to the level of superficial reportage, the relevance of technique has increased enormously. By structuring his work, the writer can hope to master the arbitrary and the individual against which Lukács so passionately inveighs. He fails to follow the insight contained in his last chapter to its logical conclusion: the purely arbitrary cannot be overcome simply by a determination to look at things in what purports to be a more objective manner. Lukács ought surely to be familiar with the key importance of the technical forces of production in history. No doubt this was more concerned with material than with cultural production. But can he really close his eyes to the fact that the techniques of art also develop in accordance with their own logic? Can he rest content with the abstract assertion that when society changes, completely different aesthetic criteria automatically come into force? Can he really persuade himself that this justifies him in nullifying the technical advance of the forces of production and providing for the canonical restoration of older, outdated forms? Does he not simply don the dictatorial mantle of socialist realism in order to expound an immutable doctrine which differs from the one he rightly repudiates only by its greater insensitivity?

Lukács places himself in the great philosophical tradition that conceives of art as knowledge which has assumed concrete shape, rather than as something irrational to be contrasted with science. This is perfectly legitimate, but he still finds himself ensnared in the same cult of immediacy of which he myopically accuses modernist literature: the fallacy of mere assertion. Art does not provide knowledge of reality by reflecting it photographically or 'from a particular perspective' but by revealing whatever is veiled by the empirical form assumed by reality, and this is possible only by virtue of art's own autonomous status. Even the suggestion that the world is unknowable, which Lukács so indefatigably castigates in writers like Eliot or Joyce, can become a moment of knowledge. This can happen where a gulf opens up between the overwhelming and unassimilable world of things, on the one hand, and a human experience impotently striving to gain a firm hold on it, on the other.

Lukács over-simplifies the dialectical unity of art and science, reducing it to bare identity, just as if works of art did nothing but apply their perspective in such a way as to anticipate some of the insights that the social sciences subsequently confirm. The essential distinction between artistic and scientific knowledge, however, is that in art nothing empirical survives unchanged; the empirical facts only acquire objective meaning when they are completely fused with the subjective intention. Even though Lukács draws a line between Realism and Naturalism, he nevertheless fails to make it clear that, if the distinction is to hold good, realist writing must necessarily achieve that synthesis with the subjective intentions which he would like to see expelled from Realism. In fact there is no way of preserving the antithesis between realist and 'formalist' approaches which, like an inquisitor, he erects into an absolute standard. On the one hand, it turns out that the principles of form which Lukács anathematizes as unrealistic and idealistic, have an objective aesthetic function; on the other, it becomes no less obvious that the novels of the early 19th century e.g. those of Dickens and Balzac, which he holds in such high esteem, and which he does not scruple to hold up as paradigms of the novelist's art, are by no means as realistic as all that. It is true that Marx and Engels might have considered them so in their polemic against the marketable romantic literature so fashionable in their day. Today, however, we not only see romantic and archaic, pre-bourgeois elements in both novelists, but even worse, Balzac's entire *Comédie Humaine* stands revealed as an imaginative reconstruction of the alienated world, i.e. of a reality no longer experienced by the individual subject. Seen in this light, the difference between it and the modernist victims of Lukács's class-justice is not very great; it is just that Balzac, in tune with his whole conception of form, thought of his monologues in terms of the plenitude of real life, while the great novelists of the 20th century encapsulate their worldly plenitude within the monologue.

This shatters Lukács's approach to its foundations. His concept of 'perspective' sinks inexorably to the level of what he strives in vain to distinguish it from in the last chapter of his book, namely an element of tendentiousness or, to use his own word, 'agitation', imposed from without. His whole position is paradoxical. He cannot escape the awareness that, aesthetically, social truth thrives only in works of art autonomously created. But in the concrete works of modern times this autonomy is accompanied by all those things which have been proscribed by the prevailing communist doctrine and which he neither could, nor can, tolerate. His hope was that obsolete and unsatisfactory aesthetic techniques might be legitimated if they could achieve a different standing in a different social system, i.e. that they might be justified from outside, from a point beyond their own internal logic. But this hope is pure superstition. It is not good enough for Lukács simply to dismiss the fact that the very products of socialist realism that have claimed to represent an advanced state of consciousness, in fact do no more than serve up the crumbling and insipid residues of bourgeois art-forms. This is a fact which stands in need of an objective explanation. Socialist realism did not simply have its origins, as communist theologians would like to believe, in a socially healthy and sound world; it was equally the product of the backwardness of consciousness and of the social forces of production. The only use they make of the thesis of the qualitative rupture between socialism and the bourgeoisie is to falsify that backwardness, which it has long been forbidden to mention, and twist it into something more progressive.

Lukács combines the charge of ontologism with that of individualism, which, following Heidegger's theory of man's existential forsakenness [*Geworfenheit*] from *Being and Time*, he interprets as a standpoint of unreflective loneliness. Lukács criticizes this stance (p. 51), showing how the literary work emerges from the poetic subject in all its adventitiousness, much as Hegel had shown in rigorous argument how philosophy emerges from the sensory certainties of the individual.[6] But as that immediacy turns out to be mediated in itself, the work of art contains within itself all the elements which Lukács finds lacking in that immediacy, while, on the other hand, the poetic subject finds it necessary to start from what is nearest to itself for the sake of that anticipated reconciliation of consciousness with the objective world. Lukács extends his denunciation of individualism to include Dostoyevsky. His story *Letters from the Underworld* is 'one of the first descriptions of the decadent individual' (p. 62). But by this junction of decadence and loneliness the process of atomization which has its source in the principle of bourgeois society itself is converted into nothing more than a manifestation of decline. Over and above this, the word 'decadent' has connotations of the biological decay of individuals: it is a parody of the fact that this

---

[6] *The Phenomenology of Mind*, trans. Baillie. See especially the end of the section on *The Unhappy Consciousness* (in Chapter IV): *Self-Consciousness passing into Reason*, which re-enacts the moves made earlier at the end of Chaps. I and II.

loneliness must have roots reaching back far beyond bourgeois society, for gregarious animals likewise form what Borchardt called a 'lonely community'; the *zoon politikon* had to be developed at a later stage. What is an historical premise of all modern art, which can only be transcended where it is fully acknowledged for what it is, appears in Lukács as an avoidable error or even as a bourgeois delusion. However, as soon as he comes to grips with the most recent Russian literature, he discovers that the structural change he had posited, has not in fact taken place. But this does not teach him to renounce such concepts as decadent loneliness. The position of the modernists he censures – or their 'transcendental situation', to use his earlier terminology – is not an ontological loneliness, but one which is historically conditioned. The ontologists of today are all too concerned with bonds which ostensibly attach Man to pure Being but in fact confer the semblance of immortality on temporal authorities of all shapes and sizes. In this they would not hit it off so badly with Lukács as one might expect. We may readily agree with him that it is illusory to think of loneliness as an *a priori* form; loneliness is a social product, and it transcends itself as soon as it reflects on itself as such.

But this is the point at which the dialectics of aesthetics rebounds against him. It is not open to the individual to transcend a collectively determined loneliness through his own decision and determination. Echoes of this can be heard distinctly enough when Lukács settles accounts with the tendentious content of the standardized Soviet novel. In general it is difficult to rid oneself of the impression one gains when reading the book, especially the impassioned pages on Kafka (vide pp. 49f.), that he reacts to the writers he anathematizes as decadent much like the legendary cab-horse which stops in its tracks on hearing the sudden sound of military music, before it goes on pulling its cart. To enable himself to resist their blandishments the more easily, Lukács joins in the chorus of censors who, ever since Kierkegaard (whom he himself classifies alongside the avant-garde), if not as far back as the furore over Friedrich Schlegel[7] and the early Romantics, have always waxed indignant over art that is merely interesting.[8] We would need to change the nature of this discussion. The fact that an insight or a work of art can be said to be interesting does not automatically mean it can be reduced to sensationalism or the cultural market, even though these

[7] Focused on his 'obscene' novel *Lucinde*.

[8] The 'interesting' developed as a concept during the Romantic period where it tended to be a defining feature of modern art and criticism, as opposed to classical beauty from which the public derived, in Kant's phrase, 'a distinterested pleasure'.

undoubtedly helped to give the concept its currency. It is certainly no seal of truth, but it has become its indispensable precondition; it is what *mea interest*, what concerns the subject, as opposed to what the over-whelming force of the powers-that-be, i.e. commodities, would like to fob us off with.

Lukács could not possibly praise what attracts him to Kafka and yet put him on his Index, were it not for the fact that, like the sceptics of late scholasticism, he secretly has a doctrine of two kinds of truth ready to hand: 'All this argues the superiority, historically speaking, of socialist realism (I cannot sufficiently emphasize that this superiority does not confer automatic success on each individual work of socialist realism). The reason for this superiority is the insights which socialist ideology, socialist perspective, make available to the writer: they enable him to give a more comprehensive and deeper account of man as a social being than any traditional ideology' (p. 115). In other words, artistic quality and the artistic superiority of socialist realism are two different things. Literature that is valid in itself is separated from literature that is valid in Soviet terms, which is supposed to be 'correct' by virtue of a sort of 'act of grace' on the part of the World Spirit.

Such a double standard ill becomes a thinker who makes such an impassioned plea in defence of the unity of reason. But if he maintains that loneliness is inescapable – and he scarcely attempts to deny that such a fate has been marked out for man by the negativity of society, by its universal reification – and if at the same time his Hegelianism makes him aware of its objective unreality, then it is scarcely possible to resist the inference that, taken to its logical conclusion, loneliness will turn into its opposite: the solitary consciousness potentially destroys and transcends itself by revealing itself in works of art as the hidden truth common to all men. This is exactly what we find in the authentic works of modern literature. They objectify themselves by immersing themselves totally, monadologically, in the laws of their own forms, laws which are aesthetically rooted in their own social content. It is this alone which gives the works of Joyce, Beckett and modern composers their power. The voice of the age echoes through their monologues: this is why they excite us so much more than works that simply depict the world in narrative form. The fact that their transition to objectivity remains contemplative and fails to become praxis is grounded in the nature of a society in which the monadological condition persists univers-ally, despite all assurances to the contrary. Moreover, Lukács's own classicism should deter him from expecting works of art to break through that contemplation. His assertion of artistic quality is incompatible with the pragmatic approach which enables him to summarily dismiss the responsible and progressive works of modern artists with the refrain 'bourgeois, bourgeois, bourgeois'.

Lukács quotes approvingly from my work on the ageing of modern music, which, paradoxically, runs parallel to the work of Sedlmayr,[9] in order to play off my reflections against modern art and against my own intentions. I do not begrudge him this: 'Only those thoughts are true which fail to understand themselves',[10] and no author can lay claim to proprietory rights over them. Nevertheless, it will need a better argument than Lukács's to take these rights away from me. The belief that art cannot survive when based on a notion of pure expression identical with *Angst* was one I committed myself to in *The Philosophy of Modern Music*, and even though I do not share Lukács's official optimism, I think that historically there might be less justification for that *Angst* nowadays and that the 'decadent intelligentsia' should perhaps have less need to feel afraid. But the ostensive gesture of expression, the 'This' in its purity, cannot be transcended either by adopting an undynamic, reified style, which was the charge I levelled at the ageing music of modernity, or by a leap into a positivity which is not substantial or authentic in a Hegelian sense, and which fails to constitute its own form prior to all reflection. Logically, the ageing of modern music should not drive composers back to obsolete forms but should lead them to an insistent self-criticism. From the outset, however, the unrelieved representation of *Angst* had a further dimension: it was a way of using speech, the power implicit in calling things by their true name, in order to stand one's ground. It was therefore the very opposite of all the associations evoked by the derogatory word 'decadent'. Lukács does indeed give credit to the art he maligns for responding negatively to a negative reality, the domination of all that is 'execrable'. 'But since', he goes on 'modernism portrays distortion without critical detachment, and since it devises stylistic techniques which emphasize the necessity of distortion in any kind of society, it may be said to distort distortions further. By attributing distortion to reality itself, it dismisses as immaterial, as ontologically irrelevant, all counter-forces and trends actually at work in reality.' (p. 75f.)

[9] Hans Sedlmayr: *Verlust der Mitte*, (trans. as *Art in Crisis*) a polemical tract on modern art which enjoyed a great vogue in the 1950s in Germany because of its despairing view of modern culture. Written from a right-wing, crypto-Fascist point of view, and positing the recovery of religious faith as a way out of the crisis, it was a significant document of the Cold War years.

[10] See Theodor Adorno, *Minima Moralia*, NLB, London 1974.

The official optimism implied in the notion of counter-forces and trends compels Lukács to do away with the Hegelian proposition that the negation of the negation – the 'distortion of the distortion' *is* the positive. This proposition alone is capable of laying bare the truth contained in the otherwise desperately irrationalist notion of the 'complex and ambiguous' nature of art, the truth namely that the expression of suffering and the pleasure taken in dissonance, scorned by Lukács as 'sensationalism, a delight in novelty for novelty's sake' (p. 105), are inextricably interwoven in authentic works of art in the modern age. This phenomenon should be linked to the problem of the dialectical tension between reality and the realm of art, which Lukács evades. Since the work of art never focuses directly on reality, it never makes the sort of statement found elsewhere in the realm of knowledge to the effect that this or that is the case. Instead it asserts: Yes, that is the way things are. Its logic, then, is not that of subject and predicate, but of internal harmony. Only by means of the latter, by means of the relationship it creates between its component parts, does it adopt a stance. It is antithetically opposed to the empirical reality which it encapsulates, as well as being encapsulated by it, because, unlike mental procedures directly concerned with reality, it does not define any portion of that reality unambiguously. It utters no propositions [*Urteil*]; it only becomes a proposition when taken as a whole. The element of untruth inherent, in Hegel's view, in every particular proposition because nothing is wholly identical with what it is supposed to be in a particular proposition, is eliminated by art in that the work of art synthesizes the elements within it in such a way that no one part is stated by any other. The very idea, so fashionable nowadays, of 'stating something' is irrelevant to art. As a synthesis which utters no propositions, art may forgo the right to make definite pronouncements on points of detail; but it more than compensates for this by its greater justice towards everything normally excised from the proposition. A work of art only becomes knowledge when taken as a totality, i.e. through all its mediations, not through its individual intentions. The latter should not be extracted from it, nor should it be judged in the light of them. Nevertheless, Lukács regularly proceeds in this manner, despite his protest against the officially licensed novelists who apply the same method in practice. Even though he very well perceives the defects of their standardized products, his own philosophy of art cannot protect him from short-circuiting the creative process, from the effects of which, the effects of an imbecility imposed from above, he then recoils.

Where the essential complexity of the work of art cannot be dismissed as a unique case of no importance, Lukács convulsively shuts his eyes to it. On the occasions when he does look at specific works, he marks in red the immediate detail and overlooks the overall meaning. He complains, for example, about an admittedly slight poem of Benn's, which goes as follows:

> O, daß wir unsere Ururahnen wären.
> Ein Klümpchen Schleim in einem warmen Moor.
> Leben und Tod, Befruchtung und Gebären
> glitte aus unseren stummen Säften vor.
> Ein Algenblatt oder ein Dünenhügel,
> vom Wind geformtes und nach unten schwer.
> Schon ein Libellenkopf, ein Möwenflügel
> wäre zu weit und litte schon zu sehr.[11]

What Lukács finds in this poem is 'the opposition of man as animal, as a primeval reality, to man as social being', and he places it in the tradition of Heidegger, Klages and Rosenberg. He sums it up as 'a glorification of the abnormal; an undisguised anti-humanist statement' (p. 32), although, even if the poem were to be identified simply with its overt content, it is clear that its final line follows Schopenhauer in its lament that the higher stage of individuation brings nothing but suffering, and Benn's nostalgia for primordial times merely reflects the intolerable burden of the present. The moralism that colours all of Lukács's critical concepts is typical of his weepings and wailings about subjectivist 'lack of reality' [*Weltlosigkeit*], just as if the modernists had literally put into practice what is known in Husserl's phenomenology, grotesquely enough, as the methodological annihilation of the world. It is in such terms that he pillories Musil: 'Ulrich, the hero of his great novel, when asked what he would do if universal power were confided into his hands, replies: "I would be compelled to abolish reality." No prolonged analysis is needed to establish the fact that the abolition of outward reality is the counterpart of a subjective existence "without qualities"' (p. 25). Yet the sentence Lukács objects to obviously points in its negativity to despair, to an uncontrollable *Weltschmerz* and to love. Lukács suppresses this and operates instead with a truly 'immediate', wholly un-

[11] [Oh, that we were our primordial ancestors. Small lumps of plasma in a sultry swamp. Life and death, conception and parturition – all emerging from those juices soundlessly.

A piece of seaweed or a dune of sand, formed by the wind and bound to the earth. Even a dragon-fly's head or the wing of a gull would be too remote and mean too much suffering.]

First published in *Die Aktion* in 1913.

critical concept of normality, complementing it with the idea of pathological disturbance that naturally accompanies it. Only a state of mind
that has been completely purged of every vestige of psychoanalysis can
fail to see the connection between this view of normality and a form of
social repression which has outlawed one-sided impulses. Any form of
social criticism which does not blush to go on talking about the normal
and the perverted, is itself still under the spell of the very ideas it claims
to have superseded. The stentorian voice of manly conviction which
Lukács employs to assert in good Hegelian fashion the primacy of the
substantial universal over the specious, untenable 'bad existence' of
mere individuals, recalls that of the public prosecutors who call for the
extermination of those unfit to live or who deviate from the norm.

His ability to appreciate lyric poetry may also be doubted. The line
'O daß wir unsere Ururahnen wären' ['Oh that we were our primordial
ancestors'] has a meaning completely at variance with that of a literal
desire. The very word 'Ururahnen' can only be uttered with a grin. The
style – which incidentally is traditional rather than modern – conveys
the sense of a poetic *persona* which is comically inauthentic; Benn is
playing a sort of melancholy game. The repulsive nature of the state to
which the poet pretends he wishes to return, but to which no return is
possible, reinforces his protest against a suffering which has historical
causes. All this, as well as the montage-like 'alienation effect' arising
from Benn's use of scientific words and motifs, has to be felt and experienced. His exaggeration undermines the very regression which
Lukács unreservedly imputes to him. Any reader who misses all these
connotations resembles that second-rate writer who diligently and
astutely set about imitating Thomas Mann's style, and of whom Mann
once said with a laugh: 'He writes just like me, only he means it seriously.'
Over-simplifications of the type found in Lukács's excursus on Benn are
not lacking in nuances, but they miss the core of the work of art itself,
which only becomes a work of art by virtue of those nuances. Such
analyses are symptomatic of the process of stultification which over-
whelms even the most intelligent as soon as they submit to regulations
like those governing socialist realism.

Earlier, in an attempt to convict modern poetry of Fascism, Lukács
triumphantly unearths a bad poem by Rilke in which he rampaged
around furiously like an elephant in the Viennese workshops.[12] It is an

[12] The Viennese workshops were established in 1903 as an offshoot of Art Nouveau.
Under the influence of Gustav Klimt they attempted to reform the style of domestic life by
applying the decorative techniques of the movement to ordinary objects. From 1908 they
organized public exhibitions of their work and it was at one of these that Oskar Kokoschka
first attracted public attention.

open question whether the retrograde movement discernible in Lukács, once one of the most progressive of minds, is itself an objective symptom of the regression which threatens to overshadow the European mind as a whole, a shadow cast over the developed nations by the underdeveloped ones which are already starting to follow the example of the former. Perhaps his position reveals to us something of the fate of a theory which seems to have diminished not just in terms of its anthropological assumptions, i.e. of the mental capacities of theoretical man, but which has also caused his substantive being to shrivel into a state of existence in which theory is at present deemed less vital than a practice whose sole task is to ward off the impending catastrophe.

Lukács's neo-naivety does not even call a halt before Thomas Mann, whom he plays off against Joyce with a fulsome flattery which would have nauseated the great chronicler of decay. The controversy about time triggered off by Bergson is treated like the Gordian Knot. Since Lukács is a good objectivist in all things, objective time always has to win out, while subjective time is merely a distortion inspired by decadence. What had induced Bergson to formulate his theory of experienced time was not the subjectivist spirit of subversiveness, as the stultified bureaucratic mind tends to believe, regardless of its political convictions, but the sheer inability to endure the meaningless passage of alienated, reified time – something which the early Lukács had once described so strikingly in his account of Flaubert's *Education Sentimentale*. But in *The Magic Mountain* Thomas Mann too paid his tribute to Bergson's concept of *temps durée*. To rescue him for Lukács's own theory of critical realism, a number of the characters in the book are given good marks because 'even subjectively, their experience of time is normal and objective'. He then writes, and I quote verbatim: 'Indeed, Ziemssen is dimly aware that the modern experience of time is simply a result of the abnormal life of the sanatorium, hermetically sealed off from everyday life' (p. 51). The irony which surrounds the whole character of Ziemssen has eluded our aestheticism; socialist realism has blunted his sensibility towards the critical realism he praises. Ziemssen is a narrow-minded officer, a sort of successor to Goethe's Valentin,[13] a man who dies a soldier's death, albeit in his bed. For Lukács Ziemssen becomes the spokesman of an authentic life, much as Tolstoy had tried and failed to achieve with Levin. In truth, Thomas Mann has depicted the relation-

---

[13] Valentin was Gretchen's brother in *Faust I*; it is he who dies 'als Soldat und brav', words echoed later in *The Magic Mountain*.

ship between the two concepts of time without reflection but with the keenest sensibility; he has represented that relationship as being as tortuous and ambivalent as is needed to reflect his own position and his dialectical attitude towards everything bourgeois: right and wrong are equally divided between the reified consciousness of time characteristic of the Philistine who vainly tries to flee from the sanatorium into his profession, and the phantasmagorical time of those who remain in the sanatorium, that allegory of Bohemianism and subjectivism. Thomas Mann wisely refrained from reconciling the two concepts of time as well as from declaring his preference for either.

The fact that Lukács can so drastically miss the aesthetic point of even his favourite text is explained by his *parti pris* for content and for the message of a work of literature, which he confuses with its nature as an artistic object. Even though he refuses to concern himself with stylistic factors, like the far from subtly disguised use of irony, to say nothing of more obvious rhetorical devices, he fails to derive any reward for this renunciation in the shape of a truth content purged of all subjective appearances. Instead he satisfies himself with the dregs, namely with the subject-matter, which of course is an essential preliminary to the discovery of the truth content of a work. Eager though Lukács is to prevent any regression in the novel, he still goes on reciting the various articles of the catechism, such as socialist realism, the ideologically sanctioned reflection theory [*Abbildtheorie*] of knowledge, and the dogma of the automatic progress of mankind, i.e. a progress independent of that spontaneity which has in the meantime been stifled – even though, in view of the nature of the irrevocable past, such a 'belief in the ultimate rationality, meaningfulness of the world and man's ability to penetrate its secrets' (p. 43) is asking rather a lot. This belief forces him to adopt something very near to those puerile ideas about art which repel him when he encounters them in literary bureaucrats less well-versed than he. His efforts to break out are in vain. The extent to which his own aesthetic perceptions have been damaged may be seen, for example, from a passage on allegory in Byzantine mosaics: in literature allegorical art of this quality can only occur in 'exceptional' cases (p. 40). He talks as if the distinction between the exception and the rule had any validity in art, outside academies and conservatories, as if he had forgotten that every aesthetic work is an individual product and so always an exception in terms of its in-dwelling principle and its general implications, whereas anything which fits in with general regulations disqualifies itself from a place in the world of art. 'Exceptional cases' are borrowed from the same vocabulary as 'top-grade performances'.

The late Franz Borkenau once said, after he had broken with the Communist Party, that he could no longer put up with the practice of discussing municipal regulations in the categories of Hegelian logic, and Hegelian logic in the spirit of meetings of the town council. Such contaminations, which date back to Hegel himself, bind Lukács to that cultural level which he would like to raise to his own. The Hegelian critique of the 'unhappy consciousness', the impulse, so powerful in speculative philosophy, to rise above the merely superficial ethos of isolated subjectivity, all this becomes in his hands an ideology for bigoted party officials who have not even reached the level of subjectivity. Their aggressive narrow-mindedness, a legacy of the backwardness of the petty bourgeoisie in the 19th century, is lent a spurious dignity by the attempt to interpret it as an adaptation to reality freed from the shackles of mere individuality. But a true dialectical leap is not one which leaps out of the dialectic itself and transforms the unhappy consciousness simply by the force of conviction into a happy collusion, at the expense of the objective social and technical factors governing artistic production. Based on such foundations the would-be loftier standpoint must necessarily remain abstract, in accordance with a proposition of Hegel's from which Lukács would hardly dissent. The desperate attempt at a profundity intended to counter the imbecility of the boy-meets-tractor literature, does not protect him from declamatory statements which are at once abstract and childish: 'The more general the significance of the theme of a work of art, and the deeper writers probe into different aspects of the laws and tendencies governing reality, the more completely will this reality be transformed into a purely or predominantly socialist society, and the closer will grow the ties between critical realism and socialist realism. In the process the negative (but: non-rejecting) perspective of critical realism will gradually be transformed into a positive (affirmative), a socialist perspective' (p. 114). The jesuitical distinction between the negative 'but non-rejecting' and the positive (affirmative) perspective shifts the problems of literary quality into that same sphere of pre-ordained convictions which Lukács wants most to escape from.

That he does wish to escape is not, of course, in any doubt. We can only do his book justice if we bear in mind that in countries where the decisive facts cannot be called by their proper names, the marks of the Terror have been branded on everything which is uttered in their place. On the other hand, and in consequence of this, even feeble, half-hearted and incomplete thoughts acquire a force in a particular context to which their literal content does not entitle them. It is with considerations of this sort in mind that we have to read the whole of Chapter 3, despite the obvious disparity between the questions treated there and the intellectual apparatus brought to bear on them. This chapter contains a large number of statements which would enable us to extricate ourselves from the morass, if only they could be thought through to their logical conclusion. Like this one: 'The mere appropriation of Marxism (to say nothing of a mere sympathy for the socialist movement or even Party membership) is not of itself sufficient. A writer may acquire useful experience in this way and become aware of certain intellectual or moral problems. This may prove to be of great value for his personality and can help to transform a possibility into a reality. But it is a grave error to suppose that the process of translating a true consciousness of reality into a valid, realistic form of art is in principle easier or more direct than in the case of a false consciousness' (pp. 96–7f.). Or again, he has this to say about the sterile empiricism of the documentary novel which flourishes everywhere nowadays: 'The emergence even in critical realism of an ideal of monographic completion, as in Zola, for example, is striking evidence of an internal problem. I shall show later that similar, and perhaps even greater problems are inherent in socialist realism' (p. 100).

When Lukács goes on, in the terminology of his youth, to insist on the primacy of intensive over extensive totality, he would only need to follow his own recommendation into the realm of the created work to find himself forced to accept the very things his ex-cathedra pronouncements find fault with in the modernists. It is grotesque that he should still persist in wanting to 'overcome' the 'anti-realism of the decadent movement'. He even comes close to perceiving that the Russian Revolution has far from created a society which requires and can sustain a 'positive' literature: 'Above all else we must not lose sight of the trivial fact that even though the seizure of power represents a tremendous leap forward, the majority of people, artists included, will not be automatically transformed' (p. 104f.). He then proceeds to let out the truth about so-called socialist realism, albeit in a somewhat muted fashion, as if he were only discussing an extreme form of it: 'The upshot is an unhealthy, diluted version of bourgeois realism, or at least a highly dubious imitation of it, which in the nature of the case is only achieved at the cost of its great virtues' (p. 116). In such literature the 'real nature of the artist's perspective' is overlooked. This means that 'many writers find themselves in the presence of really progressive tendencies, but ones which only provide guidelines to the future. If rightly viewed, they could act as the lever to bring movement into the existing situation. Instead many writers simply identify these tendencies with reality itself; something which only exists in embryonic form they represent as a fully-fledged fact, in short they mechanically equate a possible point of view, a perspective, with reality itself' (p. 116–7).

To put it in a nutshell, what this means is that the procedures of socialist realism, and the Socialist Romanticism which Lukács sees as its complement, are simply the ideological transfiguration of the prevailing unsatisfactory state of affairs. Lukács sees that the official objectivism typical of the totalitarian approach to literature ends up as pure subjectivism. He opposes to it an aesthetic concept of objectivity which is altogether more in tune with the dignity of man: 'Art too is governed by objective laws. An infringement of these laws may not have immediate practical consequences as do the infringement of economic laws, but it results no less inexorably in flawed or inferior works of art' (p. 117). Here, where he has the courage of his own convictions, his judgements are far more cogent than his philistine utterances about modern art: 'The break-up of these mediating elements leads to a false polarization. On the one hand, theory, from being a guide to practice, hardens into dogma; on the other, the element of contradiction (and even chance) disappears from the individual facts of life' (p. 118). He succinctly sums up the central issue: 'In such works, literature ceases to reflect the dynamic contradictions of social life; it becomes the illustration of abstract truth' (p. 19). The responsibility for this is put squarely at the door of 'agitation as the point of departure', as a paradigm for both art and thought, which shrivel up, ossify and degenerate into rigid schemata with an over-emphasis on praxis. 'Instead of a new dialectical structure, we find a static schematicism' (p. 121). No modernist could have put it better.

For all this, it is impossible to rid oneself of the feeling that here is a man who is desperately tugging at his chains, imagining all the while that their clanking heralds the onward march of the world-spirit. He remains dazzled by the power which would never take his insubordinate ideas to heart, even if it tolerated them. Even worse, although contemporary Russian society is oppressed and exploited, Lukács never quite manages to dispel the illusion that its contradictions are non-antagonistic in nature, to use the hair-splitting distinction worked out by the Chinese. All the symptoms at which he protests have come into being because the dictators and their hangers-on need to hammer into the masses the very thesis which Lukács implicitly endorses by his use of the term socialist realism, and to banish from their minds anything that might lead them astray. The hegemony of a doctrine which fulfils such very real functions cannot be broken merely by demonstrating its falsity. Lukács quotes a cynical sentence by Hegel which sums up the social meaning of this process as it was seen in the traditional bourgeois novel of education [*Bildungsroman*]: 'For the end of such apprenticeship consists in this: the subject sows his wild oats, educates himself with his wishes and opinions into harmony with subsisting relationships and their rationality, enters the concatenation of the world and works out for himself an appropriate attitude to it.'[14] Lukács adds this comment: 'In one sense many of the great bourgeois novels contradict Hegel's assertion; but in another sense, equally specific, they confirm his point of view. They are in conflict with it in so far as the education they have depicted does not necessarily culminate in any such recognition of bourgeois society. The struggle to realize the dreams and convictions of youth is ended by the pressures of society, the rebels are broken or driven into isolation, but the reconciliation of which Hegel speaks is not always exacted from them. No doubt, since the struggle often ends in resignation, it does not stray too far from what Hegel suggests. For on the one hand, the objective social reality does triumph over the purely subjective strivings of the individual; and on the other, the reconciliation Hegel proclaims is by no means utterly different from a feeling of resignation' (op. cit. p. 112).

The supreme criterion of his aesthetics, the postulate of a reality which must be depicted as an unbroken continuum joining subject and object, a reality which, to employ the term Lukács stubbornly adheres to, must be 'reflected' – all this rests on the assumption that the reconciliation has been accomplished, that all is well with society, that the individual has come into his own and feels at home in his world. Lukács concedes the need for all this in an anti-ascetic digression. But this would remove the resignation which Lukács discerns in Hegel and whose presence he would certainly have to acknowledge in his prototypical realist, Goethe, who actually advocated it. But the cleavage, the antagonism persists, and it is a sheer lie to assert that it has been 'overcome', as they call it, in the states of the Eastern bloc. The magic spell which holds Lukács in thrall and which prevents his return to the utopia of his youth that he longs for, is a re-enactment of that reconciliation under duress he had himself discerned at the heart of absolute idealism.

Translated by Rodney Livingstone

[14] From Hegel's *Aesthetics*, vol. I, p. 593, Oxford 1975, slightly adapted from the translation by T. M. Knox.

Theodor Adorno

Commitment

Since Sartre's essay *What is Literature?* there has been less theoretical debate about committed and autonomous literature. Nevertheless, the controversy over commitment remains urgent, so far as anything that merely concerns the life of the mind can be today, as opposed to sheer human survival. Sartre was moved to issue his manifesto because he saw – and he was certainly not the first to do so – works of art displayed side by side in a pantheon of optional edification, decaying into cultural commodities. In such coexistence, they desecrate each other. If a work, without its author necessarily intending it, aims at a supreme effect, it cannot really tolerate a neighbour beside it. This salutary intolerance holds not only for individual works, but also for aesthetic genres or attitudes such as those once symbolized in the now half-forgotten controversy over commitment.

There are two 'positions on objectivity' which are constantly at war with one another, even when intellectual life falsely presents them as at peace. A work of art that is committed strips the magic from a work of art that is content to be a fetish, an idle pastime for those who would like to sleep through the deluge that threatens them, in an apoliticism that is in fact deeply political. For the committed, such works are a distraction from the battle of real interests, in which no one is any longer exempt from the conflict between the two great blocs. The possibility of intellectual life itself depends on this conflict to such an extent that only blind illusion can insist on rights that may be shattered tomorrow. For autonomous works of art, however, such considerations, and the conception of art which underlies them, are themselves the spiritual catastrophe of which the committed keep warning. Once the life of the mind renounces the duty and liberty of its own pure objectification, it has abdicated. Thereafter, works of art merely assimilate themselves to the brute existence against which they protest, in forms so ephemeral (the very charge made against autonomous works by committed writers) that from their first day they belong to the seminars in which they inevitably end. The menacing thrust of the antithesis is a reminder of how precarious the position of art is today. Each of the two alternatives negates itself with the other. Committed art, necessarily detached as art from reality, cancels the distance between the two. 'Art for art's sake' denies by its absolute claims that ineradicable connection with reality which is the polemical *a priori* of the attempt to make art autonomous from the real. Between these two poles the tension in which art has lived in every age till now is dissolved.

Contemporary literature itself suggests doubts as to the omnipotence of these alternatives. For it is not yet so completely subjugated to the course of the world as to constitute rival fronts. The Sartrean goats and the Valéryan sheep will not be separated. Even if politically motivated, commitment in itself remains politically polyvalent so long as it is not reduced to propaganda, whose pliancy mocks any commitment by the subject. On the other hand, its opposite, known in Russian catechisms as formalism, is not decried only by Soviet officials or libertarian existentialists; even 'vanguard' critics themselves frequently accuse so-called abstract texts of a lack of provocation and social aggressivity. Conversely, Sartre cannot praise Picasso's *Guernica* too highly; yet he could hardly be convicted of formalist sympathies in music or painting. He restricts his notion of commitment to literature because of its conceptual character: 'The writer deals with meanings'.[1] Of course, but not only with them. If no word which enters a literary work ever wholly frees itself from its meaning in ordinary speech, so no literary work, not even the traditional novel, leaves these meanings unaltered, as they were outside it. Even an ordinary 'was', in a report of something that was not, acquires a new formal quality from the fact that it was not so. The same process occurs in the higher levels of meaning of a work, all the way up to what once used to be called its 'Idea'. The special position that Sartre accords to literature must also be suspect to anyone who does not unconditionally subsume diverse aesthetic genres under a superior universal concept. The rudiments of external meanings are the irreducibly non-artistic elements in art. Its formal principle lies not in them, but in the dialectic of both moments – which accomplishes the transformation of meanings within it. The distinction between artist and

---

[1] Jean-Paul Sartre, *What is Literature?*, London 1967, p. 4.

littérateur is shallow: but it is true that the object of any aesthetic philosophy, even as understood by Sartre, is not the publicistic aspect of art.
Still less is it the 'message' of a work. The latter oscillates unhappily
between the subjective intentions of the artist and the demands of an
objectively explicit metaphysical meaning. In our context, this meaning
generally turns out to be an uncommonly practicable Being.

The social function of talk about commitment has meanwhile become
somewhat confused. Cultural conservatives who demand that a work of
art should say something, join forces with their political opponents against
atelic, hermetic works of art. Eulogists of 'relevance' are more likely to
find Sartre's *Huis Clos* profound, than to listen patiently to a text whose
language challenges signification and by its very distance from meaning
revolts in advance against positivist subordination of meaning. For the
atheist Sartre, on the other hand, the conceptual import of art is the
premiss of commitment. Yet works banned in the East are sometimes
demagogically denounced by local guardians of the authentic message
because they apparently say what they in fact do not say. The Nazis
were already using the term 'cultural bolshevism' under the Weimar
Republic, and hatred of what it refers to has survived the epoch of Hitler,
when it was institutionalized. Today it has flared up again, just as it
did forty years ago at works of the same kind, including some whose
origins go a long way back and are unmistakeably part of an established
tradition.

Newspapers and magazines of the radical Right constantly stir up
indignation against what is unnatural, over-intellectual, morbid and
decadent: they know their readers. The insights of social psychology
into the authoritarian personality confirm them. The basic features of
this type include conformism, respect for a petrified façade of opinion
and society, and resistance to impulses that disturb its order or evoke
inner elements of the unconscious that cannot be admitted. This hostility
to anything alien or alienating can accommodate itself much more easily
to literary realism of any provenance, even if it proclaims itself critical
or socialist, than to works which swear allegiance to no political slogans,
but whose mere guise is enough to disrupt the whole system of rigid
coordinates that governs authoritarian personalities – to which the latter
cling all the more fiercely, the less capable they are of spontaneous
appreciation of anything not officially approved. Campaigns to prevent
the staging of Brecht's plays in Western Germany belong to a relatively
superficial layer of political consciousness. They were not even particularly vigorous, or they would have taken much crasser forms after

13 August.[2] By contrast, when the social contract with reality is abandoned, and literary works no longer speak as though they were reporting fact, hairs start to bristle. Not the least of the weaknesses of the debate on commitment is that it ignores the effect produced by works whose own formal laws pay no heed to coherent effects. So long as it fails to understand what the shock of the unintelligible can communicate, the whole dispute resembles shadow-boxing. Confusions in discussion of the problem do not indeed alter it, but they do make it necessary to rethink the alternative solutions proposed for it.

In aesthetic theory, 'commitment' should be distinguished from 'tendency'. Committed art in the proper sense is not intended to generate ameliorative measures, legislative acts or practical institutions – like earlier propagandist plays against syphilis, duels, abortion laws or borstals – but to work at the level of fundamental attitudes. For Sartre its task is to awaken the free choice of the agent which makes authentic existence possible at all, as opposed to the neutrality of the spectator. But what gives commitment its aesthetic advantage over tendentiousness also renders the content to which the artist commits himself inherently ambiguous. In Sartre the notion of choice – originally a Kierkegaardian category – is heir to the Christian doctrine 'He who is not with me is against me', but now voided of any concrete theological content. What remains is merely the abstract authority of a choice enjoined, with no regard for the fact that the very possibility of choosing depends on what can be chosen. The archetypal situation always cited by Sartre to demonstrate the irreducibility of freedom merely underlines this. Within a predetermined reality, freedom becomes an empty claim: Herbert Marcuse has exposed the absurdity of the philosophical theorem that it is always possible inwardly either to accept or to reject martyrdom.[3] Yet this is precisely what Sartre's dramatic situations are designed to demonstrate. But his plays are nevertheless bad models of his own existentialism, because they display in their respect for truth the whole administered universe which his philosophy ignores: the lesson we learn from them is one of unfreedom. Sartre's theatre of ideas sabotages the aims of his categories. This is not a specific shortcoming of his plays. It is not the office of art to spotlight alternatives, but to resist by its form alone the course of the world, which permanently puts a pistol to men's heads. In fact, as soon as committed works of art do instigate decisions at

[2] Reference to the establishment of the Berlin Wall in 1961.
[3] Reference to Marcuse's essay 'Sartre's Existentialism', included in *Studies in Critical Philosophy*, NLB, London 1972, pp. 157–90.

their own level, the decisions themselves become interchangeable. Because of this ambiguity, Sartre has with great candour confessed that he expects no real changes in the world from literature – a scepticism which reflects the historical mutations both of society and of the practical function of literature since the days of Voltaire. The principle of commitment thus slides towards the proclivities of the author, in keeping with the extreme subjectivism of Sartre's philosophy, which for all its materialist undertones, still echoes German speculative idealism. In his literary theory the work of art becomes an appeal to subjects, because it is itself nothing other than a declaration by a subject of his own choice or failure to choose.

Sartre will not allow that every work of art, at its very inception, confronts the writer, however free he may be, with objective demands of composition. His intention becomes simply one element among them. Sartre's question, 'Why write?', and his solution of it in a 'deeper choice', are invalid because the author's motivations are irrelevant to the finished work, the literary product. Sartre himself is not so far from this view when he notes that the stature of works increases, the less they remain attached to the empirical person who created them, as Hegel saw long ago. When he calls the literary work, in Durkheim's language, a social fact, he again involuntarily recalls its inherently collective objectivity, impenetrable to the mere subjective intentions of the author. Sartre therefore does not want to situate commitment at the level of the intention of the writer, but at that of his humanity itself.[4] This determination, however, is so generic that commitment ceases to be distinct from any other form of human action or attitude. The point, says Sartre, is that the writer commits himself in the present, '*dans le présent*'; but since he in any case cannot escape it, his commitment to it cannot indicate a programme. The actual obligation a writer undertakes is much more precise: it is not one of choice, but of substance. Although Sartre talks of the dialectic, his subjectivism so little registers the particular other for which the subject must first divest itself to become a subject, that he suspects every literary objectification of petrifaction. However, since the pure immediacy and spontaneity which he hopes to save encounter no resistance in his work by which they could define themselves, they undergo a second reification. In order to develop his drama and novel beyond sheer declaration – whose recurrent model is the scream of the tortured – Sartre has to seek recourse in a flat objectivity, subtracted

[4] 'Because he is a man'; *Situations* II, Paris 1948, p. 51.

from any dialectic of form and expression, which is simply a communication of his own philosophy. The content of his art becomes philosophy, as with no other writer except Schiller.

But however sublime, thoughts can never be much more than one of the materials for art. Sartre's plays are vehicles for the author's ideas, which have been left behind in the race of aesthetic forms. They operate with traditional plots, exalted by an unshaken faith in meanings which can be transferred from art to reality. But the theses they illustrate, or where possible state, misuse the emotions which Sartre's own drama aims to express, by making them examples. They thereby disavow themselves. When one of his most famous plays ends with the dictum 'Hell is other people', it sounds like a quotation from *Being and Nothingness*, and it might just as well have been 'Hell is ourselves'. The combination of solid plot, and equally solid, extractable idea won Sartre great success and made him, without doubt against his honest will, acceptable to the culture industry. The high level of abstraction of such thesis-art led him into the mistake of letting some of his best works, the film *Les Jeux sont Faits* or the play *Les Mains Sales*, be performed as political events, and not just to an audience of victims in the dark. In much the same way, a current ideology – which Sartre detests – confuses the actions and sufferings of paper leaders with the objective movement of history. Interwoven in the veil of personalization is the idea that human beings are in control and decide, not anonymous machinery, and that there is life on the commanding heights of society: Beckett's moribund grotesques suggest the truth about that. Sartre's vision prevents him from recognizing the hell he revolts against. Many of his phrases could be parroted by his mortal enemies. The idea that decision as such is what counts would even cover the Nazi slogan that 'only sacrifice makes us free'. In Fascist Italy, Gentile's absolute dynamism made similar pronouncements in philosophy. The flaw in Sartre's conception of commitment strikes at the very cause to which he commits himself.

Brecht, in some of his plays, such as the dramatization of Gorky's *The Mother* or *The Measures Taken*, bluntly glorifies the Party. But at times, at least according to his theoretical writings, he too wanted to educate spectators to a new attitude that would be distanced, thoughtful, experimental, the reverse of illusory empathy and identification. In tendency to abstraction, his plays after *Saint Joan* trump those of Sartre. The difference is that Brecht, more consistent than Sartre and a greater artist, made this abstraction into the formal principle of his art, as a didactic poetics that eliminates the traditional concept of dramatic character altogether. He realized that the surface of social life, the sphere of consumption, which includes the psychologically motivated actions of individuals, conceals the essence of society – which, as the law of exchange, is itself abstract. Brecht rejected aesthetic individuation as an ideology. He therefore sought to translate the true hideousness of society into theatrical appearance, by dragging it straight out of its camouflage. The people on his stage shrink before our eyes into the agents of social processes and functions, which indirectly and unknowingly they are in empirical reality. Brecht no longer postulates, like Sartre, an identity between living individuals and the essence of society, let alone any absolute sovereignty of the subject. Nevertheless, the process of aesthetic reduction that he pursues for the sake of political truth, in fact gets in its way. For this truth involves innumerable mediations, which Brecht disdains. What is artistically legitimate as alienating infantilism – Brecht's first plays came from the same milieu as Dada – becomes merely infantile when it starts to claim theoretical or social validity. Brecht wanted to reveal in images the inner nature of capitalism. In this sense his aim was indeed what he disguised it as against Stalinist terror – realistic. He would have refused to deprive social essence of meaning by taking it as it appeared, imageless and blind, in a single crippled life. But this burdened him with the obligation of ensuring that what he intended to make unequivocally clear was theoretically correct. His art, however, refused to accept this *quid pro quo*: it both presents itself as didactic, and claims aesthetic dispensation from responsibility for the accuracy of what it teaches.

Criticism of Brecht cannot overlook the fact that he did not – for objective reasons beyond the power of his own creations – fulfil the norm he set himself as if it were a means to salvation. *Saint Joan* was the central work of his dialectical theatre. (*The Good Woman of Szechuan* is a variation of it in reverse: where Joan assists evil by the immediacy of her goodness, Shen Te, who wills the good, must become evil). The play is set in a Chicago half-way between the Wild West fables of *Mahagonny* and economic facts. But the more preoccupied Brecht becomes with information, and the less he looks for images, the more he misses the essence of capitalism which the parable is supposed to present. Mere episodes in the sphere of circulation, in which competitors maul each other, are recounted instead of the appropriation of surplus-value in the sphere of production, compared with which the brawls of cattle dealers over their shares of the booty are epiphenomena incapable of provoking any great crisis. Moreover, the economic transactions presented as the machinations of rapacious traders are not merely puerile, which is how Brecht seems to have meant them; they are also unintelligible by the criteria of even the most primitive economic logic. The obverse of the latter is a political naiveté which could only make Brecht's opponents grin at the thought of such an ingenuous enemy. They could be as comfortable with Brecht as they are with the dying Joan in the impressive final scene of the play. Even with the broadest-minded allowance for poetic licence, the idea that a strike leadership backed by the Party could entrust a crucial task to a non-member is as inconceivable as the subsequent idea that the failure of that individual could ruin the whole strike.

Brecht's comedy of the resistible rise of the great dictator *Arturo Ui* exposes the subjective nullity and pretence of a fascist leader in a harsh and accurate light. However, the deconstruction of leaders, as with all individuals in Brecht, is extended into a reconstruction of the social and economic nexus in which the dictator acts. Instead of a conspiracy of the wealthy and powerful, we are given a trivial gangster organization, the cabbage trust. The true horror of fascism is conjured away; it is no longer a slow end-product of the concentration of social power, but mere hazard, like an accident or a crime. This conclusion is dictated by the exigencies of agitation: adversaries must be diminished. The consequence is bad politics, in literature as in practice before 1933. Against every dialectic, the ridicule to which Ui is consigned renders innocuous the fascism that was accurately predicted by Jack London decades before. The anti-ideological artist thus prepared the degradation of his own ideas into ideology. Tacit acceptance of the claim that one half of the world no longer contains antagonisms is supplemented by jests at everything that belies the official theodicy of the other half. It is not that respect for historical scale forbids laughter at housepainters, although the use of that term against Hitler was itself a painful exploitation of bourgeois class-consciousness. The group which engineered the seizure of power in Germany was also certainly a gang. But the problem is that such elective affinities are not extra-territorial: they are rooted within society itself. That is why the buffoonery of fascism, evoked by Chaplin as well, was at the same time also its ultimate horror. If this is suppressed, and a few sorry exploiters of greengrocers are mocked, where key positions of economic power are actually at issue, the attack misfires. *The Great Dictator* loses all satirical force and becomes obscene when a Jewish girl can hit a line of storm-troopers on the head with a pan without being torn to pieces. For the sake of political commitment, political reality is trivialized: which then reduces the political effect.

Sartre's frank doubt whether *Guernica* 'won a single supporter for the Spanish cause' certainly also applies to Brecht's didactic drama. Scarcely anyone needs to be taught the *fabula docet* to be extracted from it – that there is injustice in the world; while the moral itself shows few traces of the dialectical theory to which Brecht gave cursory allegiance. The trappings of epic drama recall the American phrase 'preaching to the converted'. The primacy of lesson over pure form, which Brecht intended to achieve, became a formal device itself. The suspension of form turns back against its own character as appearance. Its self-criticism in drama was related to the doctrine of objectivity [*Sachlichkeit*] in the applied visual arts. The correction of form by external conditions, with the elimination of ornament in the service of function, only increases its autonomy. The substance of Brecht's artistic work was the didactic play as an artistic principle. His method, to make immediately apparent events into phenomena alien to the spectator, was also a medium of formal construction rather than a contribution to practical efficacy. It is true that Brecht never spoke as sceptically as Sartre about the social effects of art. But, as an astute and experienced man of the world, he can scarcely have been wholly convinced of them. He once calmly wrote that, to be honest, the theatre was more important to him than any changes in the world it might promote. Yet the artistic principle of simplification not only purged politics of the illusory distinctions projected by subjective reflection into social objectivity, as Brecht intended, but it also falsified the very objectivity which didactic drama laboured to distil. If we take Brecht at his word and make politics the criterion by which to judge his committed theatre, then politics proves his theatre untrue. Hegel's *Logic* taught that essence must appear. If this is so, a representation of essence which ignores its relation to appearance must be as intrinsically false as the substitution of a lumpen-proletariat for the men behind fascism. The only ground on which Brecht's technique of reduction would be legitimate is that of 'art for art's sake', which his kind of commitment condemns as it does Lucullus.[5]

Contemporary literary Germany is anxious to distinguish Brecht the artist from Brecht the politician. The major writer must be saved for the West, if possible placed on a pedestal as an All-German poet, and so neutralized *au-dessus de la mêlée*. There is truth in this to the extent that

[5] Reference to Brecht's last play on the Roman general Lucullus.

both Brecht's artistic force, and his devious and uncontrollable intelligence, went well beyond the official credos and prescribed aesthetics of the People's Democracies. All the same, Brecht must be defended against this defence of him. His work, with its often patent weaknesses, would not have had such power, if it were not saturated with politics. Even its most questionable creations, such as *The Measures Taken*, generate an immediate awareness that issues of the utmost seriousness are at stake. To this extent Brecht's claim that he used his theatre to make men think was justified. It is futile to try to separate the beauties, real or imaginary, of his works from their political intentions. The task of immanent criticism, which alone is dialectical, is rather to synthesize assessment of the validity of his forms with that of his politics. Sartre's chapter 'Why write?' contains the undeniable statement that: 'Nobody can suppose for a moment that it is possible to write a good novel in praise of anti-semitism'.[6] Nor could one be written in praise of the Moscow Trials, even if such praise were bestowed before Stalin actually had Zinoviev and Bukharin murdered.[7] The political falsehood stains the aesthetic form. Where Brecht distorts the real social problems discussed in his epic drama in order to prove a thesis, the whole structure and foundation of the play itself crumbles. *Mother Courage* is an illustrated primer intended to reduce to absurdity Montecuccoli's dictum that war feeds on war. The camp follower who uses the Thirty Years' War to make a life for her children thereby becomes responsible for their ruin. But in the play this responsibility follows rigorously neither from the fact of the war itself nor from the individual behaviour of the petty profiteer; if Mother Courage had not been absent at the critical moment, the disaster would not have happened, and the fact that she has to be absent to earn some money, remains completely generic in relation to the action. The picture-book technique which Brecht needs to spell out his thesis prevents him from proving it. A socio-political analysis, of the sort Marx and Engels sketched in their criticism of Lassalle's play *Franz von Sickingen*, would show that Brecht's simplistic equation of the Thirty Years' War with a modern war excludes precisely what is crucial for the behaviour and fate of Mother Courage in Grimmelshausen's novel. Because the society of the Thirty Years' War was not the functional capitalist society of modern times, we cannot even poetically stipulate a

---

[6] *What is Literature?*, p. 46.

[7] Reference to *The Measures Taken*, written in 1930, which contained an implicit justification in advance of the Moscow Trials. Zinoviev and Bukharin were condemned in 1938.

closed functional system in which the lives and deaths of private individuals directly reveal economic laws. But Brecht needed the old lawless
days as an image of his own, precisely because he saw clearly that the
society of his own age could no longer be directly comprehended in
terms of people and things. His attempt to reconstruct the reality of
society thus led first to a false social model and then to dramatic im-
plausibility. Bad politics becomes bad art, and vice-versa. But the less
works have to proclaim what they cannot completely believe themselves,
the more telling they become in their own right; and the less they need
a surplus of meaning beyond what they are. For the rest, the interested
parties in every camp would probably be as successful in surviving wars
today as they have always been.

Aporia of this sort multiply until they affect the Brechtian tone itself,
the very fibre of his poetic art. Inimitable though its qualities may be –
qualities which the mature Brecht may have thought unimportant – they
were poisoned by the untruth of his politics. For what he justified was
not simply, as he long sincerely believed, an incomplete socialism, but a
coercive domination in which blindly irrational social forces returned
to work once again. When Brecht became a panegyrist of its harmony,
his lyric voice had to swallow chalk, and it started to grate. Already the
exaggerated adolescent virility of the young Brecht betrayed the borrowed courage of the intellectual who, in despair at violence, suddenly
adopts a violent practice which he has every reason to fear. The wild roar
of *The Measures Taken* drowns out the noise of the disaster that has
overtaken the cause, which Brecht convulsively tries to proclaim as
salvation. Even Brecht's best work was infected by the deceptions of his
commitment. Its language shows how far the underlying poetic subject
and its message have moved apart. In an attempt to bridge the gap,
Brecht affected the diction of the oppressed. But the doctrine he advocated needs the language of the intellectual. The homeliness and simplicity of his tone is thus a fiction. It betrays itself both by signs of
exaggeration and by stylized regression to archaic or provincial forms of
expression. It can often be importunate, and ears which have not let
themselves be deprived of their native sensitivity cannot help hearing
that they are being talked into something. It is a usurpation and almost
a contempt for victims to speak like this, as if the author were one of
them. All roles may be played, except that of the worker. The gravest
charge against commitment is that even right intentions go wrong when
they are noticed, and still more so, when they then try to conceal themselves. Something of this remains in Brecht's later plays in the linguistic

gestus of wisdom, the fiction of the old peasant sated with epic experience as the poetic subject. No one in any country of the world is any longer capable of the earthy experience of South German muzhiks: the ponderous delivery has become a propaganda device to make us believe that the good life is where the Red Army is in control. Since there is nothing to give substance to this humanity as presented, which we have to take on trust, Brecht's tone degenerates into an echo of archaic social relations, lost beyond recall.

The late Brecht was not so distant from official humanism. A journalistically minded Westerner could well praise *The Caucasian Chalk Circle* as a hymn to motherhood, and who is not touched when the splendid girl is finally held up as an example to the querulous lady beset with migraine? Baudelaire, who dedicated his work to the coiner of the motto *l'art pour l'art*, would have been less suited to such a catharsis. Even the grandeur and virtuosity of such poems as *The Legend of the Origin of the Book of Tao Te Ch'ing on Lao-Tzu's Journey into Exile* are marred by the theatricality of total plain-spokenness. What his classical predecessors once denounced as the idiocy of rural life, Brecht, like some existential ontologist, treats as ancient truth. His whole oeuvre is a Sisyphean labour to reconcile his highly cultivated and subtle taste with the crudely heteronomous demands which he desperately imposed on himself.

I have no wish to soften the saying that to write lyric poetry after Auschwitz is barbaric; it expresses in negative form the impulse which inspires committed literature. The question asked by a character in Sartre's play *Morts Sans Sépulture*, 'Is there any meaning in life when men exist who beat people until the bones break in their bodies?', is also the question whether any art now has a right to exist; whether intellectual regression is not inherent in the concept of committed literature because of the regression of society. But Enzensberger's retort also remains true, that literature must resist this verdict, in other words, be such that its mere existence after Auschwitz is not a surrender to cynicism. Its own situation is one of paradox, not merely the problem of how to react to it. The abundance of real suffering tolerates no forgetting; Pascal's theological saying, *On ne doit plus dormir*, must be secularized. Yet this suffering, what Hegel called consciousness of adversity, also demands the continued existence of art while it prohibits it; it is now virtually in art alone that suffering can still find its own voice, consolation, without immediately being betrayed by it. The most important artists of the age have realized this. The uncompromising radicalism of their works, the very features defamed as formalism, give them a terrifying power, absent from helpless poems to the victims of our time. But even Schoenberg's *Survivor of Warsaw* remains trapped in the aporia to which, autonomous figuration of heteronomy raised to the intensity of hell, it totally surrenders. There is something embarrassing in Schoenberg's composition – not what arouses anger in Germany, the fact that it prevents people from repressing from memory what they at all costs want to repress – but the way in which, by turning suffering into images, harsh and uncompromising though they are, it wounds the shame we feel in the presence of the victims. For these victims are used to create something, works of art, that are thrown to the consumption of a world which destroyed them. The so-called artistic representation of the sheer physical pain of people beaten to the ground by rifle-butts contains, however remotely, the power to elicit enjoyment out of it. The moral of this art, not to forget for a single instant, slithers into the abyss of its opposite. The aesthetic principle of stylization, and even the solemn prayer of the chorus, make an unthinkable fate appear to have had some meaning; it is transfigured, something of its horror is removed. This alone does an injustice to the victims; yet no art which tried to evade them could confront the claims of justice. Even the sound of despair pays its tribute to a hideous affirmation. Works of less than the highest rank are also willingly absorbed as contributions to clearing up the past. When genocide becomes part of the cultural heritage in the themes of committed literature, it becomes easier to continue to play along with the culture which gave birth to murder.

There is one nearly invariable characteristic of such literature. It is that it implies, purposely or not, that even in so-called extreme situations, indeed in them most of all, humanity flourishes. Sometimes this develops into a dismal metaphysic which does its best to work up atrocities into 'limiting situations' which it then accepts to the extent that they reveal authenticity in men. In such a homely existential atmosphere the distinction between executioners and victims becomes blurred; both, after all, are equally suspended above the possibility of nothingness, which of course is generally not quite so uncomfortable for the executioners.

Today, the adherents of a philosophy which has since degenerated into a mere ideological sport, fulminate in pre-1933 fashion against artistic distortion, deformation and perversion of life, as though authors, by faithfully reflecting atrocities, were responsible for what they revolt against. The best example of this attitude, still prevalent among the silent majority in Germany, is the following story about Picasso. An officer of the Nazi occupation forces visited the painter in his studio and, pointing to *Guernica*, asked: 'Did you do that?'. Picasso is said to have answered, 'No, you did'. Autonomous works of art too, like this painting, firmly negate empirical reality, destroy the destroyer, that which merely exists and, by merely existing, endlessly reiterates guilt. It is none other than Sartre who has seen the connection between the autonomy of a work and an intention which is not conferred upon it but is its own gesture towards reality. 'The work of art', he has written, '*does not have* an end; there we agree with Kant. But the reason is that it *is* an end. The Kantian formula does not account for the appeal which issues from every painting, every statue, every book.'[8] It only remains to add there is no straightforward relationship between this appeal and the thematic commitment of a work. The uncalculating autonomy of works which avoid popularization and adaptation to the market, involuntarily becomes an attack on them. The attack is not abstract, not a fixed attitude of all works of art to the world which will not forgive them for not bending totally to it. The distance these works maintain from empirical reality is in itself partly mediated by that reality. The imagination of the artist is not a creation *ex nihilo*; only dilettanti and aesthetes believe it to be so. Works of art that react against empirical reality obey the forces of that reality, which reject intellectual creations and throw them back on themselves. There is no material content, no formal category of artistic creation, however mysteriously transmitted and itself unaware of the process, which did not originate in the empirical reality from which it breaks free.

It is this which constitutes the true relation of art to reality, whose elements are regrouped by its formal laws. Even the *avant-garde* abstraction which provokes the indignation of philistines, and which has nothing in common with conceptual or logical abstraction, is a reflex response to the abstraction of the law which objectively dominates society. This could be shown in Beckett's works. These enjoy what is today the only form of respectable fame: everyone shudders at them, and yet no-one can persuade himself that these eccentric plays and novels are not about what everyone knows but no one will admit. Philosophical apologists may laud his works as sketches from an anthropology. But they deal with a highly concrete historical reality: the abdication of the subject. Beckett's *Ecce Homo* is what human beings have become. As though with eyes drained of tears, they stare silently out of his sentences. The spell they cast, which also binds them, is lifted by being reflected in them. However,

[8] *What is Literature?*, p. 34.

the minimal promise of happiness they contain, which refuses to be traded for comfort, cannot be had for a price less than total dislocation, to the point of worldlessness. Here every commitment to the world must be abandoned to satisfy the ideal of the committed work of art – that polemical alienation which Brecht as a theorist invented, and as an artist practised less and less as he committed himself more firmly to the role of a friend of mankind. This paradox, which might be charged with sophistry, can be supported without much philosophy by the simplest experience: Kafka's prose and Beckett's plays, or the truly monstrous novel *The Unnameable*, have an effect by comparison with which officially committed works look like pantomines. Kafka and Beckett arouse the fear which existentialism merely talks about. By dismantling appearance, they explode from within the art which committed proclamation sub-jugates from without, and hence only in appearance. The inescapability of their work compels the change of attitude which committed works merely demand. He over whom Kafka's wheels have passed, has lost for ever both any peace with the world and any chance of consoling him-self with the judgment that the way of the world is bad; the element of ratification which lurks in resigned admission of the dominance of evil is burnt away.

Yet the greater the aspiration, the greater is the possibility of founder-ing and failure. The loss of tension evident in works of painting and music which have moved away from objective representation and intelligible or coherent meaning, has in many ways spread to the literature known in a repellent jargon as 'texts'. Such works drift to the brink of indifference, degenerate insensibly into mere hobbies, into idle repetition of formulas now abandoned in other art-forms, into trivial patterns. It is this development which often gives substance to crude calls for com-mitment. Formal structures which challenge the lying positivism of meaning can easily slide into a different sort of vacuity, positivistic arrangements, empty juggling with elements. They fall within the very sphere from which they seek to escape. The extreme case is literature which undialectically confuses itself with science and vainly tries to fuse with cybernetics. Extremes meet: what cuts the last thread of communi-cation becomes the prey of communication theory. No firm criterion can draw the line between a determinate negation of meaning and a bad positivism of meaninglessness, as an assiduous soldiering on just for the sake of it. Least of all can such a line be based on an appeal to human values, and a curse of mechanization. Works of art which by their existence take the side of the victims of a rationality that subjugates nature, are even in their protest constitutively implicated in the process of rationalization itself. Were they to try to disown it, they would become both aesthetically and socially powerless: mere clay. The organizing, unifying principle of each and every work of art is borrowed from that very rationality whose claim to totality it seeks to defy.

In the history of French and German consciousness, the problem of commitment has been posed in opposite ways. In France aesthetics have been dominated, openly or covertly, by the principle of *l'art pour l'art*, allied to academic and reactionary tendencies.[9] This explains the revolt against it. Even extreme *avant-garde* works have a touch of decorative allure in France. It is for this reason that the call to existence and commitment sounded revolutionary there. In Germany the situation is the other way round. The liberation of art from any external end, although it was a German who first raised it purely and incorruptibly into a criterion of taste, has always been suspect to a tradition which has deep roots in German idealism. The first famous document of this tradition is that senior masters' bible of intellectual history, Schiller's *Treatise on the Theatre as a Moral Institution*. Such suspicion is not so much due to the elevation of mind to an Absolute that is coupled with it – an attitude that swaggered its way to hubris in German philosophy. It is rather provoked by the aspect that any work of art free of an ulterior goal shows to society. For this art is a reminder of that sensuous pleasure of which even – indeed especially – the most extreme dissonance, by sublimation and negation, partakes. German speculative philosophy granted that a work of art contains within itself the sources of its transcendence, and that its inner meaning is always more than the work itself – but only therefore to demand a certificate of good behaviour from it. According to this latent tradition, a work of art should have no being for itself, since otherwise it would – as Plato's embryonic state socialism classically stigmatized it – be a source of effeminacy and an obstacle to action for its own sake, the German original sin. Killjoys, ascetics, moralists of the sort who are always invoking names like Luther and Bismarck, have no time for aesthetic autonomy; and there is also an undercurrent of servile heteronomy in the pathos of the categorical imperative, which is indeed on the one hand reason itself, but on the other an absolute datum to be blindly obeyed. Fifty years ago Stefan George and his school were still being attacked as Frenchifying aesthetes.

[9] 'We know very well that pure art and empty art are the same thing and that aesthetic purism was a brilliant manoeuvre of the bourgeois of the last century who preferred to see themselves denounced as philistines rather than as exploiters.' *What is Literature?*, p. 17.

Today the curmudgeons whom no bombs could shake out of their complacency have allied themselves with the philistines who rage against the alleged incomprehensibility of the new art. The underlying impulse of these attacks is petty-bourgeois hatred of sex, the common ground of Western moralists and ideologists of Socialist Realism. No moral terror can prevent the side the work of art shows its beholder from giving him pleasure, even if only in the formal fact of temporary freedom from the compulsion of practical goals. Thomas Mann called this quality of art 'high spirits', a notion intolerable to people with morals. Brecht himself, who was not without ascetic traits – which reappear transmuted in the resistance of any great autonomous art to consumption – rightly ridiculed culinary art; but he was much too intelligent not to know that pleasure can never be completely ignored in the total aesthetic effect, no matter how relentless the work. The primacy of the aesthetic object as pure refiguration does not smuggle consumption, and thus false harmony, in again through the back door. Although the moment of pleasure, even when it is extirpated from the effect of a work, constantly returns to it, the principle that governs autonomous works of art is not the totality of their effects but their own inherent structure. They are knowledge as non-conceptual objects. This is the source of their nobility. It is not something of which they have to persuade men, because it has been given into their hands. This is why today autonomous rather than committed art should be encouraged in Germany. Committed works all too readily credit themselves with every noble value, and then manipulate them at their ease. Under fascism too, no atrocity was perpetrated without a moral veneer. Those who trumpet their ethics and humanity in Germany today are merely waiting for a chance to persecute those whom their rules condemn, and to exercise the same inhumanity in practice of which they accuse modern art in theory. In Germany, commitment often means bleating what everyone is already saying or at least secretly wants to hear. The notion of a 'message' in art, even when politically radical, already contains an accommodation to the world: the stance of the lecturer conceals a clandestine entente with the listeners, who could only be rescued from deception by refusing it.

The type of literature that, in accordance with the tenets of commitment but also with the demands of philistine moralism, exists for man, betrays him by traducing that which could help him, if only it did not strike a pose of helping him. But any literature which therefore concludes that it can be a law unto itself, and exist only for itself, degenerates into ideology no less. Art, which even in its opposition to society remains

194

a part of it, must close its eyes and ears against it: it cannot escape the shadow of irrationality. But when it appeals to this unreason, making it a *raison d'être*, it converts its own malediction into a theodicy. Even in the most sublimated work of art there is a hidden 'it should be otherwise'. When a work is merely itself and no other thing, as in a pure pseudo-scientific construction, it becomes bad art – literally pre-artistic. The moment of true volition, however, is mediated through nothing other than the form of the work itself, whose crystallization becomes an analogy of that other condition which should be. As eminently constructed and produced objects, works of art, including literary ones, point to a practice from which they abstain: the creation of a just life. This mediation is not a compromise between commitment and autonomy, nor a sort of mixture of advanced formal elements with an intellectual content inspired by genuinely or supposedly progressive politics. The content of works of art is never the amount of intellect pumped into them: if anything, it is the opposite.

Nevertheless, an emphasis on autonomous works is itself sociopolitical in nature. The feigning of a true politics here and now, the freezing of historical relations which nowhere seem ready to melt, oblige the mind to go where it need not degrade itself. Today every phenomenon of culture, even if a model of integrity, is liable to be suffocated in the cultivation of kitsch. Yet paradoxically in the same epoch it is to works of art that has fallen the burden of wordlessly asserting what is barred to politics. Sartre himself has expressed this truth in a passage which does credit to his honesty.[10] This is not a time for political art, but politics has migrated into autonomous art, and nowhere more so than where it seems to be politically dead. An example is Kafka's allegory of toy guns, in which an idea of non-violence is fused with a dawning awareness of the approaching paralysis of politics. Paul Klee too has a place in any debate about committed and autonomous art; for his work, *écriture par excellence*, had its roots in literature and would not have been what it was without them – or if it had not consumed them. During the First World War or shortly after, Klee drew cartoons of Kaiser Wilhelm as an inhuman iron-eater. Later, in 1920, these became – the development can be shown quite clearly – the *Angelus Novus*, the angel of the machine, who, though he no longer bears any emblem of caricature or commitment, flies far beyond both. The machine angel's enigmatic eyes force the onlooker to try to decide

[10] See Jean-Paul Sartre, *L'Existentialisme est un Humanisme*, Paris 1946, p. 105.

whether he is announcing the culmination of disaster or salvation hidden within it. But, as Walter Benjamin, who owned the drawing, said, he is the angel who does not give, but takes.

Translated by Francis McDonagh.

Fredric Jameson

Reflections in Conclusion

It is not only political history which those who ignore are condemned to repeat. A host of recent 'post-Marxisms' document the truth of the assertion that attempts to 'go beyond' Marxism typically end by reinventing older pre-Marxist positions (from the recurrent neo-Kantian revivals, to the most recent 'Nietzschean' returns through Hume and Hobbes all the way back to the Pre-Socratics). Even within Marxism itself, the terms of the problems, if not their solutions, are numbered in advance, and the older controversies – Marx versus Bakunin, Lenin versus Luxemburg, the national question, the agrarian question, the dictatorship of the proletariat – rise up to haunt those who thought we could now go on to something else and leave the past behind us.

Nowhere has this 'return of the repressed' been more dramatic than in the aesthetic conflict between 'Realism' and 'Modernism', whose navigation and renegotiation is still unavoidable for us today, even though we may feel that each position is in some sense right and yet that neither is any longer wholly acceptable. The dispute is itself older than Marxism, and in a longer perspective may be said to be a contemporary political replay of the 17th century *Querelle des anciens et des modernes*, in which, for the first time, aesthetics came face to face with the dilemmas of historicity.

Within the Marxism of this century, the precipitant of the controversy over Realism and Modernism was the living fact and persisting influence of Expressionism among the writers of the German Left in the 1920s and 30s. An implacable ideological denunciation by Lukács in 1934 set the stage for the series of interconnected debates and exchanges between Bloch, Lukács, Brecht, Benjamin and Adorno published in this volume. Much of the fascination of these jousts, indeed, comes from the internal dynamism by which all the logical possibilities are rapidly generated in turn, so that it quickly extends beyond the local phenomenon of Expressionism, and even beyond the ideal type of realism itself, to draw within its scope the problems of popular art, naturalism, socialist realism, avant-gardism, media, and finally modernism – political and non-political – in general. Today, many of its fundamental themes and concerns have been transmitted by the Frankfurt School, and in particular by Marcuse, to the student and anti-war movements of the 1960s, while the revival of Brecht has ensured their propagation among political modernisms of the kind exemplified by the Tel Quel group.

The legacy of German Expressionism provided a more propitious framework for the development of a major debate within Marxism than its contemporary French counterpart, surrealism, was to do. For in the writings of the surrealists, and in particular of Breton, the problem of realism largely fails to arise – in the first instance owing to their initial repudiation of the novel as a form. While for their principal adversary, Jean-Paul Sartre – the only important writer of his generation not to have passed through surrealism's tutelage, and whose notion of 'commitment' (*engagement*) Adorno was later to take as the very prototype of a political aesthetic, the realism/modernism dilemma did not arise either, but for the opposite reason: because of Sartre's preliminary exclusion of poetry and the lyric from his account of the nature and function of literature in general (in *What is Literature?*). Thus in France, until that second wave of modernism (or post-modernism) represented by the *nouveau roman* and the *nouvelle vague*, Tel Quel and 'structuralism', the terrain for which realism and modernism were elsewhere so bitterly to contend – that of *narrative* – was effectively divided up between them in advance, as though in amicable separation. If the problem of narrative does not loom large in the texts collected here, that is in part because Lukács's principal exhibits were novels, while Brecht's main field of activity was the theatre. The increasing importance, in turn, of film in artistic production since the time of·these debates (witness the frequent juxtapositions of Brecht and Godard) likewise suggests that structural differences in medium and in genre may play a larger part in compounding the dilemmas of the Realism/Modernism controversy than its earliest participants were willing to admit.

More than this, the history of aesthetics itself suggests that some of the more paradoxical turns in the Marxist debate within German culture spring from contradictions within the very concept of realism, an uneasily different quantity from such traditional aesthetic categories as comedy and tragedy, or lyric, epic and dramatic. The latter – whatever social functionality may be invoked for them in this or that philosophical system – are purely aesthetic concepts, which may be analysed and evaluated without any reference outside the phenomenon of beauty or the activity of artistic play (traditionally the terms in which the 'aesthetic' has been isolated and constituted as a separate realm or function in its own right). The originality of the concept of realism, however, lies in its claim to cognitive as well as aesthetic status. A new value, contemporaneous with the secularization of the world under capitalism, the ideal of realism presupposes a form of aesthetic experience which yet lays claim to a binding relationship to the real itself, that is to say, to those realms of knowledge and praxis which had traditionally been differentiated from the realm of the aesthetic, with its disinterested judgements and its constitution as sheer appearance. But it is extremely difficult to do justice to both of these properties of realism simultaneously. In practice, an over-emphasis on its cognitive function often leads to a naïve denial of the necessarily fictive character of artistic discourse, or even to iconoclastic calls for the 'end of art' in the name of political militancy. At the other pole of this conceptual tension, the emphasis of theorists like Gombrich or Barthes on the 'techniques' whereby an 'illusion' of reality or *'effet de réel'* is achieved, tends surreptitiously to transform the 'reality' of realism into appearance, and to undermine that affirmation of its own truth – or referential – value, by which it differentiates itself from other types of literature. (Among the many secret dramas of Lukács's later work is surely to be counted the adeptness with which he walks this particular tightrope, from which, even at his most ideological or 'formalistic', he never quite falls).

This is not to say that the concept of modernism, realism's historical counterpart and its dialectical mirror-image, is not equally contradictory,[1] and in ways which it will be instructive to juxtapose to the contradictions of realism itself. For the moment, suffice it to observe that neither of these sets of contradictions can be fully understood, unless they are replaced within the broader context of the crisis of historicity itself, and numbered among the dilemmas a dialectical criticism faces when it tries to make ordinary language function simultaneously on two mutually exclusive registers: the absolute (in which case realism and modernism veer towards timeless abstractions like the lyric or the comic), and the relative (in which case they inexorably revert to the narrow confines of an antiquarian nomenclature, restricted to use for specific

[1] For a complementary analysis of the internal contradictions of the idea of modernism, see Paul de Man, 'Literary History and Literary Modernity', in *Blindness and Insight*, New York, 1971.

literary movements in the past). Language, however, does not submit peacefully to the attempt to use its terms dialectically – that is, as relative and sometimes even extinct concepts from an archaeological past, that nonetheless continue to transmit faint but absolute claims upon us.

Meanwhile, post-structuralism has added yet a different kind of parameter to the Realism/Modernism controversy, one which – like the question of narrative or the problems of historicity – was implicit in the original exchange but scarcely articulated or thematized as such. The assimilation of realism as a value to the old philosophical concept of mimesis by such writers as Foucault, Derrida, Lyotard or Deleuze, has reformulated the Realism/Modernism debate in terms of a Platonic attack on the ideological effects of representation. In this new (and old) philosophical polemic, the stakes of the original discussion find themselves unexpectedly elevated, and their issues – once largely political in focus – lent metaphysical (or anti-metaphysical) implications. Such philosophical artillery is, of course, intended to increase the defensiveness of the defenders of realism; yet my own feeling is that we will not fully be able to assess the consequences of the attack on representation, and of post-structuralism generally, until we are able to situate its own work within the field of the theory of ideology itself.

It is at any rate clear that the Realism/Modernism controversy loses its interest if one side is programmed to win in advance. The Brecht–Lukács debate alone is one of those rare confrontations in which both adversaries are of equal stature, both of incomparable significance for the development of contemporary Marxism, the one a major artist and probably the greatest literary figure to have been produced by the Communist movement, the other a central philosopher of the age and heir to the whole German philosophical tradition, with its unique emphasis on aesthetics as a discipline. It is true that in recent accounts of their opposition,[2] Brecht has tended to get the better of Lukács, the former's 'plebeian' style and Schweikian identifications proving currently more attractive than the 'mandarin' culture to which the latter appealed.[3] In these versions, Lukács is typically treated as a professor, a revisionist,

---

[2] See Werner Mittenzwei, 'Die Brecht-Lukács Debatte' *Das Argument* 46, (March 1968), Eugene Lunn, 'Marxism and Art in the Era of Stalin and Hitler: A Comparison of Brecht and Lukács', *New German Critique*, 3 (Fall, 1974), 12–44; and, for the somewhat earlier period of the review *Die Linskskurve* (1928–1932), Helga Gallas, *Marxistische Literaturtheorie-Kontroversen im Bund proletarisch-revolutionärer Schriftsteller*, Neuwied, 1971.

[3] See Lunn, op. cit., pp. 16–18.

200

a Stalinist – or in general 'in the same way as the brave Moses Mendelssohn in Lessing's time treated Spinoza as a "dead dog",' as Marx described the standard view of Hegel current among his radical contemporaries.

To the degree to which Lukács single-handedly turned the Expressionism debate around into a discussion of Realism, and forced the defenders of the former to fight on his own ground and in his own terms, their annoyance with him was understandable (Brecht's own animosity towards him comes through particularly vividly in these pages). On the other hand, such meddling interference was at one with everything that made Lukács a major figure in 20th century Marxism – in particular his lifelong insistence on the crucial significance of literature and culture in any revolutionary politics. His fundamental contribution here was the development of a theory of mediations that could reveal the political and ideological content of what had hitherto seemed purely formal aesthetic phenomena. One of the most famous instances was his 'decoding' of the static descriptions of naturalism in terms of reification.[4] Yet at the same time, it was precisely this line of research – itself an implicit critique and repudiation of traditional content analysis – which was responsible for Brecht's characterization of Lukács's method as *formalistic*: by which he meant the latter's unwarranted confidence in the possibility of deducing political and ideological positions from a protocol of purely formal properties of a work of art. The reproach sprang from Brecht's experience as a man of the theatre, in which he constructed an aesthetic of performance and a view of the work of art in situation that was in diametric contrast to the solitary reading and individualized bourgeois public of Lukács's privileged object of study, the novel. Can Brecht then be enlisted in current campaigns against the very notion of mediation? It is probably best to take Brecht's attack on Lukács's formalism (along with the Brechtian watchword of *plumpes Denken*) at a somewhat less philosophical and more practical level, as a therapeutic warning against the permanent temptation of idealism present in any ideological analysis as such, the professional proclivity of intellectuals for methods that need no external verification. There would then be *two* idealisms: one the common-or-garden variety to be found in religion, metaphysics or literalism, the other a repressed and unconscious danger of idealism within Marxism itself, inherent in the very ideal of science itself in a world so deeply marked by the division of mental and manual

[4] See in particular 'Narrate or Describe?' in Georg Lukács, *Writer and Critic*, London 1970.

labour. To that danger the intellectual and the scientist can never sufficiently be alerted. At the same time, Lukács's work on mediation, rudimentary as at times it may have been, can on another reading be enlisted as a precursor of the most interesting work in the field of ideological analysis today – that which, assimilating the findings of psychoanalysis and of semiotics, seeks to construct a model of the text as a complex and symbolic ideological act. The reproach of 'formalism', whose relevance to Lukács's own practice is only too evident, may consequently have a wider extension to present-day research and speculation.

The charge of 'formalism' was only one item of Brecht's attack on Lukács's position; its corollary and obverse was indignation at the ideological judgements the latter used his method to substantiate. The primary exhibit at the time was Lukács's denunciation of alleged links between Expressionism and trends within Social-Democracy (in particular the USPD), not to speak of fascism, which launched the Realism debate in the German emigration and which Ernst Bloch's essay was designed to refute in some detail. Nothing has, of course, more effectively discredited Marxism than the practice of affixing instant class labels (generally 'petty bourgeois') to textual or intellectual objects; nor will the most hardened apologist for Lukács want to deny that of the many Lukács's conceivable, this particular one – epitomized in the shrill and outrageous postcript to *Die Zerstörung der Vernunft* – is the least worthy of rehabilitation. But abuse of class ascription should not lead to over-reaction and mere abandonment of it. In fact, ideological analysis is inconceivable without a conception of the 'ultimately determining instance' of social class. What is really wrong with Lukács's analyses is not too frequent and facile a reference to social class, but rather too incomplete and intermittent a sense of the relationship of class to ideology. A case in point is one of the more notorious of Lukács's basic concepts, that of 'decadence' – which he often associates with fascism, but even more persistently with modern art and literature in general. The concept of decadence is the equivalent in the aesthetic realm of that of 'false consciousness' in the domain of traditional ideological analysis. Both suffer from the same defect – the common presupposition that in the world of culture and society such a thing as pure error is possible. They imply, in other words, that works of art or systems of philosophy are conceivable which have no content, and are therefore to be denounced for failing to grapple with the 'serious' issues of the day, indeed distracting from them. In the iconography of the political art of the 1920s and 30s, the 'index' of such culpable and vacuous decadence was the champagne glass and top hat of the idle rich, making the rounds of an eternal night-club circuit. Yet even Scott Fitzgerald and Drieu la Rochelle are more complicated than that, and from our present-day vantage point, disposing of the more complex instruments of psychoanalysis (in particular the concepts of repression and denial or *Verneinung*), even those who might wish to sustain Lukács's hostile verdict on modernism would necessarily insist on the existence of a repressed social content even in those modern works that seem most innocent of it. Modernism would then not so much be a way of avoiding social content – in any case an impossibility for beings like ourselves who are 'condemned' to history and to the implacable sociability of even the most apparently private of our experiences – as rather of managing and containing it, secluding it out of sight in the very form itself, by means of specific techniques of framing and displacement which can be identified with some precision. If so, Lukács's summary dismissal of 'decadent' works of art should yield to an interrogation of their buried social and political content.

The fundamental weakness in Lukács's view of the relationship of art and ideology surely finds its ultimate explanation in his politics. What is usually called his 'Stalinism', can on closer examination, be separated into two quite distinct problems. The charge that he was complicit with a bureaucratic apparatus and exercised a kind of literary terrorism (particularly against political modernists, for example, of the Proletkult variety), is belied by his resistance in the Moscow of the 30s and 40s to what was later to be known as Zhdanovism – that form of socialist realism which he disliked as much as Western modernism, but was obviously less free to attack openly. 'Naturalism' was his pejorative code-word for it at the time. Indeed, the structural and historical identification for which he argued between the symbolic techniques of modernism and the 'bad immediacy' of a photographic naturalism was one of his most profound dialectical insights. As for his continuing party membership, what he called his 'entry ticket to history', the tragic fate and wasted talents of so many oppositional Marxists of his generation, like Korsch or Reich, are powerful arguments for the relative rationality of Lukács's choice – one, of course, that he shared with Brecht. A more serious problem is posed by the 'popular frontism' of his aesthetic theory. That betokened a formal mean between a modernistic subjectivism and an overly objectivistic naturalism which, like most Aristotelian strategies of moderation, has never aroused much intellectual excitement. Even Lukács's most devoted supporters failed to evince much enthusiasm for it. So far as the political alliance between revolutionary forces and the progressive sections of the bourgeoisie went, it was rather Stalin who belatedly authorized a version of the policy that Lukács had advocated in the 'Blum Theses' of 1928–29, which foresaw a first-stage, democratic revolution against the fascist dictatorship in Hungary, prior to any socialist revolution. Yet it is precisely that distinction, between an anti-fascist and an anti-capitalist strategy, that seems less easy to maintain today and less immediately attractive a political pro-gramme, over wide areas of a 'free world' in which military dictatorships and 'emergency regimes' are the order of the day – indeed multiplying precisely to the degree that genuine social revolution becomes a real possibility. From our present perspective, Nazism itself, with its charismatic leader and unique exploitation of a nascent communications technology in the widest sense of the term (including transportation and autobahns as well as radio and television), now seems to represent a transitional and special combination of historical circumstances not likely to recur as such; while routine torture and the institutionalization of counter-insurgency techniques have proved perfectly consistent with the kind of parliamentary democracy that used to be distinguished from fascism. Under the hegemony of the multinational corporations and their 'world system', the very possibility of a progressive bourgeois culture is problematic – a doubt that obviously strikes at the very foundation of Lukács's aesthetic.

Finally, the preoccupations of our own period have seemed to reveal in Lukács's work the shadow of a literary dictatorship somewhat different in kind from the attempts to prescribe a certain type of production which were denounced by Brecht. It is Lukács as a partisan, less of a specific artistic style than of a particular critical method, who is the focus of new polemics today – an atmosphere in which his work has found itself regarded by admirers and opponents alike as a monument to old-fashioned content-analysis. There is some irony in this transformation of the name of the author of *History and Class Consciousness* into a signal not unlike that emitted by the names of Belinsky and Chernyshevsky in an earlier period of Marxist aesthetics. Lukács's own critical practice is in fact very much genre-oriented, and committed to the mediation of the various forms of literary discourse, so that it is a mistake to enlist him in the cause of a naïve mimetic position that encourages us to discuss the events or characters of a novel, in the same way we would look at 'real' ones. On the other hand, insofar as his critical practice implies the ultimate possibility of some full and non-problematical 'representation of reality', Lukácsian realism can be said to give aid and comfort to a documentary and sociological approach to literature which is correctly enough felt to be antagonistic to more recent methods of construing the narrative text as a free-play of signifiers. Yet these apparently irreconcilable positions may prove to be two distinct and equally indispensable moments of the hermeneutic process itself – a first naïve 'belief' in the density or presence of novelistic representation, and a later 'bracketting' of that experience in which the necessary distance of all language from what it claims to represent – its substitutions and displacements – are explored. At any rate, it is clear that as long as Lukács is used as a rallying cry (or bogeyman) in this particular methodological conflict, there is not much likelihood of any measured assessment of his work as a whole.

Brecht, meanwhile, is certainly much more easily rewritten in terms of the concerns of the present, in which he seems to address us directly in an unmediated voice. His attack on Lukács's formalism is only one aspect of a much more complex and interesting stand on realism in general, to which it is surely no disservice to observe a few of the features which must seem dated to us today. In particular, Brecht's aesthetic, and his way of framing the problems of realism, are intimately bound up with a conception of science which it would be wrong to identify with the more scientistic currents in contemporary Marxism (for example the work of Althusser or Colletti). For the latter, science is an epistemological concept and a form of abstract knowledge, and the pursuit of a Marxian 'science' is closely linked to recent developments in the historiography of science – the findings of scholars like Koyré, Bachelard and Kuhn. For Brecht, however, 'science' is far less a matter of knowledge and epistemology than it is of sheer experiment and of practical, well-nigh manual activity. His is more an ideal of popular mechanics, technology, the home chemical set and the tinkering of a Galileo, than one of 'epistemes' or 'paradigms' in scientific discourse. Brecht's particular vision of science was for him the means of annulling the separation between physical and mental activity and the fundamental division of labour (not least that between worker and intellectual) that resulted from it: it puts knowing the world back together with changing the world, and at the same time unites an ideal of praxis with a conception of production. The reunion of 'science' and practical, change-oriented activity – not without its influence on the Brecht-Benjamin analysis of the media, as we shall see in a moment – thus transforms the process of 'knowing' the world into a source of delight or pleasure in its own right; and this is the fundamental step in the construction of a properly Brechtian aesthetics. For it restores to 'realistic' art that principle of play and genuine aesthetic gratification which the relatively more passive and cognitive aesthetic of Lukács had seemed to replace with the grim duty of a proper reflection of the world. The age-old dilemmas of a didactic theory of art (to teach *or* to please?) are thereby also overcome, and in a world where science is experiment and play, knowing and doing alike are forms of production, stimulating in their own right, a didactic art may now be imagined in which learning and pleasure are no longer separate from each other. In the Brechtian aesthetic, indeed, the idea of realism is not a purely artistic and formal category, but rather governs the relationship of the work of art to reality itself, characterizing a particular stance towards it. The spirit of realism designates an active, curious, experimental, subversive – in a word, *scientific* – attitude towards social institutions and the material world; and the 'realistic' work of art is therefore one which encourages and disseminates this attitude, yet not merely in a flat or mimetic way or along the lines of imitation alone. Indeed, the 'realistic' work of art is one in which 'realistic' and experimental attitudes are tried out, not only between its characters and their fictive realities, but also between the audience and the work itself, and – not least significant – between the writer and his own materials and techniques. The three-fold dimensions of such a practice of 'realism' clearly explode the purely representational categories of the traditional mimetic work.

What Brecht called science is thus in a larger sense a figure for non-alienated production in general. It is what Bloch would call a Utopian emblem of the reunified and satisfying praxis of a world that has left alienation and the division of labour behind it. The originality of the Brechtian vision may be judged by juxtaposing his figure of science with the more conventional image of art and the artist which, particularly in bourgeois literature, has traditionally had this Utopian function. At the same time, it must also be asked whether Brecht's vision of science is still available to us as a figure today, or whether it does not itself reflect a relatively primitive stage in what has now come to be known as the second industrial revolution. Seen in this perspective, the Brechtian delight in 'science' is rather of a piece with Lenin's definition of communism as 'the soviets plus electrification', or Diego Rivera's grandiose Rockefeller Centre mural (repainted for Bellas Artes) in which, at the intersection of microcosm and macrocosm, the massive hands of Soviet

New Man grasp and move the very levers of creation.

Together with his condemnation of Lukács's formalism and his conception of a union of science and aesthetics in the didactic work of art, there is yet a third strain in Brecht's thinking – in many ways the most influential – which deserves attention. This is, of course, his fundamental notion of *Verfremdung*. It is the so-called 'estrangement effect' which is most often invoked to sanction theories of political modernism today, such as that of the Tel Quel Group.[5] The practice of estrangement – staging phenomena in such a way that what had seemed natural and immutable in them is now tangibly revealed to be historical, and thus the object of revolutionary change – has long seemed to provide an outlet from the dead end of agitational didacticism in which so much of the political art of the past remains confined. At the same time it allows a triumphant reappropriation and a materialist regrounding of the dominant ideology of modernism (the Russian Formalist 'making strange', Pound's 'make it new', the emphasis of all of the historical varieties of modernism on the vocation of art to alter and renew perception as such) from the ends of a revolutionary politics. Today, traditional realism – the canon defended by Lukács, but also old-fashioned political art of the socialist realist type – is often assimilated to classical ideologies of representation and to the practice of 'closed form'; while even bourgeois modernism (Kristeva's models are Lautréamont and Mallarmé) is said to be revolutionary precisely to the degree to which it calls the older formal values and practices into question and produces itself as an open 'text'. Whatever objections may be made to this aesthetic of political modernism – and we will reserve a fundamental one for our discussion of similar views of Adorno – it would seem most difficult to associate Brecht with it. Not only was the author of 'On Abstract Painting'[6] as hostile to purely formal experimentation as was Lukács himself: that might be held to be a historical or generational accident, and simply to spell out the limits of Brecht's personal tastes. What is more serious is that his attack on the formalism of Lukács's literary

[5] For a persuasive yet self-critical statement of such a Brechtian modernism, see Colin McCabe, 'Realism and the Cinema: notes on some Brechtian theses', *in Screen*, XV, 2 (Summer, 1974), pp. 7–27.

[6] 'You say that you are communists, people intent on changing a world no longer fit for habitation . . . Yet were you in reality the cultural servants of the ruling classes, it would be cunning strategy on your part to make material things unrecognizable, since the struggle concerns things and it is in the world of things that your masters have the most to answer for.' 'Über gegenstandslose Malerei', in *Schriften zur Literatur und Kunst*, II, Frankfurt, 1967, pp. 68–69.

analyses remains binding on the quite different attempts of the political modernists to make ideological judgments (revolutionary/bourgeois) on the basis of the purely formal characteristics of closed or open forms, 'naturality', effacement of the traces of production in the work, and so forth. For example, it is certainly the case that a belief in the natural is ideological and that much of bourgeois art has worked to perpetuate such a belief, not only in its content but through the experience of its forms as well. Yet in different historical circumstances the idea of nature was once a subversive concept with a genuinely revolutionary function, and only the analysis of the concrete historical and cultural conjuncture can tell us whether, in the post-natural world of late capitalism, the categories of nature may not have acquired such a critical charge again.

It is time, indeed, to make an assessment of those fundamental changes which have taken place in capitalism and its culture since the period in which Brecht and Lukács spelled out their options for a Marxist aesthetics and a Marxian conception of realism. What has already been said about the transitional character of Nazism – a development which has done much to date many of Lukács's basic positions – is not without its effect on those of Brecht as well. Here it is necessary to emphasize the inextricable relationship between Brecht's aesthetic and the analysis of the media and its revolutionary possibilities worked out jointly by him and Walter Benjamin, and most widely accessible in the latter's well-known essay on 'The Work of Art in the Age of Mechanical Reproduction'.[7] For Brecht and Benjamin had not yet begun to feel the full force and constriction of that stark alternative between a mass audience or media culture, and a minority 'elite' modernism, in which our thinking about aesthetics today is inevitably locked. Rather, they foresaw a revolutionary utilization of communications technology such that the most striking advances in artistic technique – effects such as those of 'montage', for instance, which today we tend to associate almost exclusively with modernism as such – could at once be harnessed to politicizing and didactic purposes. Brecht's conception of 'realism' is thus not complete without this perspective in which the artist is able to use the most complex, modern technology in addressing the widest

---

[7] See *Illuminations*, London, 1970, also 'The Author as Producer', in *Understanding Brecht*, London, 1973; and for further developments in a radical theory of the media, Jürgen Habermas, *Strukturwandel der Öffentlichkeit*, Neuwied, 1962; Hans-Magnus Enzensberger, *The Consciousness Industry*, New York, 1974; and Oskar Negt and Alexander Kluge, *Öffentlichkeit und Erfahrung*, Frankfurt, 1973.

popular public. Yet if Nazism itself corresponds to an early and still relatively primitive stage in the emergence of the media, then so does Benjamin's cultural strategy for attacking it, and in particular his conception of an art that would be revolutionary precisely to the degree to which it was technically (and technologically) 'advanced'. In the increasingly 'total system' of the media societies today, we can unfortunately no longer share this optimism. Without it, however, the project of a specifically political modernism becomes indistinguishable from all the other kinds – modernism, among other things, being characterized by its consciousness of an absent public.

In other words the fundamental difference between our own situation and that of the thirties is the emergence in full-blown and definitive form of that ultimate transformation of late monopoly capitalism variously known as the *société de consommation* or as post-industrial society. This is the historical stage reflected by Adorno's two post-war essays, so different in emphasis from the pre-war materials in the present volume. It may appear easy enough in retrospect to identify his repudiation of *both* Lukács *and* Brecht, on the grounds of their political praxis, as a characterstic example of an anti-communism now outmoded with the Cold War itself. More relevant in the present context, however, is the Frankfurt School's premise of a 'total system', which expressed Adorno's and Horkheimer's sense of the increasingly closed organization of the world into a seamless web of media technology, multinational corporations, and international bureaucratic control.[8] Whatever the theoretical merits of the idea of the 'total system' – and it would seem to me that where it does not lead out of politics altogether, it encourages the revival of an anarchist opposition to Marxism itself, and can also be used as a justification for terrorism – we may at least agree with Adorno that in the cultural realm, the all-pervasiveness of the system, with its 'culture-' or (Enzensberger's variant) its 'consciousness-industry', makes for an unpropitious climate for any of the older, simpler forms of oppositional art, whether it be that proposed by Lukács, that produced by Brecht, or indeed those celebrated in their different ways by Benjamin and by Bloch. The system has a power to co-opt and to defuse even the most potentially dangerous forms of political art by transforming them into cultural commodities (witness, if further proof be needed, the grisly example of the burgeoning Brecht-Industrie itself!). On the other hand, it cannot be said that Adorno's rather astonishing 'resolution' of the

[8] The more recent French variant on this position – as for example in Jean Baudrillard – enlarges the model to include the 'socialist bloc' within this new dystopian entente.

problem – his proposal to see the classical stage of high modernism itself as the very prototype of the most 'genuinely' political art ('this is not a time for political art, but politics has migrated into autonomous art, and nowhere more so than where it seems to be politically dead') and his suggestion that it is Beckett who is the most truly revolutionary artist of our time – is any more satisfactory. To be sure, some of Adorno's most remarkable analyses – for instance, his discussion of Schoenberg and the twelve-tone system in the *Philosophy of Modern Music* – document his assertion that the greatest modern art, even the most apparently un- or anti-political, in reality holds up a mirror to the 'total system' of late capitalism. Yet in retrospect, this now seems a most unexpected revival of a Lukács-type 'reflection theory' of aesthetics, under the spell of a political and historical despair that plagues both houses and finds praxis henceforth unimaginable. What is ultimately fatal to this new and finally itself once more anti-political revival of the ideology of modernism is less the equivocal rhetoric of Adorno's attack on Lukács or the partiality of his reading of Brecht,[9] than very precisely the fate of modernism in consumer society itself. For what was once an oppositional and anti-social phenomenon in the early years of the century, has today become the dominant style of commodity production and an indispensable component in the machinery of the latter's ever more rapid and demanding reproduction of itself. That Schoenberg's Hollywood pupils used their advanced techniques to write movie music, that the master-pieces of the most recent schools of American painting are now sought to embellish the splendid new structures of the great insurance companies and multinational banks (themselves the work of the most talented and 'advanced' modern architects), are but the external symptoms of a situation in which a once scandalous 'perceptual art' has found a social and economic function in supplying the styling changes necessary to the *société de consommation* of the present.

The final aspect of the contemporary situation relevant to our subject has to do with the changes that have taken place within socialism itself since the publication of the Expressionism debate in *Das Wort* some forty years ago. If the central problem of a political art under capitalism is that of co-optation, one of the crucial issues of culture in a socialist framework must surely remain that of what Ernst Bloch calls the *Erbe*:

---

[9] For a path-breaking Marxian corrective to Adorno's reading of the *Caucasian Chalk Circle*, see Darko Suvin, 'Brecht's *Caucasian Chalk Circle* and Marxist Figuration: Open Dramaturgy as Open History', in Norman Rudick, ed., *The Weapons of Criticism*, Palo Alto, California, 1976.

the question of the uses of the world's cultural past in what will increasingly be a single international culture of the future, and of the place and effects of diverse heritages in a society intent on building socialism. Bloch's formulation of the problem is obviously a strategic means of transforming Lukács's narrow polemics – which were limited to the realistic novelists of the European bourgeois tradition – and of enlarging the framework of the debate to include the immense variety of popular or peasant, pre-capitalist or 'primitive' arts. It should be understood in the context of his monumental attempt to reinvent the concept of Utopia for Marxism and to free it from the objections correctly made by Marx and Engels themselves to the 'utopian socialism' of Saint-Simon, Owen or Fourier. Bloch's Utopian principle aims at jarring socialist thought loose from its narrow self-definition in terms which essentially prolong the categories of capitalism itself, whether by negation or adoption (terms like industrialization, centralization, progress, technology, and even production itself, which tend to impose their own social limitations and options on those who work with them). Where Lukács's cultural thinking emphasizes the continuities between the bourgeois order and that which is to develop out of it, Bloch's priorities suggest the need to think the 'transition to socialism' in terms of radical difference, of a more absolute break with that particular past, perhaps of a renewal or recovery of the truth of more ancient social forms. The newer Marxist anthropology, indeed, reminds us – from within our 'total system' – of the absolute difference of older pre-capitalist and tribal societies; and at a historical moment in which such an interest in a much more remote past seems less likely to give rise to the sentimentalizing and populistic myths which Marxism had to combat in the late nineteenth and early 20th centuries, the memory of pre-capitalist societies may now become a vital element of Bloch's Utopian principle and of the invention of the future. Politically, the classical Marxian notion of the necessity, during the transition to socialism, of a 'dictatorship of the proletariat' – that is, a withdrawal of effective power from those with a vested interest in the re-establishment of the old order – has surely not become outmoded. Yet it may emerge conceptually transformed when once we think of it together with the necessity for a cultural revolution that involves collective re-education of all the classes. This is the perspective in which Lukács's emphasis on the great bourgeois novelists seems most inadequate to the task, but it is one in which the anti-bourgeois thrust of the great modernisms also appears inappropriate. It is then that Bloch's meditation on the *Erbe*, on the repressed cultural difference of the past and the Utopian principle of the invention of a radically different future, will for the first time come into its own, at a point when the conflict between Realism and Modernism recedes behind us.

But surely in the West, and perhaps elsewhere as well, that point is still beyond us. In our present cultural situation, if anything, both alternatives of realism and of modernism seem intolerable to us: realism because its forms revive older experiences of a kind of social life (the classical inner city, the traditional opposition city/country) which is no longer with us in the already decaying future of consumer society: modernism because its contradictions have proved in practice even more acute than those of realism. An aesthetic of novelty today – already enthroned as the dominant critical and formal ideology – must seek desperately to renew itself by ever more rapid rotations of its own axis: modernism seeking to become post-modernism without ceasing to be modern. Thus today we witness the spectacle of a predictable return, after abstraction has itself become a tired convention, to figurative art, but this time to a figurative art – so-called hyperrealism or photorealism – which turns out to be the representation, not of things themselves, but of the latter's photographs: a representational art which is really 'about' art itself! In literature, meanwhile, amidst a weariness with plotless or poetic fiction, a return to intrigue is achieved, not by the latter's redis-covery, but rather by pastiche of older narratives and depersonalized imitation of traditional voices, similar to Stravinsky's pastiche of the classics criticized by Adorno's *Philosophy of Music*.

In these circumstances, indeed, there is some question whether the ultimate renewal of modernism, the final dialectical subversion of the now automatized conventions of an aesthetics of perceptual revolution, might not simply be . . . realism itself! For when modernism and its accompanying techniques of 'estrangement' have become the dominant style whereby the consumer is reconciled with capitalism, the habit of fragmentation itself needs to be 'estranged' and corrected by a more totalizing way of viewing phenomena.[10] In an unexpected dénouement,

[10] See, for example, the instructive comments of Stanley Aronowitz on the cinema. 'Unlike the important efforts of Japanese and European film-makers to fix the camera directly on the action and permit the scene to work "itself" out, American films are charac-terized by rapid camera work and sharp editing whose effect is to segment the action into one- or two-minute time slots, paralleling the prevailing styles of television production. The American moviegoer, having become accustomed in TV watching to commercial breaks in the action of a dramatic presentation, is believed to have become incapable of sustaining longer and slower action. Therefore the prevailing modes of film production rely on conceptions of dramatic time inherited from the more crass forms of commercial culture.

212

it may be Lukács – wrong as he might have been in the 1930s – who has some provisional last word for us today. Yet this particular Lukács, if he be imaginable, would be one for whom the concept of realism has been rewritten in terms of the categories of *History and Class Consciousness*, in particular those of reification and totality. Unlike the more familiar concept of alienation, a process that pertains to activity and in particular to work (dissociating the worker from his labour, his product, his fellow workers and ultimately from his very 'species being' itself), reification is a process that affects our cognitive relationship with the social totality. It is a disease of that mapping function whereby the individual subject projects and models his or her insertion into the collectivity. The reification of late capitalism – the transformation of human relations into an appearance of relationships between things – renders society opaque: it is the lived source of the mystifications on which ideology is based and by which domination and exploitation are legitimized. Since the fundamental structure of the social 'totality' is a set of class relationships – an antagonistic structure such that the various social classes define themselves in terms of that antagonism and by opposition with one another – reification necessarily obscures the class character of that structure, and is accompanied, not only by anomie, but also by that increasing confusion as to the nature and even the existence of social classes which can be abundantly observed in all the 'advanced' capitalist countries today. If the diagnosis is correct, the intensification of class consciousness will be less a matter of a populist or ouvrierist exaltation of a single class by itself, than of the forcible reopening of access to a sense of society as a totality, and of the reinvention of possibilities of cognition and perception that allow social phenomena once again to become transparent, as moments of the struggle *between* classes.

Under these circumstances, the function of a new realism would be clear; to resist the power of reification in consumer society and to reinvent that category of totality which, systematically undermined by existential fragmentation on all levels of life and social organization today, can alone project structural relations between classes as well as

The film-maker who subordinates the action and the characters to this concept of dramatic time reveals a politics inside technique that is far more insidious than "reactionary" content When viewed from this perspective, the film-maker such as Howard Hawks, who refuses to subordinate art to the requirements of segmented time, becomes more resistant to authoritarianism than the liberal or left-wing film-makers who are concerned with the humanitarian content of film but have capitulated to techniques that totally reduce the audience to spectators.' *False Promises*, New York 1973, p. 116–17.

class struggles in other countries, in what has increasingly become a world system. Such a conception of realism would incorporate what was always most concrete in the dialectical counter-concept of modernism – its emphasis on violent renewal of perception in a world in which experience has solidified into a mass of habits and automatisms. Yet the habituation which it would be the function of the new aesthetic to disrupt would no longer be thematized in the conventional modernistic terms of desacralized or dehumanizing reason, of mass society and the industrial city or technology in general, but rather as a function of the commodity system and the reifying structure of late capitalism.

Other conceptions of realism, other kinds of political aesthetics, obviously remain conceivable. The Realism/Modernism debate teaches us the need to judge them in terms of the historical and social conjuncture in which they are called to function. To take an attitude of partisanship towards key struggles of the past does not mean either choosing sides, or seeking to harmonize irreconcilable differences. In such extinct yet still virulent intellectual conflicts, the fundamental contradiction is between history itself and the conceptual apparatus which, seeking to grasp its realities, only succeeds in reproducing their discord within itself in the form of an enigma for thought, an aporia. It is to this aporia that we must hold, which contains within its structure the crux of a history beyond which we have not yet passed. It cannot of course tell us what our conception of realism ought to be; yet its study makes it impossible to us not to feel the obligation to reinvent one.

Index

216

220

Zinoviev, Grigori, 186 and n
Zola, Emile, 25n, 174
Zur Metakritik des Erkenntnistheorie.
   Studien über Husserl und die

phänomenologischen Antinomien
   (Adorno), 120
Zweig, Arnold, 47
Zweig, Stefan, 18